PALESTINE
AND
INTERNATIONAL LAW

Palestine
and
International Law

The Legal Aspects of the Arab-Israeli Conflict

HENRY CATTAN

Licencié en Droit (Paris)
LL.M.(London), of the Middle Temple
Barrister-at-Law

Formerly Member of the
Palestine Bar Association
and Tutor at the Jerusalem Law School

With a Foreword by Dr W. T. Mallison, Jr

LONGMAN

LONGMAN GROUP LTD
LONDON

*Associated companies, branches and representatives
throughout the world*

© Longman Group Ltd 1973

First published 1973

ISBN 0 582 78038 1

Set in Monotype Fournier

Printed in Great Britain by
Western Printing Services Ltd Bristol

FOREWORD

by Dr W. T. Mallison, Jr

UNIVERSAL INTERNATIONAL LAW AS THE CONSTRUCTIVE ALTERNATIVE FOR PALESTINE

The methodology of this book is both factual and juridical rather than political and polemical. In the sense that it supports the people of Palestine in their conflict with Zionist nationalism, it may be deemed to be pro-Palestinian. However, those who are informed on the Palestine problem know that Henry Cattan is a distinguished international lawyer who has played a constructive rôle in attempting to solve, rather than merely to deplore, the conflict. He accomplishes this in the larger context of universal international law in which the law applicable to Palestine appears.

An examination of the detailed table of contents will provide the thoughtful reader with a much better indication of the scope of the book than should be attempted in this Foreword. The chapters are carefully inter-related and the subsequent ones build upon the preceding ones. Each chapter, however, stands on its own and it may be examined independently by a reader who is seeking facts and analysis on a particular issue.

In the first chapter, the author appraises the Balfour Declaration of 1917 and, after applying the relevant legal criteria, reaches the conclusion that it is invalid in international law. It is believed that this analysis has made the position unassailable from a juridical standpoint. It is interesting to consider that even if, in spite of the overwhelming case to the contrary, it were to be assumed for purposes of legal analysis only that the Declaration is valid, the net result in law is the same conclusion: that it does not provide a juridical basis to support the Zionist claim to Palestine. The Declaration, which is set forth in the text, provides only that the British Government views "with favour" the Zionist national home enterprise, which is limited by the words "in Palestine", and further that the Government "will use their best endeavours" to facilitate it. It is clear beyond doubt that words such as "favour" and "best endeavours" are merely precatory and not legally obligatory. In contrast, the safeguard clauses refer unequivocally to the existing "rights" and expressly add "it being clearly understood that nothing shall be done which might prejudice" these rights. Dr Weizmann, the chief Zionist negotiator of the Declaration, regarded the final text as "a painful recession from what the Government itself was prepared to offer" before the intervention of the anti-Zionist Jews led by Edwin Montagu, the only Jewish member of the Cabinet.[1]

---

[1] The textual statements are based upon W. T. Mallison, Jr, "The Balfour Declaration:

It is inappropriate to appear to pick and choose among the succeeding chapters, since each one is an integral part of the comprehensive legal analysis. It may, nevertheless, be relevant to make a brief commentary upon Chapter VII, which considers the UN Security Council Resolution No. 242 of 22 November 1967. This commentary may be justified by the misconception, widely held in Western Europe and in the United States, that this resolution presents a balanced, just, and workable approach to a solution of both the causal Zionist-Palestine conflict and the derivative Arab-Israeli one. The author's analysis reveals it to be another attempt by the Great Powers to "solve" the Palestine problem based on the assumption that the people of Palestine either do not exist as a factual matter or are a non-people as a legal matter. The incompatibility of this approach both with the fundamental principles of the Charter and with those of international law are fully explained. Article 1 of the United Nations Charter specifies that peace is to be achieved "in conformity with the principles of justice and international law" and is to be "based on respect for the principle of equal rights and self-determination of peoples". It does not provide for the maintenance of "international peace and security" by any means whatsoever.

Further support for Mr Cattan's theme that political decisions have been substituted for legal ones concerning Palestine appears in the most recently published volume of the *Foreign Relations of the United States*. Ambassador Loy W. Henderson, then serving as the director of the Office of Near Eastern and African Affairs in the US Department of State, consistently sought to promote justice under law and, in keeping with that objective, the long-range legitimate interests of the United States in the Middle East. In a then top-secret memorandum to the Secretary of State of 22 September 1947 he stated:

> "These proposals [of the majority of the United Nations Special Committee on Palestine], for instance, ignore such principles as self-determination and majority rule. They recognize the principles of a theocratic racial state and even go so far in several instances as to discriminate on grounds of religion and race against persons outside of Palestine."[2]

In another top-secret memorandum addressed to the Under Secretary of State, Mr Lovett, on 24 November 1947 Ambassador Henderson stated, *inter alia*:

> "By our Palestine policy, we are not only forfeiting the friendship of the Arab world, but we are incurring long-term Arab hostility towards us. What is important is that the Arabs are losing confidence in the integrity of the United States and the sincerity of our many pronouncements that our foreign policies are based on the principles of the Charter of the United Nations."[3]

An Appraisal in International Law" in Ibrahim Abu-Lughod (ed.), *The Transformation of Palestine: Essays on the Origin and Development of the Arab-Israeli Conflict*, pp. 60–111, Northwestern University Press, 1971.

2 *Foreign Relations of the United States 1947*, Vol. V, p. 1157, US Government Printing Office, 1971.   3 *Ibid.*, pp. 1281–1282.

An editorial note provides the information that Mr Lovett, in a marginal notation on the memorandum, stated that he read it to President Truman.

Mr Cattan calls particular attention to the most relevant of the recent UN General Assembly resolutions which have been adopted by the two-thirds vote required by the Charter for important questions. The resolution of 10 December 1969 affirming "the inalienable rights of the people of Palestine" is demonstrated to be a sound and practical approach to the Palestine problem. In the same way, the General Assembly resolution of 6 December 1971 which, *inter alia*, confirms "the legality of the peoples' struggle for self-determination and liberation from colonial and foreign domination and alien subjugation" is appraised as far more constructive than the Security Council resolution. This resolution does not leave the applicability of its provisions to inference or implication. It applies them specifically to "the Palestinian people" as well as to named African peoples. Finally, the author discusses the all-important General Assembly resolutions adopted on 8 and 13 December 1972. These resolutions have gone much further than any previous resolutions in affirming certain guiding principles relevant to a settlement of the conflict. It is significant to observe that in these resolutions the international organization has called not only upon Israel to desist from certain actions and practices that are in violation of international law, but has also called upon all States not to recognize changes and measures carried out by Israel in the occupied territories and to avoid actions, including aid that could constitute recognition of Israel's occupation.

It should be added that the General Assembly resolutions just mentioned are set forth in full in the appendices. These appendices, which provide a wealth of source material, add to the juridical analysis the principal primary sources upon which that analysis is based. The author sets these materials out in full so that the reader may appraise them for himself rather than limiting the reader to those portions which are quoted in the text.

The implicit assumption made in the book that international law is relevant to a just solution of both the causal Zionist-Palestinian conflict and the derivative Arab-Israeli confrontation may be an unproven one to many readers. But the answer is that if international law were to be conceived as an exclusive Western system which excludes the vast majority of mankind, it has no creative potential for solving difficult problems. The United Nations Charter, as the fundamental law of the organized world community, repudiates such an exclusivist conception of international law. Its affirmation of self-determination and its repudiation of discrimination do not except the people of Palestine and other victims of colonialism from its world-wide scope.

The Palestine problem, as Mr Cattan demonstrates so persuasively, is not a failure of international law, since universal international law has never been applied to Palestine. Mr Cattan strongly recommends the application of such law as the way to solve the Palestine problem with the justice and humanity that are indispensable to an enduring and constructive peace. This book is a profound commitment to law as an instrument for the protection of human and national rights. From this perspective, international law is not something merely to be admired and laid aside; it is to be implemented as the only way of redressing wrongs without creating further injustices.

The struggle between universal humanitarianism and particular privilege and preference for some at the expense of justice to others is as old as mankind. Mr Cattan makes the case for universalism with deep insight and profound conviction. Others, regardless of their national or religious identifications, are challenged to raise their objectives to the high plane set forth in this book. If this challenge is met, justice for the Palestinians and for all mankind will be achieved.

W. T. Mallison, Jr.,
The Law Center,
George Washington University,
Washington, D.C., U.S.A.

ACKNOWLEDGEMENT

Some of the historical material in this book has already appeared in the author's previous work *Palestine, the Arabs and Israel*, published by Longman in 1969. A restatement of some facts, however, was unavoidable in order to give the reader the historical background of the issues discussed and to make possible their legal appraisal. Moreover, Chapter IV, entitled Sovereignty over Palestine, was the subject of an Appendix to the author's previous work; because of its legal nature it is substantially reproduced here.

The author is indebted to Longman for permission to reproduce this material.

H.C.

CONTENTS

CONTENTS

APPENDICES[1]

---

1 Appendices III, IV, and VI to XXXIII set out the principal UN
resolutions on the Palestine Question and the Arab-Israeli conflict
that have a bearing on the legal issues discussed in this book. There
exist scores of other resolutions adopted by the General Assembly
and the Security Council, which have not been included herein,
dealing with Palestine refugees, UNRWA, cease-fire orders, and
condemnation of Israel for breaches of the armistice agreements.

ABBREVIATIONS

AJIL   American Journal of International Law
BYIL   British Year Book of International Law
Cmd.   Command: statement issued by the British Government
G.A.   General Assembly
ICJ   International Court of Justice
RGDIP   Revue Générale de Droit International Public
S.C.   Security Council
UNEF   United Nations Expeditionary Force
UNRWA   United Nations Relief and Works Agency for Palestine Refugees

PREFACE

The object of this book is to discuss the legal issues that arise in the Arab-Israeli conflict, and in its underlying cause, the Palestine Question. The equities involved in this conflict have been buried under a mass of distortion, misinformation and insidious propaganda which have misrepresented the facts and veiled the truth to the extent that the victims are made to appear as being the wrongdoers and the wrongdoers as the victims.

The writer has subjected to a critical legal analysis the principal facts and developments in the evolution of the Arab-Israeli conflict from the time of its inception until the present day. A legal scrutiny of the Balfour Declaration, the mandate over Palestine, the UN resolution for the partition of Palestine, the proclamation of the State of Israel and its conduct since its emergence shows in no uncertain manner the grave deviations from right and justice that have occurred and their rôle as contributory causes to the crisis that has convulsed the Middle East for a number of years.

The present situation in Palestine is the result of an extraordinary accumulation of injustices, illegalities and violations of all kinds: violations of international law, violations of UN resolutions, violations of human rights and fundamental freedoms. The people of Palestine have been dispersed and scattered. Even Palestine itself has seen its historic name obliterated and its land torn apart into two territories, now called Israel and the West Bank of Jordan. The whole structure of right, law and justice has crumbled down in the country that was once the cradle of civilization and the birthplace of three great religions of the world.

Until now no solution has been found or suggested for the Arab-Israeli conflict that takes into account the principles of law and justice. One might perhaps wonder whether any useful purpose is served by an examination of the legal aspects of a situation created by power politics and maintained by military force. Are legal considerations of any use in undoing what has been done? It would be most frustrating to concede that the function of international law today is to protect and maintain, rather than to redress, wrongful situations. The writer ventures to hope that an analysis of the legal issues involved in the Arab-Israeli conflict will not simply be a matter of historical or academic interest. He firmly believes that such an analysis enables a fresh appraisal of the situation to be made and furnishes a scale of values which is essential for a proper understanding of the problem, and when the time comes, for its just and equitable solution. Without an understanding of the real nature of the problem, and without an appraisal of the situation in the light of the principles of law and justice, regardless of conditions created by force, the efforts that are being exerted to secure peace in the Middle East will remain futile. In order to be effective and durable, the solution of the Arab-Israeli conflict should attempt to bridge the gap, one would even say the abyss, between reality and legality in Palestine.

CHAPTER I
THE ZIONIST CLAIMS
TO PALESTINE

Section 1
The claim to an historic title

Before examining the Zionist claim to an historic title to Palestine, it is necessary to consider briefly what has been the Jewish association with Palestine, and to put this in its true perspective within the framework of the history of the country.

The Jews were not the earliest inhabitants of Palestine. Long before they came to Palestine the country was inhabited. Reliable evidence points to the existence of early civilizations in Palestine going back at least some 10,000 years. Jericho, the oldest walled city, has been scientifically dated back to 7000 B.C.

The earliest known inhabitants of Palestine were the Canaanites. They lived in cities as a settled population and possessed an advanced civilization. They are thought to have inhabited the country from 3000 B.C., that is, some 1,800 years before the Israelite invasion. The Canaanites gave to the country its early name, for the Bible refers to it as "the land of Canaan" (*Numbers* 34:1, 35:10) and "the country of the Canaanites" (*Exodus* 3:17).

It was the Canaanites who founded Jerusalem. Josephus mentions:

> "Son fondateur fut un prince des Cananéens surnommé Le Juste à cause de sa piété. Il consacra le premier cette ville à Dieu en lui bâtissant un temple, et changea son nom de Solyme en celui de Jérusalem."[1]

According to tradition, there was a migration of several Hebrew tribes from Chaldea to the land of Canaan in about the year 1730 B.C. The Hebrew tribes, however, did not establish themselves in the land of Canaan, and they moved on to Egypt where they lived under the rule of the Pharaohs.

Again according to tradition, the Hebrews, or Israelites, left Egypt a few centuries later and wandered in the desert for several years. In or around the

---

[1] Flavius Josephus, *Histoire de la Guerre des Juifs contre les Romains*, Tome II, p. 221, Editions Berché et Tralin, Paris, 1879.

year 1200 B.C., the Israelites invaded the land of Canaan from the east and attacked Jericho. They destroyed the city and annihilated its population. The Israelite tribes then started spreading into the Canaanite country. The process was slow and lasted some two centuries.

The Israelites did not succeed in occupying the whole country, for the Philistines, from whom the name of Palestine is derived, controlled its southern coast and the maritime plain to a point north of Japho (Jaffa). On the other hand, the Phoenicians controlled what is now known as western Galilee to a point south of Acco (Acre). The Philistines were constantly at war with the Israelites, whom they fought for over two hundred years.

For a long time after their invasion of the land of Canaan, the Israelites possessed neither a Kingdom nor a central government. They lived as tribes and were ruled by the Judges. It was only in the year 1000 B.C. that David established the first Jewish Kingdom in Palestine.

What happened to the Canaanites in the wake of the Israelite invasion?

Some passages of the Bible suggest that the Canaanites were savagely exterminated. Other passages give a different version. Thus the Bible says:

> "And the children of Israel dwelt among the Canaanites, the Hittites, the Amorites, the Perizzites, the Hivites, and the Jebusites: and they took their daughters to be their wives, and gave their daughters to their sons, and served their gods." (*Judges* 3: 5 and 6)

It should not be forgotten that the Bible is a mixture of history, legend and Hebrew mythology. Modern historians reject the theory of a general massacre of the Canaanites, or of a brutal substitution of one population for another. It seems that on the whole the Israelites and Canaanites cohabited, and even merged together.

Professor Adolphe Lods states:

> "The people of Israel at the royal period were a mixture of Hebrews and Canaanites . . . In this amalgamation, the Canaanite element was by far the most numerous . . . Being more civilized, the Canaanites naturally compelled the newly-arrived to adopt their culture, and in this sense one can say that the Canaanites conquered their victors. But, on the other hand, the Hebrews possessed and preserved the consciousness of conquerors; they succeeded in imposing their social framework, their name, their God, on the entire population of Palestine."[2]

The Kingdom of David lasted less than eighty years. In 922 B.C., after the death of Solomon, it was split into the northern Kingdom of Israel and the southern Kingdom of Judah. But these two Kingdoms were also to collapse one after the other. The Kingdom of Israel was destroyed by the Assyrians in 721 B.C. and its people were carried off into oblivion. From that date the Kingdom

---

2 Translation from Adolphe Lods, *Israël, Des Origines Au Milieu Du VIIe Siècle*, p. 386, Ed. Albin Michel, Paris, 1949. See also pp. 379–385.

of Israel became politically extinct. As to the Kingdom of Judah, it was destroyed by the Babylonians in 587 B.C., and its people were carried into captivity. This represented the end of any organized Jewish rule in Palestine, and the situation was described in the following terms:

> "The twelve tribes were deported to the Caucasus, Armenia and in particular Babylonia, and disappeared; and with them the Jewish people in the plenitude of its existence as a simultaneously ethnic, national and religious community also disappeared forever."[3]

Subsequently, in 520 B.C., Cyrus, King of Persia, allowed the Jews to return to Palestine. Not all returned, but those who did return lived under Persian rule, and later under Macedonian and Roman rule. They revolted from time to time against their rulers but they never again ruled the country. Their most important revolts were the Maccabean rising against the Macedonians in 167 B.C. and their two insurrections against the Romans in A.D. 70 and A.D. 132. After this last insurrection, the Jews were either killed or dispersed.

From that time until the 20th century, when Zionism was able under the British mandate to organize a massive Jewish immigration to Palestine, very few Jews inhabited the country. For nineteen centuries the Jews had almost ceased to exist in Palestine. Even as the main element in the population the Jews largely disappeared after the wars of A.D. 70 and A.D. 132. Benjamin of Tudela, a Jewish pilgrim who visited the Holy Land about A.D. 1170–1171, found only 1,440 Jews in all Palestine; and Nahman Gerondi, in A.D. 1267, found only two Jewish families in Jerusalem.[4]

Up to the 19th century the Jewish population of Palestine had increased very little. At the beginning of the 19th century, the Jews in Palestine numbered 8,000; in 1845 they were 11,000 and in 1880 their number did not exceed 20,000.[5] In 1918 the Jews numbered 56,000.[6] At the time of the Balfour Declaration (1917) the Jews represented less than ten per cent of the total population of Palestine.

The Israelite occupation of Palestine was only an episode in the history of that country. From 587 B.C., when Jewish rule ended in Palestine, until the 20th century – that is, during a span of some twenty-four centuries – Palestine was ruled first by pagans, then by the Christians, and finally by the Moslems.

The pagans ruled the country from 587 B.C. until the fall of paganism in Palestine in A.D. 323. Babylonian rule lasted from 587 B.C. until 538 B.C., and Persian rule from 538 B.C. until 332 B.C. In that year Alexander the Great

---

3 Georges Friedmann, *The End of the Jewish People?*, p. 266, Doubleday Anchor Books, 1968.
4 Reverend Charles T. Bridgeman's letter to the President of the Trusteeship Council, 13 January 1950, General Assembly Official Records, 5th Session, Supplement No. 9, UN Document A/1286, p. 13.
5 *Dictionnaire Diplomatique*, p. 294.
6 Government of Palestine, *Survey of Palestine*, Vol. I, p. 144.

conquered the country and the Macedonians occupied it until 63 B.C., when Pompey conquered Jerusalem for Rome. The pagan Romans continued to exercise authority in Palestine until the Christians seized power in A.D. 323.

The Christians ruled Palestine from A.D. 323 until A.D. 614. During this period they built the famous Christian churches of Jerusalem and Bethlehem. In A.D. 326 Emperor Constantine laid the foundations of the Church of the Holy Sepulchre. His mother Helena built the Church of the Nativity at Bethlehem and the Church of the Ascension on the Mount of Olives. Under Christian rule Palestine began to attract Christian pilgrims and became a centre of eremitic life. Men flocked from all quarters to live as hermits, and the country was soon dotted with a number of monasteries. Although the Christians then became the dominant element in the population, they lived side by side with the pagans.

In A.D. 614 the Persians wrested the country from the Christians. In that year Chosroes II, King of Persia, invaded Palestine, captured Jerusalem, destroyed the Christian churches and carried off the True Cross from the Holy Sepulchre. However, in A.D. 628, the Byzantines recovered Jerusalem and restored the True Cross, but nine years later, in A.D. 637, Palestine was conquered by the Moslem Arabs.

The Moslem occupation of Palestine did not put an end for all time to Christian rule, for in A.D. 1099 the Crusaders conquered the Holy City and in A.D. 1100 established the Latin Kingdom of Jerusalem. This Kingdom extended from Aqaba to Beirut and from the Mediterranean to the Jordan River. It lasted until 1187, when Jerusalem was reconquered by the Moslem Arabs. In all, Christian rule in Palestine lasted for over four centuries.

Moslem rule, by the Moslem Arabs from A.D. 637 and by the Turks from A.D. 1517, continued for almost thirteen centuries. During that time, except for the period of the Latin Kingdom of Jerusalem, and for a short period in the 13th century during which Frederick II ruled Jerusalem, Palestine was continuously under Moslem rule, either Arab or Turkish.

Turkish rule ended in 1917–1918 as a result of the military occupation of Palestine by British and Allied Forces during the First World War. Between 1922 and 1948 the British Government administered Palestine under a mandate from the League of Nations. One of the objects of the mandate was to fulfil the Balfour Declaration and to facilitate Jewish immigration into Palestine. This was done against the will of the indigenous inhabitants. The Zionists took advantage of this open door to Jewish immigration, and within a quarter of a century increased the Jewish population of Palestine more than tenfold. It was this demographic nucleus of foreign immigrants which succeeded in 1948 in establishing a Jewish State in Palestine under the name of Israel.

This brief review helps to place the historical connection of the Jews with Palestine in its true perspective. In particular, it shows the error of a current misconception, deliberately created, that the Palestinians were invaders of Palestine during the Moslem invasion of Palestine in the 7th century. This is not historically correct. The Palestinians are the earliest and the original inhabitants of Palestine. The Moslem Arab conquest of Palestine in A.D. 637 was not the starting-point of their occupation of the country. The Arabs are a pre-Islamic people. They lived in Palestine and in other parts of the Middle East before the advent of Islam. In fact, the number of the invaders at the time of the Moslem Arab conquest of Palestine in the 7th century was small, and they were assimilated by the indigenous inhabitants. Professor Maxime Rodinson points out that the Arab population of Palestine was native in all the senses of that word.[7] The Palestinians of today are the descendants of the Philistines, the Canaanites and the other early tribes which inhabited the country.[8] They have lived continuously in Palestine since the dawn of history. Their settlement in Palestine can be traced back at least forty centuries. There were infusions of other racial elements into the Palestinian stock, mainly from the Greeks, the Romans, the Moslem Arabs and the Crusaders. But this Palestinian stock, which comprises both Moslems and Christians, continued to constitute the main element of the population until the majority of the original inhabitants of Palestine were displaced by the Israelis in 1948.

After this retrospect, we shall now proceed to examine the Zionist claim to an historic title to Palestine.

The Zionist claim to an historic title to Palestine was first advanced by the Zionist Organization to the Peace Conference in Paris in 1919. In its memorandum of 3 February 1919 to the Supreme Council of the Allied Powers at the Peace Conference, the Zionist Organization suggested the adoption of a resolution whereby the Allied Powers would "recognize the historic title of the Jewish people to Palestine and the right of the Jews to reconstitute in Palestine their National Home."[9] The memorandum claimed that the country is the historic home of the Jews and that "by violence they were driven from Palestine" – totally ignoring the fact that it was by similar violence that the Israelites themselves conquered the country in times gone by. Under the heading "The Historic Title" the memorandum then proceeded to explain the basis of the Zionist claim as follows:

> "The claims of the Jews with regard to Palestine rest upon the following main considerations:
>
> (1) The land is the historic home of the Jews; there they achieved their greatest development . . .
>
> (2) In some parts of the world, and particularly in Eastern Europe, the conditions

---

7 Maxime Rodinson, *Israel and the Arabs*, p. 216, Penguin Books, 1968.
8 "The Palestinian Arab of today, then, is a descendant of the Philistines, the Canaanites and other early tribes, and of the Greeks, Romans, Arabs, Crusaders, Mongols and Turks": Moshe Menuhin, *The Decadence of Judaism in our Times*, p. 18, Exposition Press, New York, 1965.
9 J. C. Hurewitz, *Diplomacy in the Near and Middle East*, Vol. II, p. 45, Van Nostrand, 1956.

of life of millions of Jews are deplorable . . . The need for fresh outlets is urgent . . . Palestine would offer one such outlet . . .

(3) But Palestine is not large enough to contain more than a proportion of the Jews of the world . . . A Jewish National Home in Palestine will, however, be of high value to them . . .

(4) Such a Palestine would be of value to the world at large, whose real wealth consists in the healthy diversities of its civilizations.

(5) Lastly the land itself needs redemption. Much of it is left desolate . . ."[10]

Commenting on the presentation of the Zionist case at the Peace Conference in Paris, Colonel Bonsal observes in his diary:

> "If the views of the advanced Zionists prevail there is trouble ahead. Many, very many, intelligent and informed Jews admit this. It is conceded that the present inhabitants of Palestine have occupied their lands for centuries; indeed, some of the Syrian communities claim descent from the Hittites who were in possession at the dawn of history. Be that as it may, all who know the situation from actual contact and not from propaganda leaflets admit that these people have dwelt in their present homes for two thousand years, that the occupancy of the Jews does not go back to immemorial times, and that their sojourn before the Dispersion was brief. Why should these 'old settlers' be expelled, they ask, to make room for newcomers . . . ?"[11]

The Zionist claim of an historic title to Palestine has no basis in law, or in fact.

The modes of acquiring territory are well defined under international law and the claim of an historic title is not one of them.

The term "historic right" or "historic title" is used in international law in the sense of title to maritime territory that has been perfected by adverse possession, as in the case of historic bays or historic waters.[12] The term "historic title" has no connection whatsoever with a claim to recover a territory from the hands of another people on the ground of its former occupation by the claimants some time in distant history. It does not seem that international law would countenance a concept which, instead of ensuring peace, order and stability, would create the most dangerous and explosive situations. What upheavals would occur in the world if the clock of history were to be set back and present territorial situations were to be rectified and restored to what they were some ten or twenty or thirty centuries ago?

It is evident that an ancient historical connection gives no title, no rights, no claim to territory. Much less does it displace the title or justify the dispossession of the original inhabitants of the country. The Palestinians are the original

---

10 *Ibid.*, p. 46. Since we are concerned only with legal considerations, no attempt will be made here to refute the erroneous and extra-legal allegations made in the Zionist memorandum.

11 Stephen Bonsal, *Suitors and Suppliants at Versailles*, p. 45, Prentice-Hall, New York, 1946.

12 D. P. O'Connell, *International Law*, Vol. I, pp. 485–486, Stevens and Oceana, 1965.

and continuous inhabitants of Palestine from time immemorial. They survived
the transient Israelite occupation in biblical times and many other invasions.
Unlike the Israelites, their title does not rest on conquest, invasion or a transient
historical connection that ceased more than twenty centuries ago. The King-
Crane Commission, appointed in 1919 at the suggestion of President Wilson,
summed up the legal position by declaring that "the initial claim, often submitted by Zionist representatives, that they have a 'right' to Palestine based on
an occupation of two thousand years ago, can hardly be seriously considered."[13]

The Zionist claim of an "historic title" to Palestine has also no basis in fact for
two reasons.

First, Palestine is not the historic home of the Jews. In 1920, when the question of the British mandate over Palestine was discussed by the House of Lords,
Lord Sydenham declared:

> "I sympathise entirely with the wishes of the Jews to have a National Home, but
> I say that this National Home must not be given if it cannot be given without
> entailing gross injustice upon other people. Palestine is not the original home of
> the Jews. It was acquired by them after a ruthless conquest, and they have never
> occupied the whole of it, which they now openly demand. They have no more
> valid claim to Palestine than the descendants of the ancient Romans have to this
> country. The Romans occupied Britain as long as the Israelites occupied Pales-
> tine, and they left behind them in this country far more valuable and useful work.
>
> If we are going to admit claims based on conquest thousands of years ago, the
> whole world will have to be turned upside down . . . The only real claim to
> Palestine surely is that of the present inhabitants, some of whom descend from
> the pre-Jewish conquest population, and others from Israelites converted to
> Islam."[14]

Secondly, the Jews of the 20th century are mostly converts to Judaism and
have no racial link with the Israelites or Hebrews who lived in Palestine at or
before the time of Christ. The Israelis of today are not descendants of the
Israelites. Jewish historians confirm this fact. It is sufficient to cite one Jewish
source. Joseph Reinach, a French politician of Jewish origin, explains that the
Jews of today do not belong to a race and that very few of them have any
connection with Palestine. He writes:

> "The Jews of Palestinian origin constitute an insignificant minority. Like
> Christians and Moslems, the Jews have engaged with great zeal in the conversion
> of people to their faith. Before the Christian era, the Jews had converted to the
> monotheistic religion of Moses other Semites (or Arabs), Greeks, Egyptians and
> Romans, in large numbers. Later, Jewish proselytism was not less active in Asia,
> in the whole of North Africa, in Italy, in Spain and in Gaul. Converted Romans
> and Gauls no doubt predominated in the Jewish communities mentioned in the
> chronicles of Grégoire de Tours. There were many converted Iberians among the

---

13 J. C. Hurewitz, *op. cit.*, p. 70.
14 *Hansard's Reports*, House of Lords, p. 121, 21 June 1922.

Jews who were expelled from Spain by Ferdinand the Catholic and who spread to Italy, France, the East and Smyrna. The great majority of Russian, Polish and Galician Jews descend from the Khazars, a Tartar people of Southern Russia who were converted in a body to Judaism at the time of Charlemagne. To speak of a Jewish race, one must be either ignorant or of bad faith. There was a Semitic or Arab race; but there never was a Jewish race."[15]

The spiritual yearning of the Jews for Palestine and their religious belief have been the subject of political exploitation by the Zionists, even against the will and, in some cases, the concrete opposition of Orthodox Jewry. But, in any event, neither spiritual yearning nor religious belief can create rights, nor serve as a basis for taking away a territory from its inhabitants. Lord Sydenham has observed:

"We may well sympathise with the aspirations of a religion which invested with divine sanctions a return to the little region that the Jews had temporarily ruled. But it is quite impossible to admit any rights over the Holy Land to Zionists of the nineteenth and twentieth centuries who in most cases do not descend from Jews who ever saw Jerusalem."[16]

The Hebrew or Israelite occupation of Palestine was a biblical episode which came to an end centuries ago, as was the case with other invasions. It is evident that the Zionist claim to an "historical right" to Palestine was based on false historical premises and lacked any juridical basis. It was a pseudo-legal disguise designed to give a colour of right to the Zionist plan to usurp the land of Palestine from its original inhabitants. J. P. Alem has observed: "The concept of historical rights claimed by the Zionists has served the purpose for which it was conceived and is nowadays quite worn out."[17]

---

15 Translation from *Journal des Débats*, 30 March 1919, cited by Philippe de Saint Robert in *Le Jeu de la France en Mediterranée*, p. 222, Julliard, 1970.
16 Lord Sydenham of Combe, "The Tragedy of Palestine", *The Nineteenth Century and After*, May 1930, pp. 596–597.
17 Translation from J. P. Alem, *Juifs et Arabes*, p. 35, Grasset, Paris, 1968.

Section 2
The Balfour Declaration

The Balfour Declaration has been relied upon by the Zionists as if it were a document of title to Palestine. Before assessing the legal value of the document, let us first examine the circumstances in which it was made and ascertain its meaning.

On 2 November 1917, Arthur James Balfour, British Foreign Minister, addressed the following written communication to Lord Rothschild:

> "I have much pleasure in conveying to you, on behalf of His Majesty's Government, the following declaration of sympathy with Jewish Zionist aspirations which has been submitted to and approved by the Cabinet.
>
> His Majesty's Government view with favour the establishment in Palestine of a national home for the Jewish people, and will use their best endeavours to facilitate the achievement of this object, it being clearly understood that nothing shall be done which may prejudice the civil and religious rights of existing non-Jewish communities in Palestine, or the rights and political status enjoyed by Jews in any other country.
>
> I should be grateful if you would bring this declaration to the knowledge of the Zionist Federation."

This communication, which came to be known as the Balfour Declaration, created one of the most explosive problems of our times – a problem which has convulsed the Middle East for more than fifty years, and which even today has not ceased to shake the region to its very foundations. This Declaration is at the root of the Palestine tragedy and of the Arab-Israeli conflict.

The Balfour Declaration represented the culmination of Zionist efforts to secure British support for the Zionist plan to colonize Palestine and to establish there a Jewish State. The plan was originally launched by Theodor Herzl in 1896 and was adopted by the first Zionist Congress, at Basle in 1897. Zionists seized the occasion of the First World War to gain British support for the realization of their ambition by offering, in return, Jewish support for Allied war aims.

A draft declaration was prepared by the Zionists and submitted to the British Cabinet for its approval. The Zionist draft envisaged a recognition by the British Government of the whole of Palestine as "the national home of the Jewish people", and embodied no safeguard of the rights of the existing population. The concept of a Jewish national home was opposed by many British Jews who, though sympathetic to a spiritual home in Jerusalem, rejected the creation of a Jewish political entity in Palestine or the grant to the Jews of any "special rights" over the other communities existing in the country. Their opposition failed to defeat the Zionist plan, but it did succeed in reducing its scope in two respects: first, instead of recognizing Palestine as "the national home for the Jewish people", the declaration would view with favour the establishment in Palestine of such a home; secondly, a safeguard was added to provide that "nothing shall be done which may prejudice the civil and religious rights of existing non-Jewish communities in Palestine, or the rights and political status enjoyed by Jews in any other country."

The fact that the "existing non-Jewish communities in Palestine" represented, at the time, 92 per cent of the total population did not discourage the British Government from giving its support to Zionist aspirations. Nor was the British Government deterred by the fact that it had given earlier assurances and pledges to the Arabs regarding their independence after the war.

It has been said that the extent of the services of Jewry to the Allied war effort during the First World War cannot be estimated, and must always remain a matter of opinion.[18] Such uncertainty, however, does not prevail regarding the Arab contribution to the victory of the Allies during the First World War. At a secret meeting of the Supreme Council of the Allied Powers at Paris on 20 March 1919, General Allenby, Commander-in-Chief of the Expeditionary Force which wrested Palestine, Syria, and Lebanon from Ottoman control, declared that Arab help had been "invaluable".[19] At the same meeting, Lloyd George said that "on the basis of McMahon's letter to King Hussein, the latter had put all his resources into the field, which had helped us most materially to win the victory."[20]

Having obtained the British Government's declaration of sympathy with Zionist aims, the next objective of the Zionists was to secure its implementation by Great Britain. This they succeeded in doing. The mandate which the League of Nations entrusted to Great Britain in 1922 to administer Palestine provided that the Mandatory should be responsible for putting into effect the Declaration made on 2 November 1917 in favour of the establishment in Palestine of a national home for the "Jewish people".

---

18 H. W. V. Temperley, *History of the Peace Conference of Paris*, Vol. VI, p. 174, Hodder and Stoughton, 1924.
19 J. C. Hurewitz, *Diplomacy in the Near and Middle East*, Vol. II, p. 54, Van Nostrand, 1956.
20 *Ibid.*, p. 54.

It should be mentioned that the English House of Lords opposed the incorporation of the Balfour Declaration in the Palestine mandate. In a debate in the House of Lords on 21 June 1922, on a motion declaring the mandate to be unacceptable in its present form, Lord Islington said that it directly violated the pledges made by His Majesty's Government to the people of Palestine. Moreover, its provisions concerning the establishment of a Jewish national home were inconsistent with Article 22 of the Covenant of the League of Nations, which had laid down the fundamental principles of the mandatory system.[21]

Lord Islington continued:

> "The mandate imposes on Great Britain the responsibility of trusteeship for a Zionist political predominance where 90 per cent of the population are non-Zionist and non-Jewish ... In fact, very many orthodox Jews, not only in Palestine but all over the world, view with the deepest misapprehension, not to say dislike, this principle of a Zionist Home in Palestine ... The scheme of a Zionist Home sought to make Zionist political predominance effective in Palestine by importing into the country extraneous and alien Jews from other parts of the world ... This scheme of importing an alien race into the midst of a native local race is flying in the very face of the whole of the tendencies of the age. It is an unnatural experiment ... It is literally inviting subsequent catastrophe ..."[22]

Answering this criticism, the author of the Declaration, Lord Balfour, said: "Zionism may fail ... this is an adventure ... Are we never to have adventures? Are we never to try new experiments?" He then declared: "I do not think I need dwell upon this imaginary wrong which the Jewish Home is going to inflict upon the local Arabs."[23] Lord Sydenham replied that the Zionist experiment would fail,

> "but the harm done by dumping down an alien population upon an Arab country – Arab all round in the hinterland – may never be remedied ... What we have done is, by concessions, not to the Jewish people but to a Zionist extreme section, to start a running sore in the East, and no one can tell how far that sore will extend."[24]

These prophetic words still ring true today.

The motion was put to the vote and it was carried by 60 to 29.[25] This meant, in effect, the abrogation of the Balfour Declaration.

But in a subsequent debate in the House of Commons a motion asking that the mandate for Palestine should be submitted for the approval of Parliament was defeated.[26] The defeat of this motion enabled the British Government three weeks later to secure approval of the mandate by the Council of the League

---

21 *Hansard's Reports*, House of Lords, 21 June 1922, p. 997.
22 *Ibid.*, pp. 998–1004.
23 *Ibid.*, p. 1015.
24 *Ibid.*, p. 1025.
25 *Ibid.*, p. 1034.
26 *Hansard's Reports*, House of Commons, p. 342, 4 July 1922.

of Nations. Thus, in fact, the Balfour Declaration was never approved by the House of Commons, or by the House of Lords.[27]

What was the meaning of the expression "national home" in the Balfour Declaration? It is certainly vague, and it does not possess a clear, accepted meaning. But notwithstanding this vagueness, neither party to the Balfour Declaration, namely the Zionist Jews and the British Government, intended that it should convey any territorial rights to the Jews or result in their acquisition of sovereignty over Palestine. The Zionists, at least outwardly, emphatically denied that the Jewish national home envisaged the establishment of a Jewish State or the grant of sovereignty to the Jews. Writing in 1919, Sokolow, the Zionist historian, stated:

> "It has been said, and is still being obstinately repeated by anti-Zionists again and again, that Zionism aims at the creation of an independent 'Jewish State'. But this is wholly fallacious. The 'Jewish State' was never a part of the Zionist programme."[28]

Norman Bentwich, a Zionist Jew who held for several years the office of Attorney-General of Palestine during the British mandate, declared on a number of occasions that sovereignty was no part of the Jewish national home. He said:

> "State sovereignty is not essential to the Jewish national ideal. Freedom for the Jew to develop according to his own tradition, in his own environment, is the main, if not the whole demand."[29]

He also wrote:

> "It has often been made an objection to Zionist hopes that the Moslem Arabs now in possession of Palestine lands, already numbering more than a quarter of a million, cannot be ejected . . . But it is neither to be expected, nor is it desired, that the Jews should occupy and appropriate the whole country."[30]

Mr Bentwich defined the concept of the Jewish national home as not implying the grant of rights of political sovereignty, but as offering the opportunity for cultural development. He said:

> "The idea of a national home for a homeless people is now embodied in this single mandate [The Mandate for Palestine]. It signifies a territory in which a people, without receiving rights of political sovereignty, has, nevertheless, a recognized legal position and the opportunity of developing its moral, social and intellectual ideas."[31]

---

27 The official British documents relating to the Balfour Declaration and to British policy with respect to Palestine were recently compiled by Doreen Ingrams, *Palestine Papers 1917–1922, Seeds of Conflict*, John Murray, London, 1972.
28 Sokolow, *History of Zionism*, xxiv.
29 Norman Bentwich, *Palestine of the Jews*, p. 195, London, 1919.
30 *Ibid.*, pp. 206–207. It may be remarked in passing that his reference to the Moslem Arabs numbering "more than a quarter of a million" was a gross underestimate of the number of Moslem Arabs who inhabited Palestine at the time.
31 Norman Bentwich, *The Mandates System*, p. 24, Longman, London, 1930.

In 1934, Mr Bentwich distinguished between a national home and a state in the following terms:

> "A national home, as distinguished from a state, is a country where a people are acknowledged as having a recognized legal position and the opportunity of developing their cultural, social and intellectual ideals without receiving political sovereignty."[32]

Mr Bentwich thought that the Jews should integrate within Palestine with the Arab inhabitants:

> "The Jewish people on their side do not ask for political power or national sovereignty . . . They have no need or desire to rule over others. Ultimately, they would ask within the territory to form an integral part of the government of the land, together with the Arab inhabitants."[33]

Equally, the British Government as author of the Balfour Declaration did not intend to grant any political sovereignty to the Jews in Palestine. In its Statement of Policy of 1922, the British Government declared that the interpretation which His Majesty's Government placed upon the Declaration of 1917 "need not cause alarm to the Arab population of Palestine . . . His Majesty's Government have not contemplated . . . the disappearance or the subordination of the Arabic population . . . They would draw attention to the fact that the terms of the [Balfour] Declaration referred to do not contemplate that Palestine as a whole should be converted into a Jewish National Home, but that such a Home should be founded in Palestine."[34] This interpretation of the Jewish National Home was again confirmed in the Statement of Policy issued by the British Government in October 1930.[35] In the Statement of Policy of May 1939 the British Government dealt at length with the meaning it attributed to the Jewish national home:

> "The Royal Commission and previous Commissions of Enquiry have drawn attention to the ambiguity of certain expressions in the Mandate, such as the expression 'a national home for the Jewish people', and they have found in this ambiguity and the resulting uncertainty as to the objectives of policy a fundamental cause of unrest and hostility between Arabs and Jews . . .
>
> It has been urged that the expression 'a national home for the Jewish people' offered a prospect that Palestine might in due course become a Jewish State or Commonwealth. His Majesty's Government do not wish to contest the view, which was expressed by the Royal Commission, that the Zionist leaders at the time of the issue of the Balfour Declaration recognized that an ultimate Jewish State was not precluded by the terms of the Declaration. But, with the Royal Commission, His Majesty's Government believe that the framers of the Mandate in which the Balfour Declaration was embodied could not have intended that Palestine should be converted into a Jewish State against the will of the Arab

---

32 Norman Bentwich, *Palestine*, p. 101, E. Benn, London, 1934.
33 *Ibid.*, p. 288.   34 Cmd. 1700, p. 18.   35 Cmd. 3692.

population of the country. That Palestine was not to be converted into a Jewish State might be held to be implied in the passage from the Command Paper of 1922, which reads as follows:

'Unauthorized statements have been made to the effect that the purpose in view is to create a wholly Jewish Palestine. Phrases have been used such as that "Palestine is to become as Jewish as England is English." His Majesty's Government regard any such expectation as impracticable and have no such aim in view. Nor have they at any time contemplated . . . the disappearance or the subordination of the Arabic population, language or culture in Palestine. They would draw attention to the fact that the terms of the [Balfour] Declaration referred to do not contemplate that Palestine as a whole should be converted into a Jewish National Home, but that such a Home should be founded in Palestine.'

But this statement has not removed doubts, and His Majesty's Government therefore now declare unequivocally that it is not part of their policy that Palestine should become a Jewish State. They would indeed regard it as contrary to their obligations to the Arabs under the Mandate, as well as to the assurances which have been given to the Arab people in the past, that the Arab population of Palestine should be made the subjects of a Jewish State against their will."[36]

In 1922, Winston Churchill said in the House of Commons, with reference to the Balfour Declaration:

"At the same time that this pledge was made to the Zionists, an equally important promise was made to the Arab inhabitants in Palestine – that their civil and religious rights would be effectively safeguarded, and that they should not be turned out to make room for the newcomers."[37]

Herbert Samuel, who was himself a leading Zionist and the first to tackle the British Cabinet in favour of Zionism, interpreted the Balfour Declaration as not involving the creation of a Jewish State. He stated:

"The Jewish State has been the aspiration of the Jewish people for centuries. It is an aspiration which at the present day cannot be realized. It is not contained in the Balfour Declaration . . . There was no promise of a Jewish State. What was promised was that the British Government would favour the creation of a Jewish National Home – the term was most carefully chosen – in Palestine. The Declaration did not say that Palestine should be the Jewish National Home, but that it favoured a Jewish National Home in Palestine, without prejudice to the civil and religious rights of the Arab population."[38]

If one is to accept all these interpretations, it appears that the intention behind the Balfour Declaration was not to create a Jewish State in Palestine, but to establish something less, a "national home", whatever may be its precise meaning. However, even the establishment of such a national home was to be subject

---

36 Cmd. 6019, pp. 3 and 4.
37 *Hansard's Reports, op. cit.,* p. 333.
38 From Viscount Samuel's speech in the Palestine Debate in the House of Lords, 23 April 1947, p. 96, cited by J. L. Magnes, *Palestine – Divided or United,* Jerusalem, 1947.

to a safeguard in favour of the original inhabitants, namely, "that nothing shall be done which may prejudice the civil and religious rights of existing non-Jewish communities." Professor W. T. Mallison, Jr., pointing out that this safeguard was inserted by the British Cabinet despite the express objections of the Zionist negotiators, has explained its meaning as follows:

> "The most reasonable interpretation is that the clause protected the rights which were possessed and exercised by the Palestinians when Palestine was part of the Ottoman Empire. In addition to freedom of religion, such rights included a measure of political autonomy, the rights to livelihood, to own land, and to have an individual home as well as to maintain the integrity of the Palestinian community as a political entity."[39]

But even though the Balfour Declaration may be viewed as having envisioned something less than a Jewish State, its support for Jewish Zionist aspirations in Palestine was nonetheless an illegal interference with, and a trespass upon, the natural rights of the Palestinians in their homeland.

Moreover, whatever its true interpretation, the Balfour Declaration conflicted with several assurances and pledges given by the British Government to the Arabs in general, and to the Palestinians in particular, both before and after its date, concerning their independence from Turkey at the end of the war. These assurances and pledges were contained in the McMahon-Hussein Correspondence of 1915–1918, the Hogarth Message of January 1918, the Declaration to the Seven of June 1916, the Anglo-French Declaration of November 1918, and in General Allenby's assurances to the inhabitants of Palestine, Syria and Lebanon that "the Allies were in honour bound to endeavour to reach a settlement in accordance with the wishes of the peoples concerned."[40]

At the Anglo-Arab Conference of London in 1939, the Committee set up to consider the McMahon-Hussein Correspondence (1915–1916) came to the conclusion that it was evident from the statements made during and after the war that "His Majesty's Government were not free to dispose of Palestine without regard for the wishes and interests of the inhabitants of Palestine, and that these statements must all be taken into account in any attempt to estimate the responsibilities which – upon any interpretation of the Correspondence – His Majesty's Government have incurred towards those inhabitants as a result of the Correspondence."[41]

Let us now examine the validity of the Balfour Declaration.

Some have argued that the Balfour Declaration was invalid by reason of its

---

39 W. T. Mallison, Jr., "The Balfour Declaration: An Appraisal in International Law", an essay which appears in *The Transformation of Palestine*, edited by Ibrahim Abu-Lughod, p. 92, Northwestern University Press, Evanston, 1971.

40 As to the text of the British assurances and pledges given to the Arabs during the First World War, see Antonius, *The Arab Awakening*, Hamish Hamilton, London, 1938; J. C. Hurewitz, *op. cit.*, pp. 28–30; Report on correspondence between Sir Henry McMahon and Shariff of Mecca, Cmd. 5974, 16 March 1939.

41 Report of the Committee, Cmd. 5974, p. 11, 16 March 1939.

conflict with the assurances and pledges given by the British Government to the Arabs and the Palestinians. Although the Balfour Declaration might well be void by reason of its conflict with these assurances and pledges, yet, in the writer's view, its nullity depends much more upon intrinsic reasons arising from the nature of the Declaration itself and from the incapacity of its maker to make it. In other words, the Balfour Declaration is void and invalid *per se*, without the need of extraneous considerations.

Regardless of its real meaning, regardless of the real or apparent safeguard which it stipulated in favour of the inhabitants of Palestine – a safeguard which, in any event, was completely disregarded – and regardless also of its incompatibility with pledges made to the Arabs, the Balfour Declaration is legally null and void for either one of the two following reasons.

First, the British Government, as author of the Balfour Declaration, possessed no sovereignty or dominion in Palestine enabling it to make a valid promise of any rights, whatever their nature and extent, in favour of the Jews of the world. It is immaterial whether these rights were meant to be territorial, political or cultural. On the date that the Balfour Declaration was made, Palestine formed part of Turkey, and neither its territory nor its people were under the jurisdiction of the British Government. The Declaration was void on the basis of the principle that a donor cannot give away what does not belong to him. The Balfour Declaration has been described as a document in which "one nation solemnly promised to a second nation the country of a third."[42] Another writer has remarked:

> "The most significant and incontrovertible fact is, however, that by itself the [Balfour] Declaration was legally impotent. For Great Britain had no sovereign rights over Palestine; it had no proprietary interest; it had no authority to dispose of the land. The Declaration was merely a statement of British intentions and no more."[43]

Jules Basdevant, formerly President of the International Court of Justice, has observed:

> "No State has the right to extend at will its own competence at the expense of other States and other peoples. International law does not recognize the British State as having competence other than over its own territories and over its own subjects and nationals."[44]

Secondly, the Balfour Declaration is also void on the ground that it violated the natural and legitimate rights of the people of Palestine. It was immaterial whether the Balfour Declaration sought to impose the establishment in Palestine

---

42 Arthur Koestler, *Promise and Fulfilment*, p. 4, Macmillan, New York.
43 Sol M. Linowitz, "Analysis of a Tinderbox: The Legal Basis for the State of Israel", *American Bar Association Journal*, Vol. 43, pp. 522–523, 1957.
44 Cited in *The Palestine Question*, Seminar of Arab Jurists in Palestine, p. 69, Institute for Palestine Studies, Beirut, 1968.

of a Jewish State or simply of a national home for alien Jews; it was in either case invalid and could in no way affect or impair the rights of the Palestinians.

But the author of the Declaration was not concerned with the wishes or the feelings or the rights of the original inhabitants of Palestine. Arthur Balfour wrote in a memorandum to the British Government dated 11 August 1919:

> "In Palestine we do not propose even to go through the form of consulting the wishes of the present inhabitants of the country . . . The four great Powers are committed to Zionism. And Zionism, be it right or wrong, good or bad, is rooted in agelong traditions, in present needs, in future hopes, of far profounder import than the desires and prejudices of the 700,000 Arabs who now inhabit that ancient land."[45]

The Palestinians, both Moslem and Christian, and all the Arabs rejected the Balfour Declaration. But what may be little known is that the Palestinian Jews also rejected and opposed the concept of the establishment of a Jewish national home in Palestine. Ronald Storrs, the first British Military Governor of Jerusalem, wrote: "The religious Jews of Jerusalem and Hebron and the *Sephardim* were strongly opposed to political Zionism . . ."[46] The opposition of the Palestine Jews to the creation of a Jewish national home in Palestine shows that this was a foreign concept, extrinsic to Palestine and alien to the Jewish community living there. Such a concept could not be construed as a recognition of a right of self-determination in favour of the Jewish community then living in Palestine.

In a debate in the House of Lords on 21 June 1922, Lord Islington declared:

> "The Jewish people in Palestine have lived in the past in harmony with the Arab community. They have enjoyed in large measure the same privileges as their Ottoman fellow subjects and, I venture to say also as a fact, they never agitated for Zionism. I do not think – I speak subject to correction – that there has ever been a demand from the Jewish community in Palestine for the introduction of a Zionist Home in that country. The whole agitation has come from outside, from Jews in other parts of the world. I go further, and say – I think I have said it before; if so, I repeat – that a very large number of the Jewish community in Palestine today look with considerable aversion not only upon the Zionist Home but upon the Jews who are being introduced into the country from Eastern Europe."[47]

Opposition to the Balfour Declaration and to the Zionist programme was not confined to the Orthodox Jews of Palestine. Rabbi Elmer Berger has pointed out that Zionism was not only an aggression against the indigenous Palestinians, but it constituted an aggression against all Jewish nationals of other countries who did not wish to have thrust upon them "a second set of national rights

---

45 *Documents on British Foreign Policy 1919–1939*, 1st series, Vol. IV, HMSO.
46 Ronald Storrs, *Orientations*, p. 340, Nicholson and Watson, London, 1945.
47 *Hansard's Reports*, p. 1002.

and obligations in and to a territory already inhabited by a majority of people who were not Jews."[48]

It is remarkable that despite general Arab opposition to the Balfour Declaration, expressed by the General Syrian Congress at Damascus on 2 July 1919,[49] and by riots and disturbances in Palestine, an attempt was made to validate the Declaration by seeking to secure its approval *ex post facto* by the former territorial sovereign in Palestine. Article 95 of the Treaty of Sèvres, which was concluded between Turkey and the Allied Powers on 10 August 1920, provided that the administration of Palestine would be entrusted to a Mandatory who would be responsible for putting into effect the Declaration made on 2 November 1917 by the British Government in favour of the establishment in Palestine of a national home for the "Jewish people". The Treaty of Sèvres, however, was not ratified by the Turkish National Assembly, which rejected some of its provisions, including its reference to the Balfour Declaration. Three years later the Allied Powers concluded with Turkey the Treaty of Lausanne of 24 July 1923. Unlike the abortive Treaty of Sèvres, the new treaty omitted any reference to the Balfour Declaration or to its acceptance by Turkey.[50] This fact is significant because by excluding any reference in the Treaty of Lausanne to the Balfour Declaration, Turkey, as the previous sovereign over Palestine, did not, upon renunciation of its sovereignty, mortgage the future of Palestine with any obligation relating to the establishment of a Jewish national home. Thus, the attempt made in the Treaty of Sèvres to validate the Balfour Declaration by securing its acceptance by the previous territorial sovereign failed.

Such an attempt would, in any event, have been futile and ineffectual for the reason that, at the date of the Treaty of Sèvres, Turkey no longer possessed any sovereignty over Palestine. The communities living in Palestine and in other territories detached from Turkey at the end of the war had already been recognized by Article 22 of the Covenant of the League of Nations of 28 June 1919 "as independent nations".

There remains to examine an argument which has been advanced to the effect that even though the Balfour Declaration initially lacked juridical value, it was validated by its inclusion in the mandate for Palestine. Shabtai Rosenne, an

---

48 *A Just Peace in the Middle East*, p. 49, American Enterprise Institute for Public Policy Research, Washington, D.C., 1971.

49 J. C. Hurewitz, *op. cit.*, p. 59.

50 It is to be noted that although the draft text of the treaty presented to Turkey by the Allied Powers at Lausanne omitted any express reference to the Balfour Declaration, it did seek in Article 16 to secure Turkey's acceptance of "the arrangements which have been, or shall be, made regarding the attribution, independence or other régime of the territories and islands" detached from it: for the text of the treaty as originally proposed to Turkey, see *Documents Diplomatiques, Conférence de Lausanne*, Vol. II, p. 33, published by the French Ministry of Foreign Affairs in 1923. This provision could have been construed as containing an implied acceptance by Turkey of the Balfour Declaration. But Turkey rejected this provision, and the final text of Article 16 of the Treaty of Lausanne left the future of the territories detached from Turkey to be decided by "the parties concerned": see Section 2 of Chapter IV, *post*.

Israeli spokesman at the UN, said with reference to the Balfour Declaration: "Its precise legal status at the time it was made may be open to discussion but that problem is secondary in view of the fact that the Council of the League of Nations incorporated its text into the Preamble to the Mandate for Palestine."[51] The argument of an *ex post facto* validation of the Balfour Declaration by the British mandate has no legal basis. If, as is clear, Great Britain possessed no sovereignty over Palestine and no power to make the Declaration, then such a Declaration was a nullity, and the position is no better if other Powers, such as France, Italy and the USA, or any number of Powers which also possessed no sovereignty over Palestine, joined in approving the Declaration. Such approval would be a nullity and would have no validating effect. An accumulation of nullities cannot generate a valid juridical act. Rosenne argues that: "Ottoman sovereignty over the territory of Palestine, as over many other of its territories, was ceded to the Allied Powers in the Peace Treaty."[52] This statement is completely erroneous: sovereignty over Palestine was not ceded by Turkey to the Allied Powers, either under the abortive Treaty of Sèvres or under the Treaty of Lausanne, because, as already mentioned, it had no sovereignty left that it could cede.

Therefore, the inclusion of the Balfour Declaration in an international instrument, such as the mandate, did not and could not cure its invalidity. There is nothing sacrosanct about a so-called international instrument: it cannot make valid and legal what is inherently invalid and illegal. In fact, the inclusion of the Balfour Declaration in the mandate, instead of validating it, had the effect of invalidating the mandate itself, as will be explained in the next chapter.

Therefore, whether or not included in the text of the Palestine mandate, the Balfour Declaration cannot be considered to have embodied a valid grant to Zionist Jewry of any rights in Palestine. This Declaration was nothing but an illegal and mischievous promise which has brought the most disastrous consequences to Palestine and the Middle East.

---

51 *The Middle East Crisis*, edited by J. W. Halderman, p. 48, Oceana, 1969. A similar approach is made by Nathan Feinberg, *On An Arab Jurist's Approach to Zionism and the State of Israel*, pp. 22–25, Magnes Press, Jerusalem, 1971.
52 *Ibid.*, p. 48.

CHAPTER II

THE INVALIDITY OF THE MANDATE OVER PALESTINE

Section 1
Objectives
of the mandate

The concept of international mandates was inspired by the principles, propounded by President Wilson and leaders of the Russian revolution, that war settlements at the end of the First World War should not involve any annexations but should be based upon the principle of self-determination of peoples.[1] The first concrete proposal of the concept was made by General Smuts as part of a project for a League of Nations which he published in December 1918 on the eve of the Peace Conference.[2] The concept of the mandate was accepted and its basic objectives laid down in Article 22 of the Covenant of the League of Nations, which was adopted on 25 April 1919. Article 22 indicated the territories which would be subjected to mandates. These were: (a) territories detached from the Turkish Empire, (b) certain territories in central Africa, and (c) territories in South-West Africa and certain of the South Pacific Islands. The character of the mandate and the powers of the Mandatory would differ in each of these three classes of territories. The least onerous were the mandates to be granted in respect of territories detached from the Turkish Empire. As regards these territories, Article 22 (see Appendix I) provided:

> "Certain communities formerly belonging to the Turkish Empire have reached a stage of development where their existence as independent nations can be provisionally recognized subject to the rendering of administrative advice and assistance by a Mandatory until such time as they are able to stand alone. The wishes of these communities must be a principal consideration in the selection of the Mandatory."

---

1 *Le Système des Mandats, Société des Nations*, p. 14, Geneva, 1945; Stott, *Official Statements of War Aims and Peace Proposals*, pp. 188, 265 and 309, Washington, 1921; Messages of President Wilson of 8 January, 11 February and 6 April 1918.
2 General Smuts, *The League of Nations*, London, 1918.

Article 22, however, did not designate the mandatory Powers. This was done later by the Supreme Council of the Allied Powers.

Palestine, as one of the territories detached from the Turkish Empire, was one of the countries whose independence was thus provisionally recognized "subject to the rendering of administrative advice and assistance by a Mandatory." On 25 April 1920 at San Remo the Supreme Council of the Allied Powers decided to allocate the mandate over Palestine to Great Britain. But the terms of the mandate were yet to be settled.

One of the most extraordinary aspects of the Palestine mandate is that its terms were proposed by a foreign body which harboured political ambitions in respect of the country concerned. In its memorandum dated 3 February 1919, submitted by the World Zionist Organization to the Peace Conference at Paris, this body outlined its wishes and *desiderata* with respect to the future of Palestine. It is important to note that "many of the suggestions of the memorandum found their way, after revision, into a draft mandate for Palestine formulated by the Zionist Organization and circulated at the end of March 1919 . . . and, after further revision, into the mandatory instrument approved by the Council of the League of Nations."[3] Temperley mentions that the terms of the mandate over Palestine were settled by the British Government "in consultation with Zionist representatives."[4] In contrast, the parties most concerned, the Arabs of Palestine, were not even consulted. On 24 July 1922, the Palestine mandate was approved by the Council of the League of Nations substantially in the terms proposed by the Zionist Organization. The text of the Palestine mandate appears in Appendix II.

Under its terms, the mandate had two principal objectives.

The first objective was to give effect to Article 22 of the Covenant. The first recital in its preamble stated:

> "Whereas the Principal Allied Powers have agreed, for the purpose of giving effect to the provisions of Article 22 of the Covenant of the League of Nations, to entrust to a Mandatory selected by the said Powers the administration of the territory of Palestine . . ."

In fulfilment of this objective Article 2 of the mandate provided:

> "The Mandatory shall be responsible for . . . the development of self-governing institutions . . ."

The second objective was to put into effect the Balfour Declaration, and facilitate Jewish immigration. The second recital in the preamble stated:

---

3 J. C. Hurewitz, *Diplomacy in the Near and Middle East*, Vol. II, p. 45, Van Nostrand, New York, 1956.

4 H. W. V. Temperley, *History of the Peace Conference of Paris*, Vol. VI, p. 174, Hodder and Stoughton, 1924. See also John Marlowe, *The Seat of Pilate*, pp. 60–62, Cresset Press, London, 1959.

"Whereas the Principal Allied Powers have also agreed that the Mandatory should be responsible for putting into effect the declaration originally made on 2 November 1917, by the Government of His Britannic Majesty, and adopted by the said Powers, in favour of the establishment in Palestine of a national home for the Jewish people, it being clearly understood that nothing should be done which might prejudice the civil and religious rights of existing non-Jewish communities in Palestine, or the rights and political status enjoyed by Jews in any other country; and

Whereas recognition has thereby been given to the historical connexion of the Jewish people with Palestine and to the grounds for reconstituting their national home in that country . . ."

In fulfilment of this objective Article 2 provided:

"The Mandatory shall be responsible for placing the country under such political, administrative and economic conditions as will secure the establishment of the Jewish national home, as laid down in the preamble . . ."

Furthermore, Article 6 provided as follows:

"The Administration of Palestine, while ensuring that the rights and position of other sections of the population are not prejudiced, shall facilitate Jewish immigration under suitable conditions . . ."

The Palestinian Arabs rejected the mandate and took the position that it could not impair or prejudice their rights as the original inhabitants of Palestine. From this attitude they never departed throughout the whole period of the mandate. They never conceded its validity and they followed a policy of non-co-operation with the Mandatory. In fact, the history of the mandate is the history of the struggle of the Palestinians against the Balfour Declaration, Jewish immigration and the establishment of a Jewish national home in Palestine. But the struggle was between a pygmy and a giant.

Armed with the mandate, using the might of the British Empire and seconded by the forces of Zionism, the British Government implemented the Balfour Declaration in Palestine against the will and despite the opposition of its original inhabitants. Their opposition took the form of demonstrations, disturbances and an armed rebellion.[5] But the protests of the Palestinians were put down by force[6] or calmed down by promises and soothing assurances.

The mischief of the mandate was aggravated by the manner of its implementation.

---

5 Major riots and disturbances occurred in 1920, 1921, 1929, 1933 and almost continuously from 1936 until 1939, when they assumed the proportions of a rebellion.
6 The King-Crane Commission, appointed at President Wilson's suggestion in 1919 to ascertain the wishes of the Arab populations in Syria and Palestine with respect to their future government, had reported the strong feelings which existed among the local population against the Balfour Declaration, and predicted that the Zionist programme could not be carried out except by force: see Hurewitz, *op. cit.*, p. 66, and Harry N. Howard, *The King-Crane Commission*, Khayats, Beirut, 1963.

For, first, the Mandatory ignored even the tenuous safeguards laid down in favour of the original inhabitants of Palestine both in the Balfour Declaration and in the mandate itself. The Balfour Declaration had declared that "nothing should be done which might prejudice the civil and religious rights of existing non-Jewish communities in Palestine." The mandate had provided that in facilitating Jewish immigration into Palestine, the Administration should ensure that "the rights and position of other sections of the population are not prejudiced" (Article 6). The mandate was implemented without any regard to those safeguards. The prejudice caused to the Palestinians by the implementation of the Balfour Declaration and by Jewish immigration during the mandate is not only immeasurable, but is still continuing today with unforeseeable consequences.

And secondly, although under Article 2 of the mandate the Mandatory was responsible for developing self-governing institutions, there was no trace of any such institutions at any time during the mandate. Palestine was governed and administered from beginning to end directly by the British Government as if it were a colonial possession. A half-hearted attempt was made by the British Government in 1922 to grant some semblance of autonomy to the people of Palestine in the form of a Legislative Council. This attempt, however, failed because of Arab opposition to the proposed measure on the grounds that it did not recognize majority rule, and because of Jewish opposition to the grant of self-government to Palestine in any form so long as they were a minority.

Only in 1939 did the British Government finally remember that it had been charged "to secure the development of self-governing institutions" in Palestine and that it was "contrary to the whole spirit of the mandate system that the population of Palestine should remain for ever under Mandatory tutelage." It therefore announced in a White Paper[7] that Palestine would be granted its independence within ten years. At the same time the British Government recognized that the continuation of Jewish immigration into Palestine caused serious prejudice to "the rights and position" of the Palestinians which it was its duty under the terms of the mandate to safeguard. Consequently, it also announced the limitation of Jewish immigration into Palestine to 75,000 immigrants during the next five years. After this period, no Jewish immigration would be authorized except with Arab consent.

The Zionists fought this White Paper by a campaign of violence and terrorism. Their object was to intimidate the British Government and to force it to withdraw the limitation which it had imposed on Jewish immigration to Palestine.[8]

---

7 Cmd. 6019, May 1939.
8 For details about this campaign of violence, see *A Survey of Palestine*, Vol. I, pp. 56–57; The British Statement on Acts of Violence, Cmd. 6873, 1946; S. N. Fisher, *The Middle East*, p. 579, Routledge and Kegan Paul, 1960; G. Kirk, *The Middle East, 1945–1950*, pp. 209–213 and 218–223, Oxford University Press, London, 1954.

In 1947, the situation of the British Government became impossible. Unable to permit any further Jewish immigration into Palestine against the wishes of the majority of its inhabitants, plagued by Zionist demands for more and more immigrants, subjected to strong pressure by the US Government to increase Jewish immigration into Palestine despite the latter Government's having closed its own doors to Jewish immigrants, and harassed by the Zionist campaign of violence, the British Government decided to refer to the UN the question of the future government of Palestine.

When this question came up for discussion at the UN in 1947, the Arab States raised the issue of the invalidity of the mandate. They asked that the issue be referred by the General Assembly to the International Court of Justice for an advisory opinion. Sub-Committee 2 to the *Ad Hoc* Committee on the Palestine Question recommended that this legal issue, together with other issues, be referred to the International Court. The issue concerning the invalidity of the mandate was formulated as follows:

> "Whether the provisions of the Mandate for Palestine regarding the establishment of a Jewish National Home in Palestine are in conformity or consistent with the objectives and provisions of the Covenant of the League of Nations (in particular Article 22), or are compatible with the provisions of the Mandate relating to the development of self-government and the preservation of the rights and position of the Arabs of Palestine."[9]

However, the recommendation of Sub-Committee 2 was defeated in the General Assembly, where it failed to obtain the required majority.[10] As to the reasons for the negative attitude of the General Assembly of the UN in 1947 regarding the equities and legalities involved in the Palestine Question, these will appear clearly from the discussion in the following chapter.

---

9 Official Records of the 2nd Session of the General Assembly, *Ad Hoc* Committee on the Palestine Question, p. 300.
10 *Ibid.*, p. 203.

Section 2
Grounds of
invalidity of the mandate

The Palestine mandate was invalid on three grounds set out hereinafter.

1. The first ground of invalidity of the mandate is that by endorsing the Balfour Declaration and accepting the concept of the establishment of a Jewish national home in Palestine it violated the sovereignty of the people of Palestine and their natural rights of independence and self-determination.[11] Palestine was the national home of the Palestinians from time immemorial. The establishment of a national home for an alien people in that country was a violation of the legitimate and fundamental rights of the inhabitants. The League of Nations did not possess the power, any more than the British Government did, to dispose of Palestine, or to grant to the Jews any political or territorial rights in that country. In so far as the mandate purported to recognize any rights for alien Jews in Palestine, it was null and void.

2. The second ground of invalidity of the mandate is that it violated, in spirit and in letter, Article 22 of the Covenant of the League of Nations, under the authority of which it purported to be made. The mandate violated Article 22 in three respects:

(a) The Covenant had envisaged the mandate as the best method of achieving its basic objective of ensuring the well-being and development of the peoples inhabiting the mandated territories. Article 22 stated in its first two paragraphs:

> "To those colonies and territories which as a consequence of the late war have ceased to be under the sovereignty of the States which formerly governed them and which are inhabited by peoples not yet able to stand by themselves under the

---

11 Professor B. Keith has observed that the adoption of the concept of a Jewish national home ran counter to the doctrine of the right of each people to self-determination: 'Mandates', *Journal of Comparative Legislation and International Law*, Vol. IV, p. 78, 1922.

strenuous conditions of the modern world, there should be applied the principle that the well-being and development of such peoples form a sacred trust of civilization and that securities for the performance of this trust should be embodied in this Covenant.

The best method of giving practical effect to this principle is that the tutelage of such peoples should be entrusted to advanced nations who by reason of their resources, their experience or their geographical position can best undertake this responsibility, and who are willing to accept it, and that this tutelage should be exercised by them as Mandatories on behalf of the League."

Was the Palestine mandate conceived for the well-being and development of the inhabitants of Palestine? The answer is found in the provisions of the mandate itself. The mandate sought the establishment in Palestine of a national home for another people, contrary to the rights and wishes of the Palestinians. It required the Mandatory to place the country under such political, administrative and economic conditions as would secure the establishment of a Jewish national home. It required the Mandatory to facilitate Jewish immigration into Palestine. It provided that a foreign body known as the Zionist Organization should be recognized as a public body for the purpose of advising and co-operating with the Administration of Palestine in matters affecting the establishment of the Jewish national home. It is clear that although the mandate system was conceived in the interest of the inhabitants of the mandated territory, the Palestine mandate was conceived in the interest of an alien people originating from outside Palestine, and ran counter to the basic concept of mandates. As Lord Islington observed when he opposed the inclusion of the Balfour Declaration in the Palestine mandate: "The Palestine mandate is a real distortion of the mandatory system."[12] The same distinguished Lord added:

"When one sees in Article 22 . . . that the well-being and development of such peoples should form a sacred trust of civilization, and when one takes that as the note of the mandatory system, I think your Lordships will see that we are straying down a very far path when we are postponing self-government in Palestine until such time as the population is flooded with an alien race."[13]

(b) The Palestine mandate also ran counter to the specific concept of mandates envisaged by Article 22 for countries detached from Turkey at the end of the First World War. In the case of those countries, the intention was to limit the mandate to the rendering of temporary advice and assistance. It is doubtful whether the people of Palestine, as also other Arab peoples detached from Turkey, were in need of administrative advice and assistance from a Mandatory. Their level of culture was not inferior to that existing at the time in many of the nations that were members of the League of Nations. Such Arab communities had actively participated with the Turks in the government of their

---

12 *Hansard's Reports*, House of Lords, 21 June 1922, p. 1000.
13 *Ibid.*, p. 1002.

country. Their political maturity and administrative experience were comparable to the political maturity and administrative experience of the Turks, who were left to stand alone.

Be that as it may, the framers of the Palestine mandate did not restrict the Mandatory's rôle to the rendering of administrative advice and assistance, but granted the Mandatory "full powers of legislation and administration" (Article 1). Such "full powers of legislation and administration" were not laid down in the interest of the inhabitants, but were intended to be used, and in fact were used, to establish by force the Jewish national home in Palestine. Clearly this was an abuse of the purpose of the mandate under the Covenant and a perversion of its *raison d'être*.

The whole concept of the Palestine mandate stands in marked contrast to the mandate for Syria and Lebanon which was given to France on 24 July 1922. This mandate conformed to Article 22 of the Covenant. It stated in its preamble:

> "Whereas the Principal Allied Powers have agreed that the territory of Syria and the Lebanon . . . shall be entrusted to a Mandatory charged with the duty of rendering administrative advice and assistance to the population, in accordance with the provisions of Article 22 (paragraph 4) of the Covenant of the League of Nations . . ."

Article 1 provided:

> "The Mandatory shall frame, within a period of three years from the coming into force of this mandate, an organic law for Syria and the Lebanon.
>
> This organic law shall be framed in agreement with the native authorities and shall take into account the rights, interests and wishes of all the population inhabiting the said territory . . ."

(c) The grant of the Palestine mandate to Great Britain also violated the Covenant in that it ignored the wishes of the inhabitants, contrary to the provision in Article 22 which required that the wishes of the communities concerned must be a principal consideration in the selection of the Mandatory. The wishes of the Arab communities in this regard were expressed in the resolution of the General Syrian Congress of 2 July 1919[14] and were emphasized by the King-Crane Commission in its Report dated 28 August 1919.[15] The wishes of the inhabitants were that no mandate was desired, but if any mandate were to be given, their first choice was the United States, while Great Britain came second.

3. The third ground of invalidity of the mandate lies in the fact that its endorsement and implementation of the Balfour Declaration conflicted with the assurances and pledges given to the Arabs during the First World War by Great

---

14 See the text of this resolution in J. C. Hurewitz, *op. cit.*, p. 62.
15 See J. C. Hurewitz, *op. cit.*, p. 66.

Britain and the Allied Powers.[16] The denial to the Palestine Arabs of their independence and the subjection of their country to the immigration of a foreign people were a breach of those pledges.

To the inceptive illegality of the Palestine mandate one must add the illegality of its implementation. The facilitation of Jewish immigration into Palestine by the Mandatory against the wishes and despite the opposition of the original inhabitants resulted in increasing the number of Jews in Palestine more than tenfold. This forcible and unnatural alteration of the demographic character of the country constituted an illegal colonization and a grave violation of the rights of the original inhabitants.

To summarize, the Palestine mandate was nothing but a travesty of the mandate system as conceived by the Covenant of the League of Nations.

Instead of serving the interests of the original inhabitants, it served the interests of an alien people and caused a grave wrong to the Palestinians. What is remarkable is that all this was done under the colour of achieving the lofty objectives of the Covenant and promoting the well-being and development of the people of Palestine. The illegitimacy and invalidity of the Palestine mandate are obvious.

The invalidity of the Palestine mandate carries two legal consequences. On the one hand, the mandate could not, at least in theory, impair or destroy the rights of the original inhabitants. In fact, its implementation gravely injured their rights and status. On the other hand, the mandate could not confer on the Jews who emigrated to Palestine during the period of the mandate national rights that conflicted with the fundamental rights of the original inhabitants. The Palestine mandate, however, was carried out and the damage consummated. Does this mean that at present the question of the invalidity of the mandate has become academic? The answer is that the question of the invalidity of the mandate cannot be viewed as a matter of mere historical or legal interest. The implementation of the mandate has created an irregular and abnormal situation which continues at this time and even constitutes the basis of the Arab-Israeli conflict. The invalidity of the mandate and its one-sided implementation in favour of the Jews are matters that would have to be taken into account in any eventual settlement of the conflict. To ignore these facts would mean that once an illegality is committed and consummated its wrongfulness ceases to be of interest. Such a result can hardly be accepted by legal theory or by international law.

---

16 As to these assurances and pledges, see Section 2 of Chapter I.

CHAPTER III

THE UN RESOLUTION FOR THE PARTITION OF PALESTINE

Section 1
Historical background

We have seen in the preceding chapter that when the British Government's plans for the future government of Palestine were defeated by the Zionist campaign of violence, it decided in 1947 to refer this question to the UN. The question of the future government of Palestine was the subject of discussion at two sessions of the General Assembly. The General Assembly appointed a Special Committee (UNSCOP) to consider the problem. On 3 September 1947, this Committee submitted to the General Assembly two plans, a majority and a minority plan.[1] The majority plan proposed the termination of the mandate and the partition of Palestine, the creation of an Arab State and a Jewish State with economic union between them, and a *corpus separatum* for the City of Jerusalem which would be subjected to a special international régime to be administered by the UN. The minority plan also envisaged the termination of the mandate, but proposed the establishment of a federal State that would comprise an Arab State and a Jewish State with Jerusalem as the capital.

In the debate which followed, the Arabs rejected the proposal for the partition of Palestine on the ground that it violated their rights and was incompatible with law and justice and with principles of democracy. Moreover, they questioned the competence or power of the UN to recommend the partition of their homeland into two States and thus to destroy its territorial integrity.

The Zionists mobilized all their forces in order to secure a UN vote in favour of partition. As a result of political pressures which will be explained later, the General Assembly adopted on 29 November 1947, by a vote of 33 to 13 with 10 abstentions, a resolution for the partition of Palestine basically on the lines suggested by the majority plan.[2]

---

1 UN Document A/364, 3 September 1947.
2 Resolution 181 (II), 29 November 1947. See Appendix III.

The adoption of the partition resolution touched off a wave of protests, demonstrations and disturbances in Palestine. The Arabs were determined to resist the dismemberment of their country. The Jews were equally determined to create a Jewish State in Palestine. The Palestine Commission appointed by the General Assembly to implement the partition plan was unable to exercise its functions.[3] The UN was powerless to prevent the explosion of the conflict which had been brewing since the adoption of the partition resolution. On 16 April a special session was convened "to consider further the question of the future government of Palestine." However, the session ended on 14 May 1948 with the appointment of a Mediator, but without any decision on the future government of Palestine. On the following day the mandate ended in complete chaos and confusion.

We shall now turn to consider the principles governing UN resolutions, and, in particular, the grounds of invalidity of the resolution for the partition of Palestine.

---

3 See its reports to the Security Council, S/663, S/695, S/676, and its report to the Genera
   Assembly, A/532.

Section 2
Principles governing
UN resolutions

Three questions arise in this regard. What are the principles that govern UN resolutions? Can the vote of UN members on a resolution be exercised in accordance with an unlimited discretion, or even in an arbitrary manner? What is the legal effect of resolutions of the General Assembly?

The answer to the first question is found in the Charter. The Charter lays down various principles, such as the respect for human rights, fundamental freedoms and self-determination of peoples. But particular emphasis is laid upon the principles of justice and international law. The Preamble of the Charter proclaims the determination of the UN "to establish conditions under which justice and respect for the obligations arising from treaties and other sources of international law can be maintained." This is followed by Article 1, which prescribes that the purposes of the UN are, *inter alia*, to bring about by peaceful means, and "in conformity with the principles of justice and international law", adjustment or settlement of international disputes or situations which might lead to a breach of the peace. It is significant that the Charter mentioned the principles of justice before international law as if it intended to give the principles of justice precedence over international law. The concept of justice is not an empty one, and should not be confused with international law. "If we may judge by the wording of Article 1, paragraph 1 of the Charter, the 'principles of justice' are something distinct from 'international law'."[4] Kelsen also points out that: "If justice is identical with international law, one of the two terms is superfluous."[5] All were agreed during the debates that preceded the adoption of the Charter at San Francisco in 1945 that "the concept of justice is a norm of fundamental importance."[6] At the first meeting of Commission I (UNCIO Doc. 1006, 1/6) its President declared during the discussion of the Preamble and Article 1

---

4   P. E. Corbett, *Law and Society in the Relations of States*, p. 268, Harcourt, New York, 1951.
5   Hans Kelsen, *The Law of the United Nations*, p. 18, Praeger, 1950.   6   *Ibid.*, p. 17.

of the Charter: "We feel the need to emphasize that our first object was to be strong to maintain peace, to maintain peace by our common effort and at all costs, at all costs with one exception – not at the cost of justice."[7]

The concept of justice is universal, and, unlike international law, is much less subject to divergence of opinion or interpretation. The concept of justice introduces into the international sphere a gauge of moral and ethical values which are not conspicuous in the field of international law in its strict sense. It follows that respect for, and observance of, the principles of justice constitute an essential condition of UN resolutions.

The answer to the second question is given in the first advisory opinion delivered by the International Court of Justice on 28 May 1948 at the request of the General Assembly. The question put to the Court by the General Assembly was intended to determine whether a member of the UN, voting on the admission of a new member under Article 4 of the Charter, was juridically entitled to make its consent to the admission dependent on conditions not expressly stipulated in this Article. A majority of the judges of the Court considered that in expressing their vote UN members enjoyed freedom of judgment. This freedom, however, should be exercised within the scope of the conditions prescribed by Article 4, these conditions being the only ones to be taken into consideration. On the other hand, the minority of the Court decided that the freedom of judgment in voting is not circumscribed by the conditions set forth in Article 4, but may be exercised within the general purposes and principles of the Charter. But all the judges agreed in stressing that the discretion inherent in the right to vote must be exercised in good faith.[8] It seems useful to cite two passages from the collective dissenting opinion of Judges Basdevant, Winiarski, Sir Arnold McNair and Read which underline the guiding principles that govern UN resolutions:

"20. While the Members of the United Nations have thus the right and the duty to take into account all the political considerations which are in their opinion relevant to a decision whether or not to admit an applicant for membership or to postpone its admission, it must be remembered that there is an overriding legal obligation resting upon every member of the United Nations to act in good faith (an obligation which moreover is enjoined by paragraph 2 of Article 2 of the Charter) and with a view to carrying out the Purposes and Principles of the United Nations . . .

That does not mean the freedom thus entrusted to the members of the United Nations is unlimited or that their discretion is arbitrary.

25. . . . a Member of the United Nations does not enjoy unlimited freedom in the choice of the political considerations that may induce it to refuse or postpone its vote in favour of the admission of a State to membership in the United Nations. It must use this power in good faith, in accordance with the Purposes and Prin-

---

7 *Ibid.,* p. 2.
8 *Conditions of Admission of a State to Membership in the UN,* 1948, Adv. Op., *ICJ Reports,* pp. 63, 71, 79, 92, 93, 105 and 115.

ciples of the Organization and in such a manner as not to involve any breach of the Charter. But no concrete case has been submitted to the Court which calls into question the fulfilment of the duty to keep within these limits; so the Court need not consider what it would have to do if a concrete case of this kind were submitted to it."[9]

This advisory opinion concerned the vote of member States on the question of the admission of a new member, but the principles which it laid down appear to be generally applicable to all resolutions of the General Assembly or the Security Council.

Moreover, the respect and observance of the principles governing UN resolutions are perhaps more imperatively required when the subject of the resolution is the fate of a nation and the fundamental rights of its people. In assuming in 1947, whether rightly or wrongly, the responsibility of settling the Question of Palestine, and of deciding between the conflicting claims of the Palestinians and the Jews on this country, the General Assembly undertook the exercise of a juridical or a quasi-juridical function.[10] Accordingly, the General Assembly was required to observe strictly in this case the rules regulating the proper exercise of such a function and relating to justice and good faith.

As to the legal effect of resolutions of the General Assembly, a distinction might have to be made between resolutions that fall within the competence of the General Assembly and resolutions that are not within its competence. Resolutions of the General Assembly can be *intra vires* or *ultra vires*.[11] Resolutions which are *ultra vires* must be considered to be devoid of any legal effect.

But apart from the question of competence or incompetence of the General Assembly, conflicting opinions have been expressed concerning the question whether General Assembly resolutions possess, in fact, any legal effect. Goodrich and Hambro are emphatic that General Assembly resolutions have no obligatory legal character:

> "Although the General Assembly may make recommendations both to Members of the United Nations and the Security Council, it should be kept in mind that recommendations have no obligatory character, as has been shown in the Palestine case, although they may be of the greatest political importance. The Members of the United Nations are legally free to accept or reject them."[12]

In the following section we shall examine the resolution for the partition of Palestine, and the circumstances in which it was adopted by the General Assembly, in order to determine, first, whether it was *intra vires*, and secondly, whether it was in conformity with the principles governing UN resolutions.

---

9 *Ibid.*, pp. 91–92 and 93.
10 The General Assembly exercises legal and political functions and the admission of a new member under Article 4 is a legal function: H. Kelsen, *op. cit.*, p. 194, Praeger, New York, 1950.
11 D. H. N. Johnson, "The Effect of Resolutions of the General Assembly of the United Nations", *BYIL*, Vol. XXXII, p. 111, 1955–56.
12 Goodrich and Hambro, *Charter of the United Nations*, pp. 151–152, 2nd ed., 1949.

Section 3
Grounds of invalidity
of the resolution

Neither the Palestinians nor the Arab States have accepted the resolution for the partition of Palestine. They consider it to be invalid and of no effect. Their attitude is based upon political, historical and juridical considerations. The discussion here will, however, be limited to the juridical grounds that invalidate the resolution. These grounds are the following:

1. *Incompetence of the UN*

The first ground of invalidity of the resolution lies in the incompetence of the General Assembly of the UN to recommend the partition of Palestine or to create a Jewish State in that country.

The legal position is clear in this regard. The UN is an organization of States which was formed for certain purposes defined in the Charter. At no time did this organization possess any sovereignty or any other right over Palestine. Accordingly, the UN possessed no power to decide the partition of Palestine, or to assign any part of its territory to a religious minority of alien immigrants in order that they might establish a State of their own. The UN could not give what it did not possess. Neither individually, nor collectively, could the members of the UN alienate, reduce, or impair the sovereignty of the people of Palestine, or dispose of their territory, or destroy by partition the territorial integrity of their country.

Not only did the UN possess no sovereignty over Palestine, but it did not even possess any power to administer the country. The League of Nations had, prior to its dissolution, exercised a power given by Article 22 of its Covenant to supervise the administration of mandates. But with the dissolution of the League, this supervisory power came to an end. Such a result was recognized by the resolution adopted at its last session on 18 April 1946. This resolution stated that "on the termination of the League's existence, its functions with respect to the mandated territories will come to an end."[13]

On the other hand, the Charter of the UN did not give the organization any right of supervision over existing mandates. The trusteeship system envisaged by Article 77 of the Charter did not apply to territories held under mandate, except if they came to be placed thereunder by means of trusteeship agreements.[14] Duncan Hall summarized the position in these words:

"In the case of mandates, the League died without a testament ... There was no transfer of sovereignty to the United Nations ... Sovereignty, wherever it might lie, certainly did not lie in the United Nations."[15]

Similarly, Sub-Committee 2 to the *Ad Hoc* Committee of the UN on the Palestine Question declared in its Report dated 11 November 1947:

". . . it should be pointed out that the United Nations Organization has not inherited the constitutional and political powers and functions of the League of Nations, that it cannot be treated in any way as the successor of the League of Nations in so far as the administration of mandates is concerned, and that such powers as the United Nations may exercise with respect to mandated territories are strictly limited and defined by the specific provisions of the Charter in this regard."[16]

In 1947, the Arab States questioned the competence of the General Assembly to recommend the partition of Palestine. Sub-Committee 2 to the *Ad Hoc* Committee on the Palestine Question accepted this argument and declared in its Report dated 11 November 1947:

"A study of Chapter XII of the United Nations Charter leaves no room for doubt . . . neither the General Assembly nor any other organ of the United Nations is competent to entertain, still less to recommend or enforce, any solution other than the recognition of the independence of Palestine and that the settlement of the future government of Palestine is a matter solely for the people of Palestine . . . Moreover, partition involves the alienation of territory and the destruction of the integrity of the State of Palestine. The United Nations cannot make a disposition or alienation of territory, nor can it deprive the majority of the people of Palestine of their territory and transfer it to the exclusive use of a minority in their country."[17]

---

13 Twenty-first Ordinary Session of the Assembly of the League of Nations, Document A-33, pp. 5–6, 1946.

14 The UN may exercise direct jurisdictional and legislative powers with regard to such trust areas as, according to Article 81 of the Charter, may be placed under its administrative authority: Oppenheim, *International Law*, 8th ed., Vol. I, p. 421, Longman.

15 H. Duncan Hall, *Mandates, Dependencies and Trusteeships*, p. 274, Carnegie Endowment for International Peace, Washington, 1948.

16 *Official Records of the 2nd Session of the General Assembly*, Document A/AC 14/32, p. 276, 11 November 1947.

17 *Ibid.*, pp. 276–278.

The General Assembly, however, paid no heed to the arguments about its competence. It might possibly be argued that the General Assembly could deal with the Palestine Question since it was placed on its agenda as a result of a request made by the mandatory Power for a recommendation to be made under Article 10 of the Charter concerning the future government of Palestine. Article 10 provides as follows:

> "The General Assembly may discuss any questions or any matters within the scope of the present Charter . . . and, except as provided in Article 12, may make recommendations to the Members of the United Nations or to the Security Council or to both on any such questions or matters."

However, the power given by Article 10 to the General Assembly to discuss any question or matter within the scope of the Charter cannot be enlarged so as to imply a power to break up the territorial integrity of a State or to create new States. Neither could this Article be construed so as to give the Assembly the power to make recommendations that would be creative of rights in favour of the Jews, or would be incompatible with the fundamental rights of the people of Palestine. The General Assembly possessed no power to prescribe the future form of the government of Palestine, a matter which was the sole concern, and within the exclusive competence, of the people of Palestine. Such a recommendation, unless accepted by the original inhabitants of the country, possessed no juridical value or obligatory force. Since the majority of the inhabitants of Palestine had unequivocally expressed their opposition to partition, the resolution for the partition of Palestine was therefore *ultra vires* and invalid.

Certain writers recognize the invalidity of the partition resolution on the ground of the incompetence of the UN. P.B. Potter observes:

> "The United Nations has no right to dictate a solution in Palestine unless a basis for such authority can be worked out such as has not been done thus far.
> Such a basis might be found by holding that sovereignty over Palestine, relinquished by Turkey in the Treaty of Lausanne, passed to the League of Nations, and has been inherited by the United Nations, a proposition which involves two hazardous steps. Or it might be held that the mandate is still in force and that supervision thereof has passed to the United Nations, which is much more realistic but still somewhat hazardous juridically. The Arabs deny the binding force of the Mandate, now or ever, as they deny the validity of the Balfour Declaration on which it was based, and again they are quite correct juridically."[18]

Quincy Wright expresses the view that "the legality of the General Assembly's recommendation for partition of Palestine was doubtful"[19] and that "the

---

18 Pitman B. Potter, "The Palestine Problem Before the United Nations", *AJIL*, Vol. 42, p. 860, 1948.
19 *The Middle East Crisis*, edited by John W. Halderman, p. 12, Oceana, Dobbs Ferry, N.Y., 1969.

justifiability of the original Arab objection to partition can hardly be questioned."[20]

This view is shared by I. Brownlie, who says:

> "It is doubtful if the United Nations has 'a capacity to convey title', *inter alia* because the Organization cannot assume the rôle of territorial sovereign . . . Thus the resolution of 1947 containing a Partition plan for Palestine was probably *ultra vires*, and, if it was not, was not binding on member states in any case."[21]

Kelsen considers that the resolution of the General Assembly for the partition of Palestine went beyond the making of recommendations and that the arguments made by the Arab States in opposition to the resolution were correct from a strictly legal standpoint.[22]

2. *Encroachment on the sovereignty of the people of Palestine*

The resolution of the General Assembly for the partition of Palestine constituted an encroachment upon the sovereignty of the people of Palestine. This encroachment not only was contrary to principles of law, but also constituted a violation of Article 2(7) of the UN Charter, which declares that nothing contained therein shall authorize the UN to intervene in matters that are essentially within the domestic jurisdiction of any State. Since its detachment from Turkey and the recognition of its independence by Article 22 of the Covenant of the League of Nations, Palestine had become a separate State. Although in 1947 Palestine was still subject *de facto* to a mandate that had legally terminated as a result of the dissolution of the League of Nations, but which, in any event, did not affect its statehood or the sovereignty of its people,[23] yet the question of its future government was a matter that fell exclusively within its domestic jurisdiction and could not become the subject of adjudication by the UN.

3. *Violation of the Covenant of the League of Nations and of the Charter of the UN*

The third ground of invalidity of the partition resolution is that it violated the principles embodied in Article 22 of the Covenant of the League of Nations and in the Charter of the UN.

This violation, both of the Covenant of the League of Nations and of the Charter, was emphasized in the Report of Sub-Committee 2 to the *Ad Hoc* Committee on the Palestine Question dated 11 November 1947. This Report states:

---

20 Quincy Wright, "The Middle East Problem", *AJIL*, p. 277, 1970.
21 I. Brownlie, *Principles of Public International Law*, pp. 161–162, Clarendon Press, Oxford, 1966.
22 Hans Kelsen, *The Law of the United Nations*, p. 97, Stevens & Sons, London, 1950.
23 See further on this point Section 2 of Chapter IV, *post.*

"23. The Sub-Committee considered the legal implications of the plan recommended by the majority of the Special Committee as enumerated above, and its views are summarized below.

The question of the partition of Palestine has to be considered in the light both of the provisions of the Mandate for Palestine, as read with the general principles embodied in the Covenant of the League of Nations, and of the provisions of the Charter. The United Kingdom took over Palestine as a single unit. Under Article 5 of the Mandate, the Mandatory Power was responsible 'for seeing that no Palestine territory shall be ceded or leased to, or in any way placed under the control of, the government of any foreign power.' Article 28 of the Mandate further contemplated that at the termination of the Mandate the territory of Palestine would pass to the control of 'the Government of Palestine'. So also by virtue of Article 22 of the Covenant, the people of Palestine were to emerge as a fully independent nation as soon as the temporary limitation on their sovereignty imposed by the Mandate had ended.

The above conclusion is by no means vitiated by the provisions for the establishment of a Jewish National Home in Palestine. It was not, and could not have been, the intention of the framers of the Mandate that the Jewish immigration to Palestine should result in breaking up the political, geographic and administrative economy of the country. Any other interpretation would amount to a violation of the principles of the Covenant and would nullify one of the main objectives of the Mandate.

24. Consequently the proposal of the majority of the Special Committee that Palestine should be partitioned is, apart from other weighty political, economic and moral objections, contrary to the specific provisions of the Mandate and in direct violation of the principles and objectives of the Covenant. The proposal is also contrary to the principles of the Charter, and the United Nations has no power to give effect to it. The United Nations is bound by Article 1 of the Charter to act 'in conformity with the principles of justice and international law' and to respect 'the principle of equal rights and self-determination of peoples.' Under Article 73, concerning non-self-governing territories and mandated areas, the United Nations undertakes 'to promote to the utmost . . . the well-being of the inhabitants of these territories' and to 'take due account of the political aspirations of the peoples.' The imposition of partition on Palestine against the express wishes of the majority of its population can in no way be considered as respect for or compliance with any of the above-mentioned principles of the Charter."[24]

In accordance with the principle of self-determination of peoples recognized by the Charter, the people of Palestine were entitled to affirm their national identity and to preserve the integrity of their territory. The carving out of a substantial area of Palestine for the creation of a Jewish State and the subjection of part of the original inhabitants to its dominion was a patent violation of this principle.

---

24 Official Records of the 2nd Session of the General Assembly, Document A/AC 14/32, pp. 278–279, 11 November 1947.

One might perhaps argue that the existence of a Jewish minority in Palestine changed the situation. The answer is obvious. What country does not possess in its midst a religious or racial minority? Nowhere in the world can the dismemberment of a country be recognized as a legitimate method for guaranteeing the rights of a minority.

4. *Denial of justice*

In 1947, the Arab States requested the General Assembly to refer the legal issues affecting the Palestine Question, including the question of its competence to recommend or enforce any plan of partition of Palestine, to the International Court of Justice for an advisory opinion. But the political forces which were then attempting to secure a favourable vote on partition were not anxious to have their efforts hampered by an adverse judicial ruling. They were able each time to vote down every proposal to refer a legal issue to the International Court.[25]

The legal issues which the Arabs sought unsuccessfully to refer to the International Court for an advisory opinion were outlined by Sub-Committee 2 to the *Ad Hoc* Committee on the Palestine Question in a draft resolution worded as follows:

"*The General Assembly,*

Considering that the Palestine question raises certain legal issues connected, *inter alia*, with the inherent right of the indigenous population of Palestine to their country and to determine its future, the pledges and assurances given to the Arabs in the First World War regarding the independence of Arab countries, including Palestine, the validity and scope of the Balfour Declaration and the Mandate, the effect on the Mandate of the dissolution of the League of Nations and of the declaration by the Mandatory Power of its intention to withdraw from Palestine,

Considering that the Palestine question also raises other legal issues connected with the competence of the United Nations to recommend any solution contrary to the Covenant of the League of Nations or the Charter of the United Nations, or to the wishes of the majority of the people of Palestine,

Considering that doubts have been expressed by several Member States concerning the legality under the Charter of any action by the United Nations, or by any Member State or group of Member States, to enforce any proposal which is contrary to the wishes or is made without the consent of the majority of the inhabitants of Palestine,

---

25 For the several denials in 1947 by the General Assembly of requests for an advisory opinion by the International Court of Justice on the Palestine Question, see UN documents A/AC 14/21, 14 October 1947; A/AC 14/24, 16 October 1947; A/AC 14/25, 16 October 1947; and A/AC 14/32, 11 November 1947.

Considering that these questions involve legal issues which so far have not been pronounced upon by any impartial or competent tribunal, and that it is essential that such questions be authoritatively determined before the United Nations can recommend a solution of the Palestine question in conformity with the principles of justice and international law,

Resolves to request the International Court of Justice to give an advisory opinion under Article 96 of the Charter and Chapter IV of the Statute of the Court on the following questions:

(*a*) Whether the indigenous population of Palestine has not an inherent right to Palestine and to determine its future constitution and government;

(*b*) Whether the pledges and assurances given by Great Britain to the Arabs during the First World War (including the Anglo-French Declaration of 1918) concerning the independence and future of Arab countries at the end of the war did not include Palestine;

(*c*) Whether the Balfour Declaration, which was made without the knowledge or consent of the indigenous population of Palestine, was valid and binding on the people of Palestine, or consistent with the earlier and subsequent pledges and assurances given to the Arabs;

(*d*) Whether the provisions of the Mandate for Palestine regarding the establishment of a Jewish National Home in Palestine are in conformity or consistent with the objectives and provisions of the Covenant of the League of Nations (in particular Article 22), or are compatible with the provisions of the Mandate relating to the development of self-government and the preservation of the rights and position of the Arabs of Palestine;

(*e*) Whether the legal basis for the Mandate for Palestine has not disappeared with the dissolution of the League of Nations, and whether it is not the duty of the Mandatory Power to hand over power and administration to a government of Palestine representing the rightful people of Palestine;

(*f*) Whether a plan to partition Palestine without the consent of the majority of its people is consistent with the objectives of the Covenant of the League of Nations, and with the provisions of the Mandate for Palestine;

(*g*) Whether the United Nations is competent to recommend either of the two plans and recommendations of the majority or minority of the United Nations Special Committee on Palestine, or any other solution involving partition of the territory of Palestine, or a permanent trusteeship over any city or part of Palestine, without the consent of the majority of the people of Palestine;

(*h*) Whether the United Nations, or any of its Member States, is competent to enforce or recommend the enforcement of any proposal concerning the constitution and future government of Palestine, in particular any plan of partition which is contrary to the wishes, or adopted without the consent, of the inhabitants of Palestine;

Instructs the Secretary-General to transmit this resolution to the International

Court of Justice, accompanied by all documents likely to throw light upon the questions under reference."[26]

The Sub-Committee's recommendation to refer the above questions to the International Court was rejected by the *Ad Hoc* Committee on 24 November 1947 by 25 votes to 18, but the last question (*h*), concerning the competence of the UN to recommend partition, was rejected by the narrow margin of 21 votes to 20.

Pitman Potter has observed that the rejection of the Arab requests to refer the question of UN jurisdiction over the Palestine situation to the International Court of Justice "tends to confirm the avoidance of international law" in this regard.[27] Such avoidance of international law constituted a denial of justice which deprives the partition resolution of any juridical value.

5. *Undue influence*

It is no secret that the resolution for the partition of Palestine was obtained by means of Zionist influence and American political pressure. The Zionists gained to their cause President Truman, who put the weight of the US Government in support of partition. In his *Memoirs* President Truman complains about Zionist pressure:

> "The facts were that not only were there pressure movements around the United Nations unlike anything that had been seen there before but that the White House, too, was subjected to a constant barrage. I do not think that I ever had as much pressure and propaganda aimed at the White House as I had in this instance . . . Some of the extreme Zionist leaders were even suggesting that we pressure sovereign nations into favourable votes in the General Assembly."[28]

However, President Truman does not disclose his own rôle and his own pressures in favour of Zionism and of the partition plan, except to mention concisely: "I instructed the State Department to support the partition plan."[29]

American influence played a great rôle in the adoption of the partition resolution. The evidence is ample in this regard. A few days before the final vote it had become fairly clear that the partition plan would not obtain the majority of two-thirds required for its adoption. Many countries had openly declared their opposition to partition or had abstained in the Committee vote. Thus, General Carlos Romulo, the representative of the Philippines, declared that he would defend the fundamental rights of a people to decide its political future and to preserve the territorial integrity of the land of its birth.[30] But he

---

26 Official Records of the 2nd Session of the General Assembly, *op. cit.*, pp. 299–301.
27 Pitman B. Potter, *op. cit.*, p. 860.
28 Harry S. Truman, *Memoirs*, Vol. II, p. 158, Doubleday, New York, 1965.
29 *Ibid.*, p. 155.
30 Official Records of the General Assembly, 1947, Vol. II, p. 1426.

was soon to change his attitude, like many others, because the pressures began to be felt.

"From that time on the representatives of the United States impressed upon every delegation the necessity to adopt a 'positive attitude'; the means employed was more often intimidation than persuasion. In this way Belgium, France, Haiti, Liberia, Luxembourg, the Netherlands, New Zealand, Paraguay and the Philippines found themselves obliged to reconsider their vote at the plenary session."[31]

Let us listen to American testimony. Kermit Roosevelt has written:

"Our delegation declared itself . . . in favour of the plan for partition . . . After its decision was made, the delegation proceeded on the principle that other countries should be allowed to make up their own minds. This principle was modified, however, when it became apparent that if it were followed the partition plan would be defeated . . . Haiti, Liberia, the Philippines, China, Ethiopia were overnight either won to voting for partition or persuaded to abstain . . . The delegates of those six nations and their home governments as well were swamped with telegrams, phone calls, letters and visitations. Many of the telegrams, particularly, were from Congressmen, and others as well invoked the name and prestige of the US Government. An ex-Governor, a prominent Democrat with White House and other connections, personally telephoned Haiti urging that its delegation be instructed to change its vote. (The same thing happened to Liberia.) Both States reversed themselves and voted for partition."[32]

A witness of great weight is James Forrestal, then US Secretary for Defence. James Forrestal was anxious to lift the Palestine Question out of American internal politics, but in this he failed. His *Diaries* abound with information about manoeuvres designed to secure a favourable UN vote for the partition of Palestine. He said:

"There was a feeling among the Jews that the United States was not doing what it should to solicit votes in the UN General Assembly in favour of the Palestine partition . . . I thought it was a most disastrous and regrettable fact that the foreign policy of this country was determined by the contributions a particular bloc of special interests might make to party funds . . . Forrestal heard from Loy Henderson more about the 'very great pressure' that had been put on him as well as Mr Lovell to get active American solicitations for UN votes for the Palestine partition . . . I thought that the methods that had been used by people outside of the Executive branch of the government to bring coercion and duress on other nations in the General Assembly bordered closely onto scandal . . . Mr Forrestal said that our [US] Palestine policy had been made for 'squalid political purposes' . . ."[33]

---

31 Seminar of Arab Jurists on Palestine, *The Palestine Question*, p. 77, Algiers, July 22–27, 1957.
32 Kermit Roosevelt, *The Middle East Journal*, pp. 13–15, 1948.
33 *The Forrestal Diaries*, pp. 345, 347, 357, 358, 363 and 508, Viking Press, New York, 1951.

Sumner Welles, a former US Secretary of State, also throws light upon the pressures exercised by the White House in 1947 in order to ensure adoption of the partition resolution. He said:

"Jewish support for the partition plan became overwhelming. In several of the larger cities the political influence of this body of American citizens was considerable and their allegiance was a matter of more than passing concern to a President whose desire for re-election was well-known . . .

When the partition plan was finally introduced in a plenary meeting of the General Assembly on November 26 the outcome suddenly looked uncertain. Under the provisions of the Charter and the regulations of the Assembly a two-thirds majority was required for approval. It was known that among the Latin-American Republics Cuba was adamant in her opposition. It was also known that Argentina, Colombia and Mexico would abstain from voting, and that certain other republics, notably Haiti, El Salvador and Honduras, were inclined to follow the lead taken by Cuba. Several of the smaller nations of Western Europe were reluctant to take any definite position.

In the light of later events it is important that there be no misunderstanding of the position that the United States assumed at that juncture. By direct order of the White House every form of pressure, direct and indirect, was brought to bear by American officials upon those countries outside the Moslem world that were known to be either uncertain or opposed to partition. Representatives or intermediaries were employed by the White House to make sure that the necessary majority would at least be secured."[34]

Stephen Penrose, the President of the American University of Beirut, criticized the American pressure in favour of partition in the following terms:

"The political manoeuvering which led to the final acceptance of the United Nations General Assembly of the majority report of UNSCOP provides one of the blacker pages in the history of American international politics. There can be no question but that it was American pressure which brought about the acceptance of the recommendation for Partition of Palestine with Economic Union voted by the General Assembly on 29 November 1947. It was this effective American pressure for partition which is largely responsible for the terrific drop which American prestige took in all parts of the Arab and Muslim world."[35]

Even the US Congress resounded with a note of protest. Congressman Lawrence H. Smith told Congress in 1947:

"Let's take a look at the record, Mr Speaker, and see what happened in the United Nations Assembly prior to the vote on partition. A two-thirds vote was required to pass the resolution. On two occasions the Assembly was to vote and twice it was postponed. It was obvious that the delay was necessary because the proponents (the USA and the USSR) did not have the necessary votes. In the

---

34 Sumner Welles, *We Need Not Fail*, pp. 63 and 80, Houghton Mifflin, Boston, 1948.
35 Stephen B. L. Penrose, *The Palestine Problem: Retrospect and Prospect*, p. 10, American Friends of the Middle East, New York, 1954.

meantime, it is reliably reported that intense pressure was applied to the delegates of three small nations by the United States member and by officials 'at the highest levels in Washington'. Now that is a serious charge. When the matter was finally considered on the 29th, what happened? The decisive votes for partition were cast by Haiti, Liberia and the Philippines. These votes were sufficient to make the two-thirds majority. Previously, these countries opposed the move ... The pressure by our delegates, by our officials, and by the private citizens of the United States constitutes reprehensible conduct against them and against us."[36]

The official record of the General Assembly also reflects the pressure that was brought to bear upon delegates and governments in order to vote in favour of partition. Mahmoud Fawzi, the Egyptian delegate, said:

"Let us frankly say to the whole world that, despite all the pressure exerted in favour of partition, a majority of the United Nations could not stomach this violation of the principles of the Charter."[37]

Camille Chamoun, the Lebanese delegate, declared:

"I can well imagine to what pressure, to what manoeuvres your sense of justice, equity and democracy has been exposed during the last thirty-six hours. I can also imagine how you have resisted all these attempts ... in order to preserve ... the democratic methods of our Organization. My friends, think of these democratic methods, of the freedom in voting which is sacred to each of our delegations. If we were to abandon this for the tyrannical system of tackling each delegation in hotel rooms, in bed, in corridors and ante-rooms, to threaten them with economic sanctions or to bribe them with promises in order to compel them to vote one way or another, think of what our Organization would become in the future."[38]

Sir Mohammed Zafrullah Khan, the delegate for Pakistan, stated:

"It is with satisfaction that one notes, Mr President, that you are anxious to secure ... an undisturbed and uninfluenced discussion. Whether the vote is going to be equally free and uninfluenced is no longer a matter for satisfaction ... Those who have no access to what is going on behind the scenes have known enough from the Press that ... the deliberations ... will not be left free."[39]

Mr Dihigo, the Cuban delegate, concluded his speech against partition in these words:

"For these reasons, we feel bound to vote against the plan of partition ... and to adhere firmly to our stand despite the negotiations and despite the pressure which has been brought to bear upon us."[40]

Fadel Jamali, the delegate of Iraq, stated:

"Great pressure is being brought upon members who have already formulated their point of view, pressure designed to have them change their minds, and

---

36 US Congressional Record, p. 1176, 18 December 1947.
37 Official Records of the General Assembly, 2nd Session, 1947, Vol. II, p. 1330.
38 *Ibid.*, p. 1341.   39 *Ibid.*, p. 1366.   40 *Ibid.*, p. 1385.

power politics is playing havoc with the independence of judgment of the members of this General Assembly . . .

It is no secret that some great Powers are bringing pressure upon member States to have this plan adopted. If the United Nations adopts this plan, we know very well that it will not be a United Nations plan, but a plan imposed by power politics."[41]

Mr Lopez, the Colombian delegate, said:

"The plan of partition will remain a minority proposal in our minds. It will not lose that character even if it succeeds in securing the votes of three or four more delegations; and the scanty strength of the proposal becomes all the more evident if we consider the great international importance of the problem and the distinction that this solution enjoys of having the joint backing of the United States and the USSR. It would seem to all unprejudiced observers that, but for that all-powerful backing, the proposal would never have made its way to the General Assembly. Here it may eventually be adopted, but we submit that reluctant votes, recruited with irrelevant eleventh-hour appeals, will not improve its position in the opinion of the outside world."[42]

Even after the resolution was adopted, complaints about the pressure used to secure its adoption were again voiced at the General Assembly. His Royal Highness Amir Faisal Al Saud, delegate of Saudi Arabia, declared:

"We have felt, like many others, the pressure exerted on various representatives of this Organization by some of the big Powers in order that the vote should be in favour of partition. For these reasons, the Government of Saudi Arabia registers on this historic occasion the fact that it does not consider itself bound by the resolution adopted today by the General Assembly."[43]

Sir Mohammed Zafrullah Khan speaking for Pakistan said:

"Partition totally lacks legal validity. We entertain no sense of grievance against those of our friends and fellow representatives who have been compelled, under heavy pressure, to change sides and to cast their votes in support of a proposal the justice and fairness of which do not commend themselves to them. Our feeling for them is one of sympathy that they should have been placed in a position of such embarrassment between their judgment and conscience, on the one side, and the pressure to which they and their Governments were being subjected, on the other."[44]

At the second special session of the General Assembly which was convened on 16 April 1948 at the request of the USA to consider a temporary trusteeship over Palestine, the pressure used to secure the vote on partition was again the subject of criticism. Mr Gromyko for the USSR declared that "the United States had originally used all its influence to encourage the adoption of the partition plan . . ."[45]

---

41 *Ibid.*, p. 1389. 42 *Ibid.*, pp. 1396–1397.
43 *Ibid.*, p. 1425. 44 *Ibid.*, p. 1426.
45 Official Records of the 2nd special session of the General Assembly, Vol. II, p. 17, 1948.

Mr Vilfan, the Yugoslav delegate, observed that the United States had become "the principal sponsor of partition".[46]

Sir Mohammed Zafrullah Khan for Pakistan said:

> "It was also strange that on 29 November a certain number of representatives had voted for partition, whereas on 26 November they had declared that they were opposed to partition as unjust . . . The representatives who had changed their minds during those three days . . . were caught between the dictates of their conscience and the strong pressure which was being put on them and their Governments. Those facts were so well-known that the partition plan could be called a United States rather than a United Nations decision."[47]

Charles Malek for Lebanon observed:

> "When the Special Committee's recommendation was made to the General Assembly, it was extremely difficult for the Assembly to decide upon any solution other than partition. Mr Malik did not wish to comment on the circumstances which attended that decision beyond remarking that he had first-hand knowledge of certain shameful pressures which were exerted."[48]

What is the legal value of a resolution which was obtained only by means of political pressures? Pitman Potter has observed: "The United States came close to exercising undue influence to get the partition plan adopted . . ."[49] It seems, however, that the existence of undue influence is more than amply demonstrated, and without such undue influence the partition resolution would never have been adopted. In fact, the partition resolution was "steamrollered" through the General Assembly by the United States.[50] On the basis of the general principles of law recognized by civilized nations and the jurisprudence of the International Court of Justice requiring members of the UN to conform, in the exercise of their vote, to the principles of the Charter and of good faith, the partition resolution must be considered to be null and void on the ground, amongst others, of having been obtained by the exercise of undue influence.

6. Iniquity of partition

In discussing in Section 2 above the principles that govern UN resolutions, we have noted the emphasis placed by the Charter on the principles of justice.

Let us now examine whether in adopting the partition resolution the General Assembly has observed the principles of justice prescribed by the Charter. In order to answer this question, one must recall the facts, with respect both to population and to land ownership.

---

46 *Ibid.*, p. 33.   47 *Ibid.*, p. 51.   48 *Ibid.*, p. 66.
49 Pitman B. Potter, *op. cit.*, p. 861.
50 Bassiouni and Fisher, "The Arab-Israeli Conflict", *St John's Law Review*, p. 444, note 135, January 1970.

In 1946, the total population of Palestine amounted to 1,972,000 inhabitants, comprising 1,203,000 Moslems, 145,000 Christians and 608,000 Jews.[51] Only one-tenth of these Jews were part of the original inhabitants and belonged to the country. In fact, the original Jewish Palestinian community did not, as we have seen earlier, favour partition or the establishment of a Jewish State. The rest of the Jewish population was composed of foreign immigrants originating mostly from Poland, the USSR and Central Europe.[52] Only one-third of these Jewish immigrants had acquired Palestinian citizenship.[53]

In terms of land ownership, it appears from the Palestine Government's Village Statistics that the Jews then owned 1,491,699 dunoms[54] of land – exclusive of urban property – out of a total area of 26,323,023 dunoms in Palestine.[55] Thus, Jewish land ownership amounted to 5·66 per cent of the total area of the country.[56] In contrast, the Palestine Arabs owned 12,574,774 dunoms, i.e. 47·77 per cent of the area of the country. The rest comprised public domain.

What did the partition plan do? It attributed to the Jews – who were less than one-third of the population and owned less than six per cent of the land – an area exceeding 14,500 square kilometres and representing 57 per cent of the area of Palestine. This meant that the Jews were given a territory which was ten times the area owned by them in the whole of Palestine.[57] Moreover, the territory allocated to the Jewish State included the coastal plain extending from Acre to Isdud and other fertile lands, while the Palestinians were left with mountainous and sterile regions. In other words, this was not a partition, but a spoliation. Its iniquity is obvious.

---

51 UN Document A/AC 14/32, p. 304, 11 November 1947.
52 Government of Palestine, *Statistical Abstract 1944–1945*, p. 42.
53 *Ibid.*, pp. 36 and 46. And see Section 2 of Chapter V, *post.*
54 One dunom equals one thousand square metres.
55 Appendix VI to the Report of Sub-Committee 2, UN Document A/AC 14/32, p. 270, 11 November 1947. In other words, the Jews owned an area of 1,491 square kilometres out of a total area of 26,323 square kilometres.
56 The figure of land in Jewish possession on 30 June 1947 was given by Sub-Committee No. 1 of the *Ad Hoc* Committee on the Palestinian Question as being 1,802,386 dunoms (Official Records of the Second Session of the General Assembly, 1947, A/AC 14/34). This figure, however, represents land in Jewish possession rather than in Jewish owner-ship and includes 200,000 dunoms of public lands leased by the Government of Palestine to the Jews in the Haifa Bay area. Even if one takes as a basis land in Jewish possession instead of ownership, the percentage of total Jewish land holdings still remains at the low figure of only 6·8 per cent of the area of Palestine.
57 Presumably in an attempt to reduce the abyss between Jewish land ownership in Palestine and the size of the Jewish State as delineated by the partition resolution, Israeli apologists do not hesitate to distort official figures of Arab and Jewish land ownership respectively in Palestine. Nathan Feinberg, for example, states that in May 1948, 8·6 per cent of the land belonged to the Jews, 3·3 per cent to the Arabs of Israel, and 16·9 per cent "to those Arabs who fled", and that the remainder, more than 70 per cent, was owned by the Government of Palestine: Nathan Feinberg, *On An Arab Jurist's Approach to Zionism and the State of Israel*, p. 105, footnote 296, Magnes Press, Jerusalem, 1971. These figures have no basis in fact, and they are flatly contradicted by the official statistics furnished to the UN by the Government of Palestine: see Official Records of the Second Session of the General Assembly, 1947, A/AC 14/34, p. 270.

The aftermath of the partition resolution further aggravated the injustice. The partition plan, unjust and iniquitous as it was, went with the wind, and an unimaginably more unjust and iniquitous situation was created at the end of the mandate in 1948. A Zionist racist State emerged which had nothing in common in terms of territory, population, or political structure with the Jewish State envisaged by the partition resolution, and a war broke out between the new State and the neighbouring Arab States. The Israelis ignored the frontiers fixed for the Jewish State by the partition resolution and seized four-fifths of the area of Palestine. At the same time, they uprooted one million Palestinians from their homes. Although the war ended with four Armistice Agreements concluded in 1949 between Israel, on the one hand, and Egypt, Lebanon, Jordan and Syria, on the other hand, the conflict has never been settled. In the final result, the partition resolution was never applied. All that it did was to serve as a pretext for the proclamation of the State of Israel and to open in the history of Palestine a tragic chapter whose last pages are still unwritten.

Needless to say, the Israeli-Arab War of June 1967 has further aggravated the situation, because the Israelis have occupied since that date the whole of Palestine as well as territories belonging to three neighbouring Arab States.

It is evident that the grounds of nullity of the partition resolution which we have reviewed in the preceding pages vitiate such a resolution and make it null and void. The partition resolution was essentially a political decision which was conceived, engineered and adopted through the efforts and pressures of the Zionists and their friends in violation of principles of law, justice, and democracy. The nullity of the partition resolution and the nullity of the Balfour Declaration and of the British mandate over Palestine should not be dismissed as matters of the past. Although ethically wrong, and legally void, these grave acts are still producing their effect. The present abnormal and explosive situation which exists in Palestine and the Middle East is directly related to the Balfour Declaration, to its implementation under the mandate, and to its realization in the partition plan.

In the next two chapters we shall consider the legal consequences of the nullity of the resolution, first on the title of Israel to the territories which it occupies, and then on its legitimacy as a State.

CHAPTER IV
SOVEREIGNTY
OVER PALESTINE

Section 1
Legal and political sovereignty

The term sovereignty, described by D. P. O'Connell as "the least exact of any in the literature of international law", covers a variety of concepts relating to States: *majestas, dominium, imperium*, independence, jurisdiction and other attributes of the State's supreme power. Thus sovereignty combines political and legal connotations relating to right and power. Brierly observes:

> "One result of identifying sovereignty with might instead of legal right was to remove it from the sphere of jurisprudence, where it had its origin and where it properly belongs, and to import it into political science, where it has ever since been a source of confusion."[1]

From the diversity of concepts of sovereignty, one can extract four basic meanings:

   i. the absolute and supreme power of a king in a monarchy, or of the people in a democracy;[2]

  ii. independence of any other earthly authority;[3]

 iii. a relation to other states;[4]

 iv. legal title to a territory.

Taken in this last sense, there exists an analogy between territorial sovereignty and ownership of property. Brownlie states:

> "The analogy between sovereignty and ownership is evident . . . The general power of government, administration and disposition is *imperium . . . Imperium* is thus distinct from *dominium . . ."*[5]

---

1   J. L. Brierly, *The Law of Nations*, 6th ed., p. 13, Clarendon Press, Oxford, 1963.
2   As to this meaning, see Oppenheim, *International Law*, Vol. I, 8th ed., p. 120, Longman.
3   *Ibid.*, p. 286.
4   Ian Brownlie, *International Law*, p. 250, Clarendon Press, Oxford, 1966.
5   *Ibid.*, p. 99.

The same author continues:

> "The materials of international law employ the term *sovereignty* to describe both the concept of title and the legal competence which flows from it."[6]

Brierly points out that territorial sovereignty refers not to a relation of persons to persons, nor to the independence of the State itself, "but to the nature of rights over territory . . . Territorial sovereignty bears an obvious resemblance to ownership in private law."[7] Such a resemblance has remained despite the existence of other meanings of the term sovereignty. "There is, in fact, no ground for assuming that the science of international law will discard the analogy between territorial sovereignty and property in private law, even if it does not go the length of identifying the two conceptions."[8]

The relationship between sovereignty and property has been maintained both in legal theory and in actual international practice. Van Kleffens observes: "Under the influence of Roman law sovereignty with regard to territory was long regarded and interpreted in terms of property . . . In modern times it still has had its votaries in various countries."[9] Fauchille states: "Le territoire d'une nation est sa propriété exclusive. Seule, cette nation a le droit d'en user."[10] Similarly, Hall calls territorial sovereignty "property".[11] The Italians also uphold the relationship between sovereignty and property, and Donato Donati is the strongest exponent of the doctrine.[12] It is on the basis of the principle of Roman law that sovereignty and property could exist one without the other that Grotius erected a distinction between *imperium* and *dominium* in international law.[13]

On the other hand, under international practice, the relationship between sovereignty and property has served to determine the legitimacy of title of a State to the territory that it occupies. Although in its political aspect sovereignty means the supreme power of a State over a certain territory and its people regardless of the legitimacy of its origin, in its legal aspect sovereignty involves a broader and more fundamental concept: the legal and inalienable title of a king or a nation to a territory. It was on the basis of this concept of legitimacy of title that the pre-Napoleonic sovereigns were restored to power and Europe was reconstructed after 1815.[14] It is on the basis of the same concept that the

---

6 *Ibid.*, p. 114. Brownlie speaks of "territorial sovereignty or title", p. 122.
7 Brierly, *op. cit.*, p. 162.
8 H. Lauterpacht, *Private Law Sources and Analogies of International Law*, p. 95, Archon Books, 1970.
9 E. N. Van Kleffens, "Sovereignty in International Law", *Hague Recueil*, Vol. 82, p. 94, 1953.
10 Fauchille, *Traité de Droit International Public*, T.I., Ire partie, p. 450, Rousseau, Paris, 1925.
11 Hall, *A Treatise on International Law*, 8th ed., p. 125.
12 Donato Donati, *Stato e Territorio*, pp. 59–117, 1924.
13 Grotius, II, C.3, S.42.
14 See Guglielmo Ferrero, *The Reconstruction of Europe* (translation by Jaeckel), New York, 1941, and C-M de Talleyrand, *Mémoires*, Vol. II.

nationhood of Poland was preserved during the long *interregnum* between 1795 and 1919 until it finally triumphed with the restoration of its sovereignty and of its international personality. Again, it was on the basis of the same concept that Poland's title and legal sovereignty survived the Russo-German conquest of its territory in 1939.

The same concept of legitimacy of title sustained the continuance of Ethiopia's sovereignty despite its annexation by Italy in 1936. Many States then accorded recognition, either *de facto* or *de jure*, to Italy's annexation and accredited their diplomats to the King of Italy as Emperor of Ethiopia. The fact of recognition by other States, however, did not terminate Ethiopia's legal sovereignty or extinguish its title to its territory. Neither did the Italian occupation destroy Ethiopia's personality, since it remained a member of the League of Nations for two years after its subjugation by Italy. During the whole period of Italy's annexation of Ethiopia and of the recognition of such annexation by other States, Ethiopia retained its title to its territory.

The same broad concept of legitimacy of title also explains the survival of Austria's sovereignty during the period of its forced union with Germany in 1938 until its formal re-establishment in 1945, the restoration of Czechoslovakia's personality and territory after its occupation and dismemberment by Germany in 1938, and the restoration of Albania's sovereignty after its invasion and annexation by Italy in 1939. All these States were restored despite their complete annexation and even extinction as political entities.[15]

These various cases of restoration of States and their territories can be considered as constituting applications of the modern principle that conquest is not a source of title. In the past the *fait accompli*, such as conquest or annexation, if successfully maintained, constituted a source of title to territory under international law. This situation has now changed. Guggenheim noted the recent practice according to which "modern international law is not prepared to admit lightly the validation of acts that are invalid and unlawful."[16] Since then this practice has become recognized as a firm rule of international law. The principle of no acquisition of territory by war, declares Quincy Wright:

"is implicit in the international law of the 19th century which held that military occupation of the territory of a recognized state gave no title to the occupied territory. It was affirmed in the Pan-American Conference of 1890 and in the Bogota Charter of the Organization of American States in 1948 as a principle of American international law, that territory could not be acquired by conquest; in the League of Nations Covenant which guaranteed the territorial integrity and political independence of its Members against external aggression; and in the

---

15 For a detailed review of several cases of restoration of sovereignty after conquest and annexation in recent times, see K. Marek, *Identity and Continuity of States in Public International Law*, Droz, Geneva, 1968.
16 Translated from Paul Guggenheim, "La Validité et la Nullité des Actes Juridiques Internationaux", *Hague Recueil*, 74, 1949, Vol. I, p. 232.

Kellogg-Briand Peace Pact of 1928 by which the parties renounced war as an instrument of national policy applied in the Manchurian situation by the Stimson Doctrine of 1932. The Atlantic Charter opposing territorial acquisitions in World War II, the Nuremberg Charter and Trial punishing the crime against peace on the bases of the Kellogg-Briand Pact, also affirmed this principle."[17]

Lauterpacht states that "title by conquest has been abolished."[18]

In several resolutions concerning the Arab-Israeli conflict and Israel's annexation of Jerusalem after the War of 5 June 1967, both the Security Council and the General Assembly have proclaimed "the inadmissibility of the acquisition of territory by war" or "by military conquest".[19] In other words, conquest cannot give title and this regardless of whether a conquest is or is not by itself an aggression. Referring to the principle of "the inadmissibility of the acquisition of territory by war" laid down in Security Council resolution 242 of 22 November 1967, Quincy Wright states:

"The principle goes beyond the principle 'no fruits of aggression'. It says there shall be no territorial fruits from war, using the latter term in the material sense of a considerable use of armed force. Its application, therefore, does not depend on determining who was the 'aggressor' in the 1967 hostilities, a difficult question to answer. There can be no doubt that, whether or not Israel was the aggressor, its occupations of territory were achieved by the use of armed force."[20]

The general principle of law is that a right cannot arise from a wrong. Hence, all the cases of revival or survival of State sovereignty despite conquest and annexation can also be explained by the maxim *ex injuria jus non oritur*. A claim to a territorial title which originates in an illegal act is invalid.[21] "International law" says Lauterpacht:

"will not recognize acquisition of territory accomplished in disregard of the accepted forms. Not every acquisition is a lawful one. The dictum '*Besitzstand gleicht Rechtszustand*' (possession is law) has no validity in international law. Mere force unaccompanied by a legally recognized form of acquisition does not confer a legal title."[22]

An attempt has been made in recent times to erode the maxim *ex injuria jus non oritur* by the principle of effectiveness in the exercise of power. This is expressed by another maxim: *ex facto jus oritur*. However, no one has yet openly subscribed to the principle that international law should ignore the wrongfulness of illegal acts, even though they may be effective. The principle of effectiveness

---

17 Quincy Wright, "The Middle East Crisis", *AJIL*, Vol. 64, No. 4, 1970, p. 74.
18 H. Lauterpacht, *Private Law Sources and Analogies of International Law*, p. 107, Longman. See also Oppenheim, *International Law*, Vol. 1, 8th ed., p. 574.
19 See S. C. resolutions 242 of 22 November 1967, 252 of 21 May 1968, 267 of 3 July 1969, 271 of 15 September 1969, 298 of 25 September 1971, and G.A. resolutions 2628 of 4 November 1970, 2799 of 13 December 1971 and 2949 of 8 December 1972. The texts of these resolutions can be found in the Appendices.
20 Quincy Wright, "The Middle East Problem", *AJIL*, p. 270, 1970.
21 Oppenheim, Vol. I, *op. cit.*, pp. 141–142, 574.   22 Lauterpacht, *op. cit.*, p. 100.

has been described by Charles de Visscher as a "coarse criterion" for ascertaining the existence of a new State entity.[23] Effectiveness, he observes, does not confer a valid title to an illicit act. Effectiveness produces legal results if, after a reasonable time, the illicit act is not effectively contested.[24]

The principle of effectiveness, it is submitted, has two limitations. First, it has no application where a claim of title is maintained or, at least, is not abandoned. Secondly, the principle of effectiveness has no application in the case of legal sovereignty in contradistinction to political sovereignty, for the reason that the existence or non-existence of a right cannot depend on the effectiveness of the usurpation. In all the instances where the sovereignty of a nation was revived or restored on its territory, notwithstanding its conquest and annexation, the conqueror's annexation was fully effective, and despite its effectiveness the legitimate title was restored.

A distinction, therefore, exists between legal and political sovereignty, the latter meaning factual dominion and control and the former signifying the rightful and inalienable title of a people to its territory. Such a distinction corresponds to the difference between sovereignty in law (*de jure* sovereignty) and sovereignty in fact.[25]

Professor Jèze has pointed out that the belligerent occupier acquires a "sovereignty in fact but not in law":

> "Cette prise de possession, qui repose exclusivement sur la force, n'entraîne pas au profit du vainqueur l'acquisition du territoire occupé ... Supposons d'abord que l'Etat dont le territoire est envahi se refuse à traiter, et que le vainqueur maintienne son occupation. La domination de l'Etat victorieux sera une souveraineté de fait et non de droit ... Tant que des protestations se feront entendre, il y aura bien une domination de fait, mais non un état de droit."[26]

Professor Schwarzenberger has expressed the distinction between legal and political sovereignty in these terms: "The last word is still not with law, but power. On such a level, the counterpart to legal sovereignty is political sovereignty."[27]

The distinction between legal and political sovereignty is of direct bearing on the territorial and political changes brought about by force by the Jews in Palestine since 1948. It provides the gauge for appraising the legal character of such changes.

---

23 Charles de Visscher, *Théories et Réalités en Droit International Public*, 4th ed., p. 185, Pedone, Paris, 1970.
24 *Ibid.*, p. 319.
25 For the contrast between "the assumption of powers of government" and "*de jure* sovereignty", see Ian Brownlie, *op. cit.*, pp. 100 and 102.
26 Gaston Jèze, *Etude Théorique et Pratique sur l'Occupation*, Paris, 1896, pp. 44–46. See also Ian Brownlie, *Principles of Public International Law*, Oxford, 1966, who refers to the continued existence of legal personality under international law despite the fact that the process of government in an area falls into the hands of another State, pp. 100–102.
27 G. Schwarzenberger, "The Fundamental Principles of International Law", p. 215, *Hague Recueil*, 1955.

Section 2
Sovereignty
of the original
inhabitants of Palestine

Notwithstanding the political vicissitudes in Palestine during the last fifty years, legal sovereignty still lies today in the original inhabitants of the country as they existed at the time of the detachment of Palestine from Turkey at the end of the First World War.

Prior to the occupation of Palestine by the British Army in 1917, Palestine formed an integral part of Turkey, which was a sovereign and independent State. The inhabitants of Palestine, Moslems, Christians, and Jews – all Arabic-speaking peoples – were then Turkish citizens and enjoyed equal rights with the Turks in government and administration. The Turkish Constitution made no distinction between Turk or Arab or between Moslem or Christian or Jew. Turks and Arabs, therefore, shared sovereignty over all the territories of the Turkish Empire regardless of whether such territories were Turkish or Arab provinces. This situation continued until the detachment of the Arab territories, including Palestine, from Turkey at the end of the First World War.

The British military occupation of Palestine in 1917 did not confer sovereignty on the occupying power, nor take away the sovereignty of the inhabitants. Apart from the fact that under international law the military occupation of enemy territory does not give title to the occupier, the avowed objective of the Allied Powers during the First World War was not the acquisition of territory in the Middle East. This is evident from the various pledges and assurances given to the Arabs by Great Britain and its Allies between 1915 and 1918 regarding the future of the Arab territories.[28] It should be remarked that the reference to these pledges and assurances does not signify that they are made a foundation for the Arab claim to Palestine. The title of the Palestinian Arabs to Palestine does not, and cannot, depend upon pledges and assurances of a third

---

28 These pledges and assurances were mentioned in Section 2 of Chapter I.

Power which never possessed sovereignty or any right whatsoever over Palestine. Their title rests upon their possession of the country from time immemorial. That the title of the Palestinians to Palestine dates from time immemorial is literally true, not a figure of speech. The Palestinians are the descendants of the Philistines and the Canaanites, and have lived continuously in Palestine since the dawn of history, long before the ancient Hebrews set foot in the country.[29]

The Covenant of the League of Nations, approved by the Paris Peace Conference on 28 April 1919, and incorporated into the Treaty of Versailles on 28 June 1919, also discarded any idea of annexation of the territories seized from Turkey during the First World War. Article 22 of the Covenant envisaged a new status under international law for the Arab communities detached from the Turkish Empire and, it is important to note, declared that "their existence as independent nations can be provisionally recognized."[30] The meaning of the expression "provisionally recognized" in Article 22 of the Covenant was explained by R. Erlich as follows:

> "Obviously, this does not mean that the existence as a nation, or relative independence which is expressly recognized, will be conditional; on the contrary, the inferior situation of a mandated territory constitutes a transitory phase in the development of peoples under tutelage towards real independence. This appears clearly from the last words of the sentence: 'until such time as they are able to stand alone'."[31]

Duncan Hall has observed: "Underlying Article 22 was the assumption of independent national sovereignty for mandates. The drafters of the Covenant took as their starting-point the general notions of 'no annexation' and 'self-determination'."[32] In the case concerning the International Status of South-West Africa (1950) the International Court held that in Article 22 of the Covenant "two principles were considered to be of paramount importance: the principle of non-annexation and the principle that the well-being and development of such peoples form a sacred trust of civilization."[33] The inhabitants of the mandated territories were the beneficiaries of this trust.[34]

The legal effect under international law of the detachment of Palestine from the Turkish Empire and of the recognition of its people as an independent nation was to make of this country a separate and independent State in which was vested legal sovereignty over the territory of Palestine.

But although Palestine acquired its own sovereignty as a result of its detachment *de facto* from Turkey and the recognition of its people as an independent

---

29 See Section 1 of Chapter I, above.
30 See Appendix I.
31 Translated from R. Erlich, "La Naissance et la Reconnaissance des Etats", *Hague Recueil*, T.13 (III), p. 450, 1926.
32 H. Duncan Hall, *Mandates, Dependencies and Trusteeships*, p. 80, Carnegie Endowment for International Peace, Washington, 1948.
33 *ICJ Reports*, 1950, p. 131.
34 *Ibid.*, p. 132.

nation by the Covenant of the League of Nations, the formal renunciation by Turkey of its sovereignty over its former Arab provinces occurred only some time later. The Supreme Council of the Principal Allied Powers had sought at first to impose upon Turkey the Treaty of Sèvres of 10 August 1920, which provided in Article 132 for a renunciation by Turkey "in favour of the Principal Allied Powers" of all rights and title outside her frontiers as fixed by the Treaty "which are not otherwise disposed of by the present Treaty." As we have seen earlier, the Treaty of Sèvres was not ratified by the Turkish Government. Ultimately, the Allied Powers had to negotiate with the Turkish nationalists, who in 1922 had abolished the Sultanate and declared the Ottoman Government to be no longer in existence. The Turkish nationalists accepted the separation of the Arab provinces and on 24 July 1923 concluded with the Allied Powers the Treaty of Lausanne after certain provisions of the abortive Treaty of Sèvres had been withdrawn and abandoned. It is significant that the new treaty materially altered the renunciation provision contained in the abortive Treaty of Sèvres.

Article 16 of the Treaty of Lausanne provided as follows:

> "Article 16. Turkey hereby renounces all rights and title whatsoever over or respecting the territories situated outside the frontiers laid down in the present Treaty and the islands other than those over which her sovereignty is recognized by the said Treaty, the future of these territories and islands being settled or to be settled by the parties concerned."

The new renunciation provision embodied in the Treaty of Lausanne calls for two comments. First, the Treaty left the future of Palestine, and of other Arab territories, to be decided by "the parties concerned". This expression was not defined, but it can only mean the communities which inhabited these territories, since they were the parties primarily concerned. Discussing the meaning of the expression "the parties concerned" (*intéressés*) in Article 16 of the Treaty of Lausanne, Verdross points out that Article 46 of the same treaty speaks of "States newly created on the Asiatic territories detached from the Ottoman Empire by virtue of the present Treaty." From this he concludes that these new States are included among "the parties concerned".[35]

Secondly, in contradistinction to Article 132 of the abortive Treaty of Sèvres, which envisaged Turkey's renunciation of "all rights and title" over Arab territories detached from it "in favour of the Principal Allied Powers", the Treaty of Lausanne did not provide for any such renunciation in favour of the signatory Powers. The absence of any such renunciation in favour of the Principal Allied Powers stands in contrast with the provision contained in Article 15 in the same treaty wherein "Turkey renounces in favour of Italy all rights and title" over certain specified islands. The difference between the two renunciation provisions can be ascribed to two reasons: first, it was not the in-

---

35 A. Verdross, "Droit International de la Paix", *Hague Recueil*, 1929, Vol. V, p. 403.

tention that the Principal Allied Powers or any one of them should acquire sovereignty over the Arab provinces; secondly, the Arab communities in the territories detached from Turkey were the original inhabitants and already possessed sovereignty over their own territories, a sovereignty, moreover, that Article 22 of the Covenant of the League of Nations had acknowledged by recognizing their existence as independent nations, subject only to the temporary rendering to them of administrative aid and assistance by a Mandatory. Hence, the Arab communities detached from Turkey were not in need of any renunciation of sovereignty to be made in their favour, in contrast with Italy, which needed such a renunciation in its favour to enable it to acquire sovereignty over the islands that came under its occupation. In this regard, Turkey's renunciation by the Treaty of Lausanne of its sovereignty over the Arab territories is comparable to Spain's relinquishment of its sovereignty over Cuba by the Treaty of Paris, 1898. In both cases the renunciation of sovereignty was not made in favour of the occupying Power. In the case of Cuba, Spain's renunciation was held to vest sovereignty in the inhabitants:

> "In the present case, as the United States expressly disclaimed any intention to exercise sovereignty, jurisdiction, or control over the island, 'except for the pacification thereof', the ownership of the island, upon the relinquishment by Spain of her sovereignty over it, immediately passed to the inhabitants of Cuba, who, in the resolution referred to, were declared to be free and independent, and in whom, therefore, abstractly considered, sovereignty resided.
>
> Had the language been 'Spain cedes to the United States the island of Cuba' as by Article II she did Puerto Rico, that would have divested her of all title to and, by consequence, all sovereignty over Cuba, both of which would then immediately have passed to the United States, as they did in the case of Puerto Rico; subject, however, to the rights of the people. True, when, pursuant to the treaty, the United States occupied the island, the inhabitants thereof during such occupancy undoubtedly owed allegiance to the United States, i.e. fidelity and obedience for the protection they received, but that did not divest them of their inherent rights." (*Galban and Company, A Corporation v. the United States*, 40 Ct. Cls. (1905), 495, 506–507.)[36]

Although, as a result of these developments, Palestine had become a separate and independent political entity, distinct from the political entity of which it previously formed part, and was now possessed of its own statehood and sovereignty, its people were prevented from the exercise of effective sovereignty. This was the result of two circumstances: first, the existence of a military administration, and subsequently the grant of a mandate to the British Government to administer Palestine.

It is necessary, therefore, to consider whether the grant by the League of Nations of a mandate to the British Government to administer Palestine affected the sovereignty of its inhabitants.

---

36 Hackworth, *Digest of International Law*, Vol. I, p. 425.

Conflicting views have been expressed in the past as to who possessed sovereignty in the case of a mandated territory. Some have argued that sovereignty lay in the Principal Allied Powers[37] or in the League of Nations[38] or in the Mandatory[39] or jointly in the League of Nations and the Mandatory[40] or in the inhabitants of the mandated territory.[41] All the various views which have been expressed on the point – except that which considers sovereignty to reside in the inhabitants of the mandated territory – have now been abandoned or discredited. None of the views that sought to vest sovereignty elsewhere than in the inhabitants of the mandated territory appears to rest on an acceptable legal basis.

We have seen that the Peace Treaty concluded with Turkey at the end of the First World War did not embody any renunciation in favour of the Principal Allied Powers of Turkey's sovereignty over the Arab territories. It is clear, on the other hand, that it was not the intention of the Covenant of the League of Nations or of the mandates that the League of Nations or the mandatory Power should acquire sovereignty over the mandated territories. The terms of the mandates did not involve any cession of territory or transfer of sovereignty to the mandatory Power. The International Court of Justice has recently confirmed this principle with regard to the mandate for South-West Africa. The Court said:

> "The terms of this Mandate, as well as the provisions of Article 22 of the Covenant and the principles embodied therein, show that the creation of this new international institution [i.e. the mandate] did not involve any cession of territory or transfer of sovereignty to the Union of South Africa. The Union Government was to exercise an international function of administration on behalf of the League, with the object of promoting the well-being and development of the inhabitants."[42]

The absence of any sovereignty in the mandatory Power is also to be inferred from the fact that the terms of the mandates precluded any disposition by the Mandatory of the mandated territory. Thus Article 5 of the Palestine mandate forbade the mandatory Power from alienating or leasing any part of the territory of Palestine.

The view that sovereignty over a mandated territory lies in its inhabitants received the support of several writers, and was summarized by Van Rees, Vice-President of the Permanent Mandates Commission, as follows:

---

37 Hoijer, *Le Pacte de la Société des Nations*, p. 374, Spes, Paris, 1926.
38 Redslob, *Le Système des Mandats Internationaux*, p. 196.
39 H. Rolin, "Le Système des Mandats Internationaux", *Revue de Droit International et de Législation Comparée* (1920), p. 302.
40 Quincy Wright, "Sovereignty of the Mandates", *AJIL*, 1923, p. 698.
41 P. Pic, "Le Régime du Mandat d'après le Traité de Versailles", RGDIP, Vol. 30, p. 334, 1923; Millot, *Les Mandats internationaux*, p. 91; Stoyanovski, *La théorie générale des mandats internationaux*, p. 92.
42 Advisory Opinion of the International Court of Justice regarding the Status of South-West Africa, *ICJ Reports* (1950), p. 132.

"Enfin, un dernier groupe d'auteurs – divisé en deux fractions – le seul groupe qui a tenu compte du principe de non-annexion adopté par la Conférence de la Paix, soutient que les auteurs du Pacte ont voulu tenir en suspens ou bien la souveraineté elle-même sur les territoires sous mandat pour une période équivalente à la durée des mandats respectifs (Lee D. Campbell, *The Mandate for Mesopotamia and the principle of trusteeship in English law*, p. 19; A. Mendelssohn Bartholdi, *Les mandats africains* (traduction), Archiv für Politik und Geschichte, Hamburg, 1925) ou bien l'exercice des pouvoirs souverains dont furent provisoirement chargées certaines nations en qualité de tuteurs. D'après ce dernier point de vue la souveraineté elle-même serait détenue, depuis la renonciation des anciens Empires, par les communautés et les populations autochtones des différents territoires. En d'autres termes, les anciens Empires ayant renoncé à leurs droits et titres sur les territoires en question sans qu'il y ait eu transfert de ces droits et titres à d'autres Puissances, la souveraineté, qui appartient à ces divers peuples et communautés jusqu'au moment de leur soumission à l'Allemagne et à la Turquie, renaît automatiquement du fait de la renonciation susdite. (Paul Pic, *Le régime des mandats d'après le Traité de Versailles*, RGDIP, Paris, 1923, p. 14; Albert Millot, *Les Mandats internationaux*, Paris, 1924, pp. 114–118; J. Stoyanovski, *La théorie générale des mandats internationaux*, Paris, pp. 83 and 86.)[43]

The same author pointed out that the view which held that sovereignty lies in the indigenous communities and populations of the mandated territory "is the only one which at least takes into account the principle of non-annexation unanimously adopted by the Peace Conference."[44]

The concept of sovereignty is not strained by recognizing its attribution to the inhabitants of mandated territories. Westlake has said: "The duties and rights of States are only the duties and rights of the men who compose them."[45] In Republican Rome, sovereignty belonged to the people.[46] In its resolution adopted in 1931 the Institute of International Law described the communities under mandate as subjects of international law.[47] The international personality of communities under mandate, first recognized by the Covenant of the League of Nations, has now come to be accepted as a principle of international law.[48] Pélichet has observed:

"La personnalité internationale ne fut longtemps reconnue qu'aux Etats. Ce n'est qu'à la fin du XIXe siècle, sous l'influence de Mancini et de l'école italienne, qu'on admit que certaines collectivités, étrangères aux Etats, pouvaient relever du droit des Gens et en devenir des sujets. Cette opinion a de plus en plus prévalu."[49]

---

43 D. F. W. Van Rees, *Les Mandats internationaux*, p. 20, Rousseau, Paris, 1927.
44 Translation from D. F. W. Van Rees, *Certains Aspects du Régime des Mandats Internationaux*, p. 21, Bibliotheca Visseriana, 1931.
45 Westlake, *Collected Papers*, p. 78.
46 A. Larson, C. W. Jenks, *Sovereignty Within the Law*, p. 437, Stevens (Oceana), 1965.
47 *AJIL*, 1932, p. 91.
48 See in this regard E. Pélichet, *La Personnalité Internationale Distincte des Collectivités sous Mandat*, p. 183, Rousseau, Paris, 1932.
49 E. Pélichet, *op. cit.*, p. 51.

One of the first writers who proclaimed the principle that sovereignty lies in the inhabitants of the mandated territory was Professor Pic. He said:

"Les rédacteurs du Traité de Versailles, s'inspirant avant tout d'un droit pour les peuples de disposer d'eux-mêmes, ont formellement proclamé qu'il n'y aurait aucune annexion des territoires sous-mandat par une puissance quelconque, pas plus par la collectivité des Etats ayant nom Société des Nations et siégeant à Genève, que par tel ou tel Etat particulier. Ces territoires appartiennent virtuellement aux populations ou communautés autochtones, dont la Société des Nations s'est constituée le défenseur, et au regard desquelles elle joue un peu le rôle d'un conseil de famille. Or, en droit interne, un conseil de famille n'a pas plus que le tuteur qu'il désigne, et dont il contrôle les actes, de droit privatif sur les biens du pupille."[50]

A somewhat similar view was held by Professor Quincy Wright with respect to the 'A' mandates. He observed:

"Communities under 'A' mandates doubtless approach very close to sovereignty."[51]

The Earl of Birkenhead thought that the 'A' mandated territories had a close similarity to protected States. He observed:

"The question as to the sovereignty of the mandated territory raises difficulties. It may lie in the League of Nations, in the mandatory State or in the mandated territory. With regard to the 'A' territories their close similarity to protected States would suggest a solution; but . . . the 'B' and 'C' territories may have to await the happening of some crucial event . . . before the juristic position can be unquestionably defined."[52]

Referring to Palestine and Syria in particular, the same author said:

"The position of Palestine and Syria is that they were integral portions of the Turkish Empire (which has renounced all right or title to them: Article 16 of the Treaty of Lausanne, 1923), they have become, administratively, partially dependent now upon an appointed mandatory State, but they are acknowledged – in the terms of Article 22 of the Covenant – to be entitled to provisional recognition of independence . . . The status of Palestine and Syria resembles very closely that of States under suzerainty."[53]

---

50 Professor P. Pic, *op. cit.*, p. 334.
51 Quincy Wright, *Sovereignty of the Mandates*, *AJIL*, Vol. 17, 1923, p. 696. Mandates were classified into three types: 'A', 'B' and 'C'. This classification was made in a 'descending order of political individuality' according to their international status and the degree of authority given to the Mandatory. The 'A' mandates applied to Iraq, Palestine, Syria and Lebanon. The 'B' mandates applied to German possessions in West Africa. The 'C' mandates related to German possessions in South-West Africa and to certain South Pacific Islands. It is to be remarked that only in the case of 'A' mandates were the communities concerned recognized by Article 22 of the Covenant as independent nations.
52 Earl of Birkenhead, *International Law*, 6th ed., p. 99.
53 *Ibid.*, p. 40.

The position of inhabitants of the 'A' mandated territories, observes Schoenborn, is not far from that of countries placed under a protectorate that are compelled also to be internationally represented by another power.[54]

Millot also vested sovereignty in the inhabitants of the mandated territory. He based his view upon Article 22 of the Covenant of the League of Nations and upon the intention of the Peace Conference which ended the First World War. Regarding the Arab territories detached from the Turkish Empire he said that Article 22 of the Covenant had declared these territories to be provisionally independent States and remarked that "independent" meant "sovereign".[55]

Stoyanovsky has argued that the people of a mandated territory are not deprived of the right of sovereignty but are deprived only temporarily of its *exercise*. The right of sovereignty belongs to the inhabitants of the mandated territory "by virtue of the principles of nationality and self-determination which are the foundations of modern international law."[56] The distinction between sovereignty and its exercise in the case of mandated territories is comparable to the distinction made under private law between ownership and its exercise in cases of guardianship, curatorship or other forms of tutelage.

Pélichet has advanced the view that communities under mandate enjoy real, not only virtual, sovereignty:

"La jouissance des droits de souveraineté est détenue réellement, et non point virtuellement, par les collectivités."[57]

In regard to Palestine, Pélichet pointed out that the United Kingdom, as the mandatory Power, concluded agreements with Palestine, as the mandated territory. Thus a community under a mandate can acquire rights, conclude agreements and assume international obligations. In consequence, he concluded:

"Nous estimons que la théorie de la souveraineté des peuples sous mandat est celle qui convient le mieux à l'esprit comme à la lettre de l'article 22."[58]

In his separate opinion concerning the International Status of South-West Africa, Lord McNair expressed the view that the mandate system does not fit into the old conceptions of sovereignty. According to Lord McNair sovereignty over a mandated territory is "in abeyance".[59]

The principle that sovereignty lies in the people of the mandated territory itself was recently applied to territories held under trusteeship in accordance with the Charter of the United Nations. Mandates and trusteeships possess the same legal affiliation. In the case of Società A.B.C. *v.* Fontana and Della Rocca,

---

54 W. Schoenborn, "Nature Juridique du Territoire", *Hague Recueil*, 1929, Vol. 30, p. 182.
55 Millot, *Les Mandats internationaux*, pp. 91 and 115.
56 Stoyanovsky, *La Théorie Générale des Mandats Internationaux*, p. 83.
57 E. Pélichet, *op. cit.*, p. 100.
58 *Ibid.*, p. 108.
59 Advisory Opinion of the International Court of Justice regarding the Status of South-West Africa, *ICJ Reports*, 1950, p. 150.

the Italian Court of Cassation held that "sovereignty over the territory of Somaliland is vested in its population, although, under Article 2 of the Trusteeship Agreement, the administration of the territory, for the period specified in the Agreement, has been entrusted to Italy."[60] The same view was expressed by Oppenheim, who observed:

> "In considering the question of sovereignty over trust territories – a question which is by no means of mere academic importance – the distinction must be borne in mind between sovereignty as such (or what may be described as residuary sovereignty) and the exercise of sovereignty. The latter is clearly vested with the trustee powers subject to supervision by and accountability to the United Nations."[61]

We can therefore conclude this inquiry by remarking that the grant by the Council of the League of Nations of a mandate to the British Government to administer Palestine did not deprive its people of their sovereignty, nor the State of Palestine of its own entity. The legal status of Palestine under international law during the British mandate and upon its termination on 15 May 1948 can, therefore, be summarized as follows: during the currency of the mandate the people of Palestine enjoyed an independent international status and possessed sovereignty over their land; Palestine possessed its own statehood as well as its own identity, which were distinct from those of the mandatory Power; its administration was theoretically its own though, in fact, it was exercised by the Mandatory; the Government of Palestine, theoretically as the representative of the people of Palestine, but in actual fact administered by the British Government, concluded agreements with the mandatory Power and became party, through the instrumentality of the Mandatory, to a number of international treaties and conventions; however, the full exercise of sovereignty by the people of Palestine was restricted by the powers of administration entrusted to the mandatory Power; upon the termination of the mandate the Mandatory's powers of administration came to an end and, as a result, the restrictions upon exercise of full sovereignty by the people of Palestine ceased, so that by virtue of this right, as well as by virtue of their right of self-determination, they became entitled to rule themselves and to determine their future in accordance with normal democratic principles and procedures. The first and fundamental rule in any democracy is the rule of the majority. This rule, however, was not respected by the General Assembly of the UN, which disregarded the will of the majority and recommended in 1947, in circumstances and under political pressures already mentioned, the partition of the country between Arab and Jewish States. The events which followed and the emergence of Israel have prevented the Palestinian people from exercising their right of sovereignty over their own land.

---

60 Decision dated 10 August 1954, *International Law Reports*, Vol. 22, p. 77, 1955.
61 Oppenheim, *International Law*, Vol. I, 8th ed., p. 236, Longman, London, 1955.

The question which we shall now consider is whether the emergence of Israel and its occupation in 1948 and 1949 of various territories of Palestine deprived the people of Palestine of their legal sovereignty. In other words, did Israel acquire legal sovereignty over such territories? For reasons of clarity in the discussion, rather than by reason of any difference in conclusions, this inquiry into the legitimacy or illegitimacy of Israel's title will be made separately in respect of the territory allotted to the Jewish State by the partition resolution, and in respect of the other territories which Israel seized in excess of the same resolution.

Section 3
Has Israel acquired title to the territory allocated to the Jewish State by the partition resolution?

The question of whether Israel has acquired sovereignty over the territory which was allocated to the Jewish State by the partition resolution can be examined in the light of three political developments, with a view to determining whether any one of them could have conferred title or sovereignty upon Israel. These three developments are: the Balfour Declaration of 2 November 1917; the United Nations resolution on the partition of Palestine of 29 November 1947; and the conquest or occupation by Israel in 1948 and in 1949 of the territory earmarked for the proposed Jewish State by the said resolution.

a. *No grant of sovereignty was or could have been involved in the Balfour Declaration*

The Balfour Declaration, which the Zionists have utilized almost as a document of title for the establishment of a Jewish State in Palestine, never possessed any juridical value. In Section 2 of Chapter I we have set forth the reasons for this conclusion. It is, therefore, clear that the Jews did not and could not gain any title or other right whatsoever in Palestine from the Balfour Declaration. From the juridical standpoint any claim by the Jews to Palestine on the basis of the Balfour Declaration is entirely groundless, if not plainly nonsensical.

b. *No title was derived by Israel from the partition resolution*

Neither did the Jews acquire any title under the partition resolution.

The question as to whether the General Assembly of the UN could give any title to the Jews or to a Jewish State over any part of the territory of Palestine was considered in Section 3 of Chapter III, and answered in the negative. It is evident that the partition resolution lacked all juridical basis, constituted an excess of jurisdiction, and could not confer on Israel any valid title over any part of Palestine.

In addition to the invalidating circumstances with which the partition resolution is tainted, no title could be gained by Israel under such resolution, because a General Assembly resolution cannot *per se* constitute a source of title. A General Assembly resolution, says Jennings, has no effect upon title and cannot effect any change in sovereignty.[62]

It is clear then that the partition resolution could neither take away the title of the Palestinians, nor confer title on the Jews to any part of the territory of Palestine. One can even cite in support of this conclusion the words of Israel's representative at the UN: "a General Assembly resolution," he says, "neither creates rights nor does it take rights away. It is a political settlement."[63]

Aside from the fact that the partition resolution cannot be invoked by Israel as a source of title, it is important to observe that in a subsequent resolution the General Assembly receded to some extent from the partition plan and recommended an adjustment of the situation in Palestine by means of mediation. This occurred when, as a result of grave disturbances which followed the adoption of the partition resolution, it became increasingly evident that partition could not be implemented. The Security Council considered the situation between 24 February and 1 April 1948 without any concrete results. On 19 March 1948 Warren R. Austin, the US representative at the UN, asked the Security Council to suspend action on the partition plan and to call a special session of the General Assembly to work on a new solution. He advocated a temporary trusteeship for Palestine under the Trusteeship Council until the establishment of a Government approved by Arabs and Jews. On 30 March he presented to the Security Council a resolution asking that the General Assembly be convened "to consider further the question of the future government of Palestine." On 16 April 1948 a second special session of the General Assembly was convened to consider further the question of Palestine. Discussions both at the Security Council and at the second special session of the General Assembly revealed that some Governments questioned the wisdom of the partition plan. The United Kingdom, as the retiring mandatory Power, declared that it was not prepared to participate in the enforcement of a settlement which was not acceptable to both Arabs and Jews, and further asserted that lack of co-operation on its part sprang from the fact that the partition had not been impartially conceived. Eventually, the General Assembly ended its second special session on 14 May 1948 with a resolution appointing a Mediator to promote, *inter alia*, "a peaceful adjustment of the future situation in Palestine."[64]

The legal effect of this resolution was to withdraw from the partition resolution its character of finality and to make it subject to the mediation mission of

---

62 R. Y. Jennings, *The Acquisition of Territory in International Law*, p. 85, Manchester University Press, 1963.
63 Shabtai Rosenne in *The Middle East Crisis*, edited by H. W. Halderman, p. 66, Oceana, 1969.
64 Resolution 186 (S-2) of 14 May 1948 (Appendix IV).

Count Folke Bernadotte. This was, in fact, the attitude adopted by the late Mediator. In a letter to Count Bernadotte dated 5 July 1948 the Provisional Government of Israel had objected to his suggestions for a peaceful solution as constituting "deviations from the General Assembly resolution of 29 November 1947." On 6 July 1948, Count Bernadotte replied as follows:

> "In paragraph 1 of your letter it is stated that my suggestions 'appear to ignore the resolution of the General Assembly of 29 November 1947 . . .' I cannot accept this statement. As United Nations Mediator, it is true that I have not considered myself bound by the provisions of the 29 November resolution, since, had I done so, there would have been no meaning to my mediation. The failure to implement the resolution of 29 November 1947, and the open hostilities to which the Arab opposition to it led, resulted in the convoking of the second special session of the General Assembly 'to consider further the future Government of Palestine'. This special Assembly, taking into account the new situation, adopted on 14 May 1948 the resolution providing for a Mediator."[65]

Dr Bunche has pointed out that the UN Mediator for Palestine did not accept "the Jewish view that the territory provided for the Jewish State in the General Assembly's recommendation of 29 November was beyond the jurisdiction of the Mediator because it was now the territory of a sovereign State."[66]

The functions of the UN Mediator for Palestine were transferred after his assassination to the Conciliation Commission for Palestine by resolution 194 (III) of the General Assembly dated 11 December 1948. Although the Conciliation Commission for Palestine has not been conspicuous for its achievements, the resolution making provision for "a peaceful adjustment of the future situation in Palestine" is still on the records of the UN and constitutes its basic mandate.

The conclusion is obvious, therefore, that the partition resolution was called in question and its finality was impaired by subsequent resolutions. Hence, the question of the future of Palestine cannot be considered to have been finally settled since, in accordance with the record of the UN, it is still "subject to a peaceful adjustment". In these circumstances, and under the partition resolution itself, Israel cannot be considered to have acquired any definitive right, of whatever value.

c. No title was gained by Israel as a result of conquest or occupation

Israel cannot under international law invoke conquest or occupation in order to claim title to the territories of the Jewish State, as defined by the partition resolution, which it seized in 1948 and 1949.

The right of conquest does not exist any more. It is now established by the

---

65 Progress Report of the UN Mediator for Palestine, 16 September 1948, UN Document A/648, p. 9.
66 Official Records of the 3rd session of the G.A., Part I, First Committee, 1948, p. 770.

consensus of the civilized community that military conquest is not a ground of acquisition of territory. War cannot give title. There is no need to repeat here what was said in this regard in the first section of this chapter.

Neither can Israel derive any title by occupation. In accordance with accepted principles of international law, occupation as a means of acquiring territory can only be conceived in the case of a *res nullius*.[67] Palestine was at no time *terra nullius*, so that it was not open for occupation nor capable of acquisition by any State or any group of alien settlers.

---

67 Oppenheim, *op. cit.*, Vol. I, p. 555.

Section 4
Has Israel acquired title to the territories seized in excess of the partition resolution?

The Israelis showed no respect, either before or after 15 May 1948, for the territorial boundaries fixed by the partition resolution for the proposed Arab and Jewish States. They not only occupied the territory of the proposed Jewish State but also seized a substantial portion of the territory reserved for the proposed Arab State. The areas seized by Jewish forces before and after 15 May 1948, in excess of the territorial limits of the Jewish State as fixed by the partition resolution, include Western Galilee, the New City of Jerusalem, the area west of Jerusalem to the Mediterranean, the Arab cities of Jaffa, Acre, Lydda and Ramleh, and several hundred Arab towns and villages. The total areas which the Israelis seized in 1948 and 1949 amounted to 20,850 square kilometres[68] out of 26,323 square kilometres representing the total area of Palestine. This meant that Israel increased the territory of the Jewish State as proposed by the UN from 14,500 square kilometres to 20,850 square kilometres and by the same act reduced the territory of the proposed Arab State by 54 per cent, that is, from 11,800 square kilometres to about 5,400 square kilometres. The total area which thus fell under Israeli control amounted to almost 80 per cent of the territory of Palestine.

The legal position with respect to the territories which Israel seized in 1948 and 1949 in excess of the territorial limits fixed by General Assembly resolution 181 (II) of 29 November 1947 is quite obvious. Primarily, neither conquest nor occupation can give Israel any valid legal title to such territories. And, moreover, Israel's seizure of such territories gives it no title for the added reason that it constituted a violation of the terms of the resolution. Israel can have no possible claim to the territories which it seized in excess of the partition resolution, for it is inconceivable that it could acquire rights by violating a General Assembly resolution.

---

68 Israel Government, *Government Year-book*, English edition, 5712 (1951/1952), p. 315.

Israel has both invoked the partition resolution to justify its occupation of the territory envisaged for the Jewish State, and has violated the same resolution by its seizure of territories earmarked for the Arab State.[69] In 1948 Count Bernadotte made it plain to Israel that it was not entitled to consider provisions of the partition resolution which were in its favour as effective and to treat certain others of its provisions which were not in its favour as ineffective. In his reply dated 6 July 1948 to the Israeli Government's letter of the preceding day, wherein it objected to the Mediator's suggestions for a peaceful settlement of the Palestine Question on the ground of their "deviations from the General Assembly resolution of 29 November 1947",[70] Count Bernadotte stated as follows:

"2. . . . You have not taken advantage of my invitation to offer counter-suggestions, unless I am to understand that your reference in paragraphs 1 and 2 of your letter to the resolution of the General Assembly of 29 November 1947 implies that you will be unwilling to consider any suggestions which do not correspond to the provisions of that resolution.

3. In paragraph 1 of your letter it is stated that my suggestions 'appear to ignore the resolution of the General Assembly of 29 November 1947' . . .

6. As regards paragraph 4 of your letter, I note that your Government no longer considers itself bound by the provisions for Economic Union set forth in the 29 November resolution for the reason that the Arab State envisaged by that resolution has not been established. In paragraphs 1 and 2, however, the same resolution is taken as your basic position. Whatever may be the precise legal significance and status of the 29 November resolution, it would seem quite clear to me that the situation is not of such a nature as to entitle either party to act on the assumption that such parts of the resolution as may be favourable to it may be regarded as effective, while those parts which may, by reason of changes in circumstances, be regarded as unfavourable are to be considered as ineffective."[71]

Israel may not have it both ways. It is elementary that Israel cannot claim title to the territory envisaged for the Jewish State under the General Assembly resolution and deny the title of the Palestinians to the territories envisaged for the Arab State under the same resolution. Such an attitude is tantamount to a denial by Israel of its birth certificate. In his Progress Report to the General Assembly, Count Bernadotte took the position, almost as a matter of course, that Israel is not entitled to retain the areas which it had occupied in excess of the partition resolution. He said:

---

69 See Ben Gurion, *Israël, Années de Lutte*, pp. 59 and 61, Flammarion, Paris, 1964.
70 UN Document, A/648, p. 9.
71 Count Bernadotte's Progress Report to the General Assembly dated 16 September 1948 (UN Document A/648) contains extracts only from the said letter. However, the full text of Count Bernadotte's letter to the Provisional Government of Israel dated 6 July 1948, which contains the passages quoted above, is set out in his diary published under the title *To Jerusalem*, pp. 153–158, Hodder and Stoughton, London, 1951.

"(C) The disposition of the territory of Palestine not included within the boundaries of the Jewish State should be left to the Governments of the Arab States in full consultation with the Arab inhabitants of Palestine, with the recommendation, however, that in view of the historical connexion and common interests of Transjordan and Palestine, there would be compelling reasons for merging the Arab territory of Palestine with the territory of Transjordan . . ."[72]

Count Bernadotte's view that Israel was not entitled to retain the areas which it seized in excess of the General Assembly's resolution was shared by the US Government. At the third session of the General Assembly held in Paris in 1948, Dr Philip C. Jessup, then US representative, indicated the position of the United States as being that if Israel desired additions to the boundaries set forth in the resolution of 29 November 1947, "it would have to offer an appropriate exchange, acceptable to the Arabs, through negotiation."[73] Similarly, Mr Rusk for the United States declared at the same session that "any modifications in the boundaries fixed by the resolution of 29 November 1947 could only be made if acceptable to the State of Israel. That meant that the territory allocated to the State of Israel could not be reduced without its consent. If, on the other hand, Israel wished to enlarge that territory, it would have to offer an exchange through negotiation."[74]

The US Government maintained its view that Israel cannot keep territory seized in excess of the partition resolution when it appeared during the meetings of the Conciliation Commission for Palestine, in Lausanne in 1949, that Israel's obdurate attitude was preventing any settlement on the basis of the Lausanne Protocol. On 29 May 1949, the US Government addressed through its Ambassador, James G. McDonald, a note to Israel which

"expressed disappointment at the failure of Eytan (Israel's representative) at Lausanne to make any of the desired concessions on refugees and boundaries; interpreted Israel's attitude as dangerous to peace and as indicating disregard of the UN General Assembly resolutions of 29 November 1947 (partition and frontiers) and 11 December 1948 (refugees and internationalization of Jerusalem); reaffirmed insistence that territorial compensation should be made for territory taken in excess of the 29 November resolution and that tangible refugee concessions should be made now as an essential preliminary to any prospect for general settlement."[75]

Israel's attitude concerning the territories which it seized in 1948 and 1949 in excess of the partition resolution has fluctuated in accordance with prevailing circumstances. Before its admission to membership of the UN, Israel's position

---

72 UN Document A/648, p. 18.
73 Official Records of the 3rd Session of the General Assembly, Part I, 1948, First Committee, pp. 682 and 727.
74 Official Records of the 3rd Session of the General Assembly, 1949, *supra*, p. 836.
75 James G. McDonald, *My Mission to Israel*, pp. 181–182, Simon and Schuster, New York, 1951. And see Section 2 of Chapter VI, *post*.

with regard to such territories was flexible. On 1 December 1948 Israel's representative declared at the UN:

> "The State of Israel claimed full rights over the whole of the territory assigned to it under the resolution of 29 November. The territories occupied by the forces of Israel as a result of its struggle to defend its territory were a fit matter for negotiations, in which the views and claims of the State of Israel should receive due consideration."[76]

It is evident that Israel was not then asserting any claim of title to these territories. During the debate in 1949 on its application for admission to membership of the UN, Israel explained the discrepancy between the territory which it held at that time and the territory envisaged for the Jewish State by the resolution of 29 November 1947 as follows:

> "All the areas occupied by Israel's forces at this time are so occupied with the agreement concluded with Arab States under the resolution of 16 November."[77]

The "resolution of 16 November" to which reference was made was resolution No. 62 of the Security Council dated 16 November 1948. This resolution took note that "the General Assembly is continuing its consideration of the future Government of Palestine in response to the request of the Security Council in its resolution 44 (1948) of 1 April 1948", and called upon the parties involved in the conflict to seek agreement with a view to the immediate establishment of the armistice. The "agreement" mentioned by Israel's representative as a basis for its occupation can, therefore, refer only to the Armistice Agreements which had then been concluded with Egypt, Lebanon, Syria and Jordan. Israel's occupation of Palestinian territory under the Armistice Agreements is not and cannot be a source of title. In fact, the Armistice Agreements specifically provided that "the armistice lines are not to be construed as political or territorial boundaries and are delineated without prejudice to the ultimate settlement of the Palestine Question."[78]

After its admission to the UN, Israel hardened its attitude. It did not consider any longer that the areas which it had seized in excess of the partition resolution were "a fit matter for negotiations", but asserted a claim of title to them based on conquest. Such a claim is obviously inadmissible.

In conclusion it can be said that Israel did not and could not gain title to the territories which it seized in 1948 and 1949 whether within or in excess of the boundaries of the partition resolution. Neither did Israel acquire title to the territories which it seized in 1967. Its legal status in both cases is identical: it is the status of a belligerent occupier. And it is immaterial whether Israel is

---

76 Official Records of the 3rd Session of the General Assembly, First Committee, p. 832, 1948.
77 Official Records of the 3rd Session of the General Assembly, Part II, p. 347, 1949.
78 See Article V(2) of the Egyptian-Israeli Armistice Agreement of 24 February 1949. The Armistice Agreements with Lebanon, Jordan and Syria embody a similar provision.

considered a belligerent occupier or a conqueror. In neither case can it acquire sovereignty. "Israel," says Hedley V. Cooke, "alone among all the countries of the world, possesses not a single square inch of territory which she could assuredly proclaim to be her own in perpetuity."[79] The title of the Palestinians to their homeland remains unaltered. Their sovereignty survives despite the situation created by force in Palestine. "Sovereignty," declared the French Constitution of 3 September 1791, "is one, indivisible, inalienable and imprescriptible." These principles are immutable and they are as valid today as they were in the past.

---

79 Hedley V. Cooke, *Israel, A Blessing and A Curse*, p. 186, Stevens and Sons ,London 1960.

CHAPTER V
THE ILLEGITIMACY
OF ISRAEL

Section 1
Three aspects
of Israel's illegitimacy

Israel does not fulfil the normal requirements of statehood under international law. These requirements are: a people, a defined territory, and a Government.

In their great majority the present Jewish inhabitants of Palestine do not belong to the country. They are aliens who came to Palestine from the four corners of the world against the will of the original inhabitants whom they displaced by force and terror. In no way can they be considered to be a "people", much less the people of Palestine.

Turning to territory, and apart from the fact that Israel has no recognized frontiers, it is the entirety of the territory that Israel occupies which is in dispute with the original inhabitants of Palestine and with the neighbouring Arab States. As Dr Zaki Hashem observes: "A territorial dispute over the entire surface claimed for a State to be created is evidently a matter which raises questions which go to the root of the existence of the new entity."[1]

As to the Government, it is evident that it should, as a matter of definition, be representative of the people of the country. It can hardly be said that the Israeli Government is representative of the people of Palestine whom it has uprooted.

In addition to not fulfilling the normal requirements of statehood, the State of Israel is tainted with an inherent illegitimacy. This illegitimacy has three aspects:

   i. the usurpation of political power;
  ii. the usurpation of territory;
 iii. the absence of any legal basis in international law for its proclamation as a State.

The usurpation of political power needs no explanation. The establishment

---

1   Zaki Hashem, "International Law Aspects of the Palestine Question", *Revue Egyptienne de Droit International*, Vol. 23, 1967, p. 71.

of a Government in Palestine in 1948 by a group of alien immigrants, whether or not claiming to act under the authority of an invalid UN resolution, was an unlawful usurpation of political power that legitimately belonged to the original inhabitants.

Similarly, the forcible seizure of a large area of Palestine by such a Government, whether such area fell within or outside the boundaries fixed by an invalid UN resolution, was an unlawful usurpation of a territory that legitimately belonged to the original inhabitants.

The third aspect of Israel's illegitimacy, namely, the absence of any legal basis in international law for its establishment and for its proclamation of statehood, will be considered in the next section.

Section 2
The proclamation of the State of Israel had no basis under international law

The British mandate over Palestine ended on 15 May 1948. On the eve of that day the State of Israel was proclaimed. In its operative part, the Proclamation of the State of Israel declared the following:

> "Accordingly we, the members of the National Council, representing the Jewish people in Palestine and the World Zionist Movement, are met together in solemn assembly today, the day of termination of the British Mandate for Palestine; and by virtue of the natural and historic right of the Jewish people and of the Resolution of the General Assembly of the United Nations,
>
> We hereby proclaim the establishment of the Jewish State in Palestine, to be called Medinath Yisrael (The State of Israel)."

Two questions here arise: the competence or legal capacity of the parties that made the Proclamation, and the validity of the grounds on which the Proclamation was based.

Let us first consider the competence of the parties. The Proclamation was made by "the members of the National Council, representing the Jewish people in Palestine and the World Zionist Movement." At the time of the Proclamation, "the Jewish people in Palestine" were in their majority alien immigrants. Only one-tenth of them were indigenous inhabitants of the country. The bulk of the Jews who on 14 May 1948 proclaimed the State of Israel and seized a large area of Palestine were foreign immigrants, some of whom had been admitted by the mandatory Power as "legal immigrants" while others had come in illegally,[2] and who in all cases had entered the country against the will of its original inhabitants.[3] The majority of the indigenous Jews who lived in Palestine in

---

2 The Palestine Government estimated the number of Jewish illegal immigrants in 1945 to have been between 50,000 and 60,000: Government of Palestine, *A Survey of Palestine*, Vol. I, p. 210.
3 Most of Israel's political leaders, past and present, heve come from Russia, Poland,

1948 were opposed to the concept and establishment of a Jewish State.[4] Moreover, the majority of the Jews who proclaimed the State of Israel in 1948 had not even become citizens of Palestine. Although the mandatory Power facilitated the acquisition of Palestinian citizenship by Jewish immigrants and did not require more than two years' residence in order to give them Palestinian nationality, the total number of certificates of naturalization granted by the Government of Palestine between 1925 and 1945 to all categories of immigrants – Jews and others – did not exceed 91,350.[5] The number of Jewish immigrants who had acquired Palestinian citizenship up to 1945 was 132,616 persons.[6] Thus the total number of Jews who possessed Palestinian citizenship in 1948, comprising both indigenous Jewish inhabitants of Palestine and naturalized Jewish immigrants, hardly reached one-third of the Jewish population[7] or one-ninth of the total population. The Palestine Government statistics indicated the provenance of immigrants into Palestine.[8] According to these statistics the Jewish immigrants came largely from Poland, Germany, Rumania and Czechoslovakia. Accordingly, when the Proclamation of the State of Israel states that it was made by the "Jewish people in Palestine", it does not mean the indigenous Jewish inhabitants of Palestine, who in any event, as we have seen, were opposed to the establishment of a Jewish State, but means, in effect, the Jews and nationals of Poland, Germany, Rumania and Czechoslovakia and other countries who had emigrated to Palestine and who did not even possess Palestinian citizenship or the political rights or status of Palestinian citizens. In these circumstances, the proclamation of the State of Israel by a minority of alien settlers, foreign both in origin and nationality, possessing no power or authority to proclaim a Jewish State in Palestine, had no legal basis. Their action could not even be viewed as a secession from the mother country by a section of the original inhabitants.

Turning to the co-author of the Proclamation, namely the "World Zionist Movement", it is obvious that such a Movement had not the slightest power or competence to proclaim the establishment of a State in Palestine. Any argument that a foreign body or movement, such as the "World Zionist Movement",

---

South Africa and other countries, and cannot even claim to belong to the country by birth on its soil. Ben Gurion, Israel's former Prime Minister, has taken pride in asserting that he came to Palestine in 1906 as a Russian tourist on a three-months' visa and simply overstayed: Ben Gurion, *Israël, Années de Lutte*, p. 9, Flammarion, Paris, 1964.

4 As to the opposition of the Orthodox Jews of Palestine to the establishment of a Jewish State, see Ronald Storrs, *Orientations*, p. 340, Nicholson and Watson, London, 1945, and Section 2 of Chapter I, *ante*.

5 Government of Palestine, *A Survey of Palestine*, Vol. I, p. 208; Government of Palestine, *Statistical Abstract*, 1944–1945, pp. 36 and 46.

6 Government of Palestine, *A Survey of Palestine*, Vol. I, p. 208.

7 Official Records of the 3rd Session of the General Assembly, First Committee, Part I, p. 849. The total number of the inhabitants of Palestine in 1946 amounted to 1,972,560, divided as follows: 1,203,780 Moslems, 145,060 Christians, 608,240 Jews, 15,490 others. (Official Records of the 2nd Session of the General Assembly, 1947, Appendix I to report of Sub-Committee 1, p. 270.)

8 *Statistical Abstract of Palestine*, 1941, p. 33.

possessed any legal capacity or competence to create a State in the territory of Palestine would be simply ridiculous.

It follows, therefore, that the parties which purported to proclaim the State of Israel in 1948 possessed no power under the internal law of Palestine or under international law to proclaim a Jewish State in Palestine and their action must be considered null and void.

If we now turn to the grounds upon which the Proclamation was based we find them as invalid as the parties that made it were incompetent.

The first of those grounds was stated to be "the natural and historic right of the Jewish people." There is no need to repeat here what was said in Section 1 of Chapter I about this claim being spurious in law and false in fact. This ground entirely collapses under an historical and legal scrutiny.

With the collapse of one of the two legs which supported its statehood, Israel cannot even limp along on the other leg, namely, the partition resolution. This second ground has no more legal basis than the first. We have seen, in Chapter III, the grounds which invalidate this resolution and it is clear that it gave the Jews neither a legal basis for establishing a State in Palestine, nor title to the territory which they occupied.

The view that the State of Israel derived no valid root of title from the partition resolution is further reinforced by the consideration that Israel was established not in conformity with, but in "flagrant violation" of, the UN resolution.[9] Neither territorially, nor demographically, nor organically does the State of Israel correspond to the concept of the Jewish State that was envisaged by the UN.

Thus, territorially, Israel is not the Jewish State which was envisaged by the UN resolution. We have already described in Section 4 of Chapter IV the areas which Israel seized in excess of the partition plan. Such seizure was no accident, but was deliberate, and the ground for it was prepared by the complete omission in the Proclamation of the State of Israel of any reference to boundaries. David Ben Gurion states that the question of boundaries was considered at the time of drafting the Proclamation. There were then two conflicting possibilities: to create a State without defining its frontiers, or to fix its frontiers as determined by the UN. Ben Gurion opposed the fixing of any frontiers for the Jewish State, thus preparing the ground for its expansion. By five votes to four it was decided that the question of frontiers should not be mentioned in the Declaration of Independence.[10]

Likewise, neither demographically nor organically could Israel be considered to be the Jewish State contemplated by the UN. The Jewish State as envisaged by the General Assembly resolution was Jewish only in name, for in fact it would have had an Arab majority. The proposed Jewish State would have had

---

9 See statement of Fuad Ammoun, Lebanese Delegate to the UN, Official Records of the 3rd Session of the General Assembly, 1948, First Committee, p. 238.
10 David Ben Gurion, *Israël, Années de Lutte*, pp. 49–50, Flammarion, Paris, 1964.

a total population of 1,008,800, consisting of 509,780 Arabs and 499,020 Jews.[11] Israel, however, planned to be a Jewish State undiluted by Gentiles, and it therefore forcibly reduced its Arab population to about ten per cent of its original number. (See Section 1 of Chapter VI, *post*.)

Thus, by their seizure of a large part of the territory earmarked for the proposed Arab State and by displacing the majority of the Arab population, the Israelis completely distorted the concept of the Jewish State as originally envisaged by the UN and created something entirely and radically different. It is evident that the UN never intended to create a racist and theocratic state from which the original inhabitants of the country, both Moslems and Christians, would be ousted. Hence Israel cannot lay claim to the territorial and political rights which were intended by the partition resolution for a materially different demographic entity.

In conclusion, it can be said that neither of the two grounds invoked for the establishment of Israel is sustainable either under the internal law of Palestine or under international law. This conclusion affects, and even destroys, the very foundations of the State of Israel.

Sensing the absence of any legal grounds for the establishment of the State of Israel, Zionist advocacy now falls back on fanciful grounds to justify Israel's creation. Thus, the partition resolution is presented as "an act of international legislation" on the part of the General Assembly of the UN.[12] Such a dogmatic assertion of the existence of an international legislative power in the General Assembly is, of course, devoid of any legal basis. The UN does not possess, nor was it ever intended to possess, any legislative power either to create or to dismember States.

Another fanciful and imaginative ground to clothe the creation of Israel with some kind of legitimacy was advanced by Mrs Golda Meir. In an interview published in *Le Monde*, Israel's Prime Minister declared that she feels no concern over the non-recognition of Israel by the Arabs: "This country," she said, "exists as a result of a promise made by God himself. It would be ridiculous to ask for the recognition of its legitimacy."[13] Needless to say, the concept of the creation and legitimacy of States by divine promise is unknown in international law.

Israel's illegitimacy is self-evident. Neither the parties that proclaimed its statehood, nor the grounds upon which the proclamation was made can withstand legal scrutiny. Fanciful explanations of its creation under a divine promise or by an act of international legislation cannot obliterate its illegitimate origin. The stigma of illegitimacy will continue to attach to Israel, with all its legal and political consequences.

---

11 UN Document A/AC 14/32, 11 November 1947, Official Records of the 2nd Session of the General Assembly, *Ad Hoc* Committee, 1947, p. 291.
12 Louis Blom-Cooper in a letter to *The Times*, London, 4 September 1970.
13 Translated from *Le Monde*, 15 October 1971.

Section 3
Was the illegitimacy of Israel cured by recognition, by admission to the UN, or by prescription?

Since the emergence of Israel, certain jurists have searched for some ground to legitimate its creation and to cover up the illegality of its origin. Some have found a ground for its legitimation in the fact of its recognition by a number of other States; others have found such a ground in the fact of its admission to membership of the UN. These two arguments in favour of Israel's legitimation were summarized by Quincy Wright as follows:

> "The Arab claims that the Balfour Declaration and the partition of Palestine violated their rights were probably originally valid, but became moot after the general recognition of Israel and its admission to the United Nations."[14]

Clarifying his thought further, the same writer declared that the admission of Israel to the UN and its recognition by most States "gave legal effectiveness to the partition resolution."[15] At this point suffice it to remark generally that one fails to see on what legal basis a UN resolution which is *ab initio* void and of no effect could subsequently and retroactively acquire legal effectiveness. If, as is clear, the General Assembly was incompetent to partition Palestine, then it is difficult to understand how it could have subsequently acquired any such competence. Similarly, one also fails to see how the invalidating effect of the various grounds that nullify the resolution, namely the encroachment on the sovereignty of the people of Palestine, the violation of the Covenant of the League of Nations and of the Charter of the UN, the denial of justice, the exercise of undue influence, and the iniquity of partition, has ceased and come to an end just because some states have recognized Israel or because Israel was admitted to membership of the UN. If the partition resolution was null and void, then

---

14 Quincy Wright, "Legal Aspects of the Middle East Situation", *The Middle East Crisis*, p. 28, Oceana, 1969.
15 Quincy Wright, "The Middle East Problem", *AJIL*, 1970, p. 271.

such nullity remains for all time and cannot be removed by extraneous and irrelevant circumstances.

The difficulties involved in the validation of the defective title of a State in international law are mentioned by D. P. O'Connell:

> "The problem of reconciling, no matter how ardently we desire it, the theory of the invalidity of title founded on aggression with the necessity of acknowledging the juridical implications of the fact of power in a given territory is quite as acute as the problem of defining aggression . . . Jurisprudentially, resort to recognition or to prescription for validation of title is fraught with difficulties."[16]

In the following pages we shall examine specifically the two grounds that have been suggested for the legitimation of the State of Israel. In addition, we shall consider whether this State's illegitimacy and the wrong done in Palestine could be buried under a plea of prescription.

a. *Recognition of Israel by other States*

Israel is recognized either *de jure* or *de facto* by over two-thirds of the States of the world. About forty States, including all the Arab States, refuse to accord it their recognition. Of greater legal significance is the fact that Israel is not recognized by the Palestinians.

Let us now examine what is the legal effect of Israel's recognition by a number of States. This leads to the question: what is the function of the recognition of a State under international law? "The primary function of recognition," says Brierly, "is to acknowledge as a fact something which has hitherto been uncertain, namely the independence of the body claiming to be a State, and to declare the recognizing State's readiness to accept the normal consequences of that fact, namely the usual courtesies of international intercourse."[17] Oppenheim mentions the more important consequences that flow from recognition. These are, principally, the capacity for the new State to enter into diplomatic relations, the right to sue in the courts of the recognizing State, and immunity from jurisdiction.[18] It is obvious, therefore, that the function of recognition is not the legitimation of the State which is recognized.

On the other hand, the recognition of a State is not determined by considerations relating to its legitimacy. Philip C. Jessup has observed that the practice of basing recognition on constitutional legitimacy instead of on actual existence and control of the country has not as yet been widely enough accepted to be acknowledged as having the force of customary law.[19] Neither *de jure* recognition nor *de facto* recognition implies the legitimacy or the legitimation of the recognized State. Philip Brown states:

---

16 D. P. O'Connell, *International Law*, Vol. I, p. 262, Stevens, London.
17 J. L. Brierly, *The Law of Nations*, 6th ed., p. 139, Clarendon Press, 1963.
18 Oppenheim, *International Law*, Vol. I, 8th ed., pp. 137–139.
19 *AJIL*, 1931, p. 721.

> "*De jure* recognition means full complete recognition. It does not refer to the legality of the recognized Government. *De facto* recognition means the situation created by the continuance or the establishment of diplomatic relations with a new Government, irrespective of its origin."[20]

In the Tinoco arbitration, Chief Justice Taft laid down the principle that recognition of a Government is determined by inquiry into "its *de facto* sovereignty and complete governmental control," but not into "its illegitimacy or irregularity of origin."[21]

De Visscher states:

> "One might be inclined to think that State recognition is strictly a juridical institution governed by precise legal criteria . . . Observation demonstrates that this is far from being the case, and the matter, in varying degrees, depends on politics much more than on law."[22]

The same author remarks that "recognition is based on effectiveness of power, not on the internal constitutional legality of its origins."[23] Again, Lauterpacht declares that "legitimacy of origin as a criterion of recognition was rejected in favour of the principle of effectiveness of governmental power."[24] Rousseau observes that recognition does not entail moral approbation, but solely an ascertainment of effectiveness.[25]

Recognition, then, is neither evidence of the legitimacy nor a means of legitimation of the recognized State.

Just as recognition has no effect upon the legitimacy or illegitimacy of the recognized State, so also recognition has no effect upon the question of title of the recognized State to the territory under its occupation. As an example among many, in 1936 a large number of States accorded *de facto* or *de jure* recognition to Italy's annexation of Ethiopia, but this recognition did not legalize Italy's occupation of Ethiopian territory nor vest Italy with title over such territory. Recognition by other States does not remove the vice with which an occupation is tainted:

> "La reconnaissance par les Puissances ne peut avoir au point de vue juridique aucune influence sur la validité de l'occupation . . . La reconnaissance du fait accompli par les Puissances civilisées est impuissante à couvrir le vice qui entache la prise de possession."[26]

The rule that recognition has no bearing on the title of the recognized State to the territory under its occupation is, however, subject to one qualification.

20 Philip M. Brown, "The Legal Effects of Recognition", *AJIL*, Vol. 44, 1950, p. 617.
21 *AJIL*, 1924, p. 152.
22 Translation from De Visscher, *Théories et Réalités en Droit International Public*, 4th ed., pp. 254–255, Pedone, Paris, 1970.
23 *Ibid.*, p. 321.
24 H. Lauterpacht, *Recognition in International Law*, p. 102, University Press, Cambridge, 1947.
25 Charles Rousseau, *Le Conflit Italo-Ethiopien*, p. 235, Pedone, Paris, 1938.
26 Gaston Jèze, *Etude Théorique et Pratique sur l'Occupation*, p. 298, Paris, 1896.

Where the recognizing State itself possesses a claim over such territory, then in such an event recognition would be tantamount to a waiver on its part of its claim. "Recognition," states Dr Schwarzenberger, "estops the State which has recognized the title from contesting its validity."[27]

Some writers have thought that where a large number of States recognize a new State, the cumulative effect of the recognitions might presumably affect the question of title. Thus Jennings states:

> "On the other hand, where the recognition in question is on the part of a third State having itself no possible title to the territory, the position, as we have already seen, is quite different. The recognition of the third State cannot affect the title unless perhaps when a considerable number of other States have likewise recognized title, in which case the cumulative effect of the recognitions may presumably form an ingredient of a process of consolidation."[28]

Although this view is only tentatively expressed, it does not seem that it could be accepted as a rule of international law. Ian Brownlie considers that it is open to considerable doubt that the vice of title can be cured by recognition by third States.[29] D. P. O'Connell also rejects the view that collective recognition could validate title. He says:

> "Various methods acceptable to law for the validation of title have been suggested. The first is multilateral recognition of the change in a general treaty of settlement. The action here is quasi-legislative and confers validity at least so far as the signatory States are concerned. Unilateral recognition by one State is similarly quasi-legislative so far as that State's courts are concerned, who may then be obliged to take cognizance of the change. This approach to the question of validation of title is open to the criticism that a mere adding up of assents is of no greater juristic value than a particular assent, and that since unanimous action is improbable, validation can never be international but can only be *vis-à-vis* the assenting States. Such a subjective rule is unsatisfactory."[30]

The question of the effect on the territorial title of the recognized State of an accumulation of recognitions remains academic so long as the title of the State is not contested. But where, as in the case of Israel, the title of the occupying State is contested by the original inhabitants of the country, it seems unreasonable to suggest that recognitions by third parties could affect, impair or destroy their rights and title. Legally, State recognition can be neither declaratory, nor translative, of a territorial title.

Recently, the possibility has arisen of the recognition of Israel by some Arab States. It is therefore necessary to consider whether such recognition would be different in its legal effect from recognition by any other State. The answer is

---

27 G. Schwarzenberger, "Title to Territory", 51 *AJIL*, 1957, p. 42.
28 R. Y. Jennings, *The Acquisition of Territory in International Law*, p. 44, Manchester University Press, 1963.
29 Ian Brownlie, *International Law*, p. 159, Clarendon Press, Oxford, 1966.
30 D. P. O'Connell, *op. cit.*, Vol. I, p. 496.

that no difference exists. Recognition by an Arab State would confer no legitimacy nor title on the State of Israel. The reason is obvious. The territory involved is the territory of Palestine, which belongs to the Palestinians, and no State, Arab or non-Arab, can alienate it.

At present, there is no Government which represents the Palestinians, or which can speak on their behalf. According to reliable estimates, the total number of Palestinians at the beginning of 1972 was 3,138,000 distributed as follows: 963,000 in the territory of the East Bank of Jordan; 717,000 in the territory of the West Bank; 389,000 in the Gaza Strip; 364,000 in Palestinian territory occupied by Israel before 1967; 257,000 in Lebanon; 174,000 in Syria; 150,000 in Kuwait; 124,000 in Egypt, Saudi Arabia, Iraq, Libya, the Gulf States and other countries.

At the first Palestinian National Congress, convened in Jerusalem between 28 May and 2 June 1964, it was resolved that "the Palestine Liberation Organization shall alone possess the right to represent the Palestinians and to speak on their behalf" (Resolution 5). Moreover, Article 4 of the Palestine National Covenant, adopted at the same Congress, declared:

> "The people of Palestine shall, after the liberation of their homeland, decide their own destiny in accordance with their own desire, will and choice."

The Palestinians have ceded their rights to no other Government; no other Government can abrogate their right to their own land.

The conclusion, therefore, is that the recognition of Israel by other States, even by an Arab State, does not remove the illegitimacy of Israel, nor impair the natural and inalienable right of the Palestinians to their homeland.

b. *Admission of Israel to the UN*

Admission to the UN did not involve recognition of Israel's legitimacy. The principle was established early in the life of the League of Nations that co-membership in the organization does not involve mutual recognition of the member States. The same principle applies in the UN.[31] Admission to membership of the UN, like recognition by other States, does not affect the status of Israel or cure its illegitimacy. Admission to the UN is not a kind of religious sacrament which, like baptism in Christianity, washes away human sin.

The UN is not vested under the Charter with any power to legitimate a State which is illegitimate. The admission of a State does not depend upon the legitimacy or otherwise of the State applying for membership. Nor does the procedure of admission involve any inquiry into the constitutional legitimacy or the manner of creation of the applicant State. All that is required under the Charter is evidence of its ability and willingness to accept and carry out the obligations

---

31 See Oppenheim, *op. cit.*, 8th ed. Vol. I, p. 134, and D. P. O'Connell, *op. cit.*, Vol. I, p. 169.

contained in the Charter. The admission of Israel to UN membership therefore cannot be construed to involve a legitimation of its creation.

Moreover, as will be explained in greater detail in Section 3 of Chapter VIII, Israel was admitted to membership of the UN only after it gave to the General Assembly formal assurances concerning the implementation of its resolutions, and, in particular, concerning the implementation of the resolutions of 29 November 1947 and 11 December 1948. Despite such assurances, Israel has violated those resolutions, as well as a very large number of other resolutions, both of the General Assembly and the Security Council. In these circumstances, any argument that Israel's admission to the UN involved a retrospective legitimation of its creation would be tantamount to rewarding it for its breach of UN resolutions and of the conditions of its admission.

c. *Prescription*

Lapse of time does not cure Israel's illegitimacy, nor make legitimate its usurpation of the land of Palestine. Professor Giraud has observed that in contrast to private law, no prescription is envisaged by international law to regularize irregular situations.[32]

Even those who consider that prescription has a place in international law must concede that Israel cannot free itself from the stain of illegitimacy so long as its title is contested. Grotius considered the basis of prescription to be the presumed voluntary abandonment of his territory by the previous sovereign. In other words, prescription is grounded in acquiescence of the rightful sovereign. Lauterpacht states:

> "The limits and conditions of acquisitive prescription in international law are not above controversy. Although its requirements are not as stringent as in the municipal sphere, the patent illegality of the purported acquisition, combined with continued protests on the part of the dispossessed State, are sufficient to rule out the legalization, in that manner, of the original illegality."[33]

Likewise, D. P. O'Connell observes:

> "Proof of actual consent to a territorial claim, or of failure to protest against it . . . is also essential in the case of prescription, for acquiescence in the possession of territory by a foreign State is a precondition of that possession being peaceful and constituting an effective reversal of the title of the definitive sovereign."[34]

In the case of Palestine, there exists no acquiescence on the part of the Palestinians to Israel's usurpation, nor any abandonment of their claim.

---

32 E. Giraud, "Le Droit International et la Politique", *Hague Recueil*, Vol. III, 1963, p. 425.
33 H. Lauterpacht, *Recognition in International Law*, p. 428, Cambridge University Press, 1947.
34 D. P. O'Connell, *op. cit.*, Vol. I, pp. 489–490.

The people of Palestine have never given their consent to any transfer of title over their country nor have they recognized any sovereignty in the occupier. "In present day international law," observes Professor Schwarzenberger, "it is by itself not sufficient to transform wartime occupation into a transfer of sovereignty. Even in the relations between belligerents, not to speak of third States, the title requires to be consolidated by positive acts of recognition or consent or, at least, by acquiescence of the former territorial sovereign."[35]

In the absence of international legal machinery available to the Palestinians to put an end to the usurpation of Palestine, one cannot really speak of laches or acquiescence or prescription. In these circumstances, neither the inalienable right of the Palestinians to their homeland nor the illegitimacy of Israel are eroded by time.

---

35 G. Schwarzenberger, *International Law*, 3rd ed., p. 302.

CHAPTER VI

ISRAEL'S
VIOLATIONS OF
UN RESOLUTIONS AND
OF INTERNATIONAL LAW

Section 1
Uprooting of the Palestinians

When in 1896 Theodor Herzl launched the idea of a Jewish State to be established either in Argentina or in Palestine, he attempted to find a solution for all the problems that were bound to arise, but he overlooked the most important one: the problem of what to do with the indigenous inhabitants of the country. When he spoke of Argentina, Herzl mentioned "its sparse population" and the fact that the infiltration of Jews into that country had "certainly produced some discontent". In the case of Palestine, his only concern was about "the sanctuaries of Christendom" which, he stated, "would be safeguarded by assigning to them an extra-territorial status."[1] There is not one word about the existing population which had lived there for tens of centuries. This significant silence about the existence of an indigenous population in Palestine became positive deception in the slogan: "A land without people for a people without land", which the Zionists then coined to promote their colonization scheme in Palestine.

If Theodor Herzl simply ignored the problem of the presence of the Palestinians in Palestine, the Zionist leaders who followed him did not ignore it. They solved it. It is clear that the Zionist concept of a politico-religious Jewish State was not compatible with the presence of Gentiles, much less with a substantial number of Palestinian Arabs as was contemplated by the partition resolution. In accordance with the partition plan the proposed Jewish State would even have had, as we have seen, a starting majority of Palestine Arabs in the proportion of 509,780 Moslems and Christians to 499,020 Jews.[2] In the Zionist concept, it would be a contradiction to describe as Jewish a State in which the Palestine

---

1   Theodor Herzl, *The Jewish State*, 5th ed., p. 30, H. Pordes, London, 1967.
2   See Appendix I to Report of Sub-Committee 2 to the *Ad Hoc* Committee on the Palestinian Question, Official Records of the 2nd Session of the General Assembly, Document A/AC 14/32, p. 304.

Arabs exceeded the number of Jews. Maxime Rodinson has observed that the Jewish character of the State is "the prime aim and postulate of Zionist ideology."[3]

In consequence, Zionist leadership resolved the problem of the presence of the Palestinians in the proposed Jewish State by recourse to a brutal and barbarous method. This was nothing other than their forcible uprooting and displacement. Georges Friedmann says that "it seems that the principal Zionist leaders, both political and military, considered a massive Arab exodus to be desirable from the point of view of the future State."[4]

The means to that end began to be applied before the end of the British mandate. The Zionist terrorist machine, operated by three para-military organizations, began to sow fear among the Palestine Arabs.[5] Among the most notorious Zionist terrorist exploits before the British mandate ended on 15 May 1948 were the blowing up of the King David Hotel at Jerusalem, which caused the death of 91 persons (22 July 1946); the dynamiting of the Semiramis Hotel at Jerusalem, which killed 20 persons (5 January 1948); and the massacre of Deir Yassin, where 300 persons – old men, women and children – were massacred "without any military reason or provocation of any kind."[6]

The Zionist objective for the Deir Yassin massacre, of terrorizing the Arab civilian population, was achieved with disastrous results. It can safely be said that the Deir Yassin massacre was the principal reason which caused the Palestine Arab exodus of 1948. Jacques de Reynier, the Chief Delegate of the International Red Cross in Palestine, commented in the following terms:

> "This action had immense repercussions. The whole press, both Jewish and Arab, strongly condemned this manner of acting, but insisted all the same upon the fact of its possible repetition and upon the need of being watchful. Thereupon terror seized the Arabs and gave rise to movements of panic which were wholly out of proportion with the real danger. The exodus began and became nearly general."[7]

The process of intimidation and terrorization of the Palestine Arabs continued after the proclamation of the State of Israel. Where terror failed to achieve the objective, Israeli armed forces resorted to actual expulsion. The expulsion of the Palestine Arab inhabitants was carried out in Haifa,[8] Lydda and Ramleh,[9] Tiberias,[10] Safad,[11] Beersheba and several other towns and villages.[12]

---

3 Maxime Rodinson, *Israel and the Arabs*, p. 228, Penguin Books, London, 1968.
4 Georges Friedmann, *The End of the Jewish People?*, p. 279, Doubleday, 1968.
5 As to Zionist terrorism in Palestine during the mandate, see *British Statement on Acts of Violence*, Cmd. 6873 (1946).
6 See the account of this massacre by the Chief Delegate of the International Red Cross, Jacques de Reynier, *A Jérusalem un drapeau flottait sur la ligne de feu*, Editions de la Baconnière, Neuchâtel, Switzerland, 1950.
7 Translation from Reynier, *op. cit.*, p. 213.   8 *Middle East Journal*, 1949, p. 325.
9 In Lydda and Ramleh 60,000 persons, many of whom were refugees from other places, were expelled by the Israelis: G. Kirk, *The Middle East 1949–50*, p. 281, Oxford University Press, London, 1954.   10 *Middle East Journal*, 1948, p. 331.
11 S. N. Fisher, *The Middle East*, p. 589, Routledge and Kegan Paul, London, 1960.
12 Ibid, p. 589.

On various occasions Israeli forces used loud-speakers to threaten the civilian population and to order it to leave.[13] Describing the occupation of Haifa, George Kirk states:

> "The Jewish combatants there and elsewhere made skilful use of psychological warfare to break their opponents' morale, and the effect upon the civilians was only what was to be expected. At a later stage, the Israeli armed forces did not confine their pressure on the Arab civilian population to playing upon their fears. They forcibly expelled them: for example the population of 'Akka (including refugees from Haifa) in May; the population of Lydda and Ramleh (including refugees from Jaffa) in July; and the population of Beersheba and Western Galilee in October."[14]

The creation of a Jewish State in Palestine has been described as a "process which either by accident or intent rid Israel of the majority of its large Arab population."[15] In fact, there was little accident in the process. I. F. Stone observed:

> "Jewish terrorism, not only by the Irgun, in such savage massacres as Deir Yassin, but in milder form by the Haganah itself, 'encouraged' Arabs to leave the areas the Jews wished to take over for strategic or demographic reasons. They tried to make as much of Israel as free of Arabs as possible."[16]

Lieutenant-General E. L. M. Burns, Chief of Staff of the UN Truce Supervision Organization in Palestine, declared that "Israelis had a record of getting rid of Arabs whose lands they desired."[17]

John H. Davis, who occupied for five years the office of Commissioner-General of the UN Relief and Works Agency for Palestine Refugees in the Near East, has remarked that "the extent to which the refugees were savagely driven out by the Israelis as part of a deliberate master-plan has been insufficiently recognized." Dr Davis went on to explain how the Zionist concept of a Jewish State called for the ousting of the indigenous Arab population from its homeland, and emphasized that this objective was achieved by means ranging from "expert psychological warfare to ruthless expulsion by force."[18]

As a result of terror, violence and expulsion, nearly a million Palestinians left or were forced in 1948 to leave their homes, towns and villages, and to seek refuge either in other parts of Palestine or in neighbouring Arab countries.[19]

---

13 As to the use of loud-speakers by Israeli forces as a means of "psychological blitz" to frighten and secure the evacuation of the civilian population of Haifa, see G. Kirk, op. cit., p. 262, and S. N. Fisher, op. cit., p. 589. As to their use in Acre, see Sacher, The Establishment of a State, p. 245.

14 G. Kirk, op. cit., p. 264.   15 Middle East Journal, 1948, p. 447.

16 I. F. Stone in New York Review of Books, 3 August 1967.

17 E. L. M. Burns, Between Arab and Israeli, p. 191, Harrap, London, 1962, and Institute for Palestine Studies, Beirut, 1969.

18 John H. Davis, The Evasive Peace, pp. 57–60, John Murray, London, 1968.

19 The present number of refugees exceeds two million. This figure is only an estimate because UNRWA's records, which show 1,506,640 refugees as on 30 June 1972 (according to the annual report of the Commissioner-General of UNRWA dated 27 October 1972), do not give the whole picture since not all refugees are registered with UNRWA.

Count Bernadotte, the UN Mediator for Palestine, exerted all his efforts to secure the repatriation of the Palestine refugees. Israel refused to allow their repatriation. The UN Mediator did not accept Israel's decision, and recommended to the General Assembly that "the right of the Arab refugees to return to their homes in Jewish-controlled territory at the earliest possible date should be affirmed by the United Nations . . ."[20]

The General Assembly accepted Count Bernadotte's recommendation, and in paragraph 11 of its resolution 194 (III) dated 11 December 1948 it declared:

> "that the refugees wishing to return to their homes and live at peace with their neighbours should be permitted to do so at the earliest practicable date, and that compensation should be paid for the property of those choosing not to return and for loss of or damage to property which, under principles of international law or in equity, should be made good by the Governments or authorities responsible."[21]

The same resolution instructed the UN Conciliation Commission for Palestine "to facilitate the repatriation, resettlement and economic and social rehabilitation of the refugees . . ."

But Israel was adamant. It refused to implement the General Assembly resolution. In its Third Progress Report, the Conciliation Commission stated that it had not succeeded in achieving the acceptance by Israel of the principle of the repatriation of the Palestine refugees.[22]

On only one occasion, as a result of pressure from the US Government, did Israel make an offer to take back a limited number of refugees. In May 1949, the US Government addressed a note to Israel in which it insisted that Israel should make tangible concessions on the question of refugees, boundaries and the internationalization of Jerusalem, failing which the US Government would reconsider its attitude towards it. The US note "interpreted Israel's attitude as dangerous to peace and as indicating disregard of the UN General Assembly resolutions of 29 November 1947 and 11 December 1948."[23] This produced an Israeli offer to the Conciliation Commission to permit the return of 100,000 refugees, subject to conditions, one of which was that Israel "reserved the right to resettle the repatriated refugees in specific locations, in order to ensure that their re-installation would fit into the general plan of Israel's economic development." Obviously, a proposal to permit the return of some 10 per cent of the refugees and to resettle them in specific locations away from their homes did not constitute a compliance with the UN repatriation resolution. The Conciliation Commission's comment was that it considered the Israeli proposal unsatisfactory.[24]

---

20 UN Document A/648, p. 14.
21 UN Document A/810 (Appendix VI).
22 UN Document A/927, 21 June 1949.
23 Don Peretz, *Israel and the Palestine Arabs*, pp. 41–42, Middle East Institute, Washington, D.C., 1958; James G. McDonald, *My Mission to Israel*, pp. 181–182, Simon and Schuster, New York, 1951.
24 UN Document A/1367, p. 14.

Since 1948, the General Assembly has annually reaffirmed its resolution calling on Israel to allow the return of the refugees, but without avail. Israel's opposition to the repatriation of the refugees has not changed or diminished.

To complete the uprooting of the Palestinians and to make difficult a reversal of the situation, Israel did not only refuse their repatriation, it took two other measures.

First, it exerted all its efforts to attract the greatest possible number of Jews from the four corners of the world. In 1950 it enacted the *Law of Return*, which granted to every Jew in the world potential citizenship and enabled any Jew who desired it to emigrate to Israel and settle there. More than one and three-quarter million Jews emigrated to Israel and were given the lands and the homes of the Palestine refugees.[25]

Secondly, the Israeli Government destroyed a great number of Arab villages. The intention was to prevent their inhabitants who had fled or had been forced to evacuate from returning to their homes. Up till November 1953 one hundred and sixty-one Arab villages had been razed to the ground after their occupation by Israeli forces.[26] Many of these villages were even destroyed after the UN resolution of 11 December 1948 calling upon Israel to permit the return of the refugees to their homes. Writing in 1966, Sabri Jiryis states that more than 250 Arab villages were demolished by Israel after the expulsion of their inhabitants.[27]

When world opinion awakened to the full significance of the tragedy of the Palestine refugees, the Israeli-Zionist propaganda machine sought to distort its real cause. Israel disavowed responsibility for what had happened and laid the blame upon the Arab States, the British, and even upon the refugees themselves.[28] Long after the tragedy, the Israelis began spreading the story that Arab broadcasts had been made to the Palestinians telling them to flee from their homes. This fabrication was exposed by Erskine B. Childers, a British journalist. As a guest of the Israeli Foreign Office, Mr Childers investigated the Israeli statement about the alleged Arab broadcasts ordering the evacuation, and could find no dates, names of stations or texts of messages. He even checked British and American monitoring units of all Middle Eastern broadcasts throughout 1948. "There was not," he concluded, "a single order or appeal or suggestion about evacuation from any Arab radio station inside or outside Palestine, in 1948. There is repeated monitored record of Arab appeals, even flat orders, to the civilians of Palestine to stay put."[29]

The Israelis have also attempted to disclaim liability for the exodus of the

---

25 In 1946 the number of Jews in Palestine amounted to 608,000. At the end of 1971 their number had increased to 2,634,000.
26 A list giving the names of these villages was published with a letter of protest to the Israeli Government in *Al Rabitah*, No. 12, November 1953, a church magazine of the Greek Catholic Episcopate in Israel.
27 Sabri Jiryis, *The Arabs in Israel*, p. 56, Institute for Palestine Studies, Beirut, 1968.
28 See Don Peretz, *op. cit.*, pp. 36 and 86.
29 *The Spectator*, 12 May 1961.

Palestinians by alleging that the refugee problem was the result of the war between the Arab States and Israel. There is nothing farther from the truth. The Palestine refugee tragedy was the consequence of Zionist terrorism and of the Deir Yassin massacre. This massacre was perpetrated several weeks *before* any war had taken place between the Arab States and Israel. In fact, the exodus had already reached considerable proportions before the outbreak of the war. It was estimated that before the outbreak of the Arab-Israeli war on 15 May 1948 the number of Palestine refugees had reached about 300,000. As Anthony Nutting has remarked: "it would be truer to say that the refugees were the cause of the first Arab-Israeli war and not the result."[30]

Israel's obstinate refusal since 1948 to permit the return of the refugees to their homes belies the pleas of innocence which have been invented by Zionist apologists. Had there been any substance in the claim that the Israelis were not responsible for the exodus of the Palestinians, they would certainly have been less adamant in opposing their repatriation.

During the War of 5 June 1967, Israeli armed forces again sought the displacement of the Palestinians from the areas which they planned to annex, and, in particular, from Jerusalem and its surroundings. For this purpose they resorted to some of the methods which they had successfully applied in 1948. Thus, in Jerusalem, loud-speakers announced on 6 June 1967 the capture of the city and asked the Arab inhabitants to leave for Amman while the road was still open. They were told that their safety could not be guaranteed if they remained. In other places, such as in Bethlehem, the people were ordered to leave within two hours, failing which their houses would be blown up over their heads. Some heeded the threats, others did not. In his report to the Security Council, N. G. Gussing, the Special Representative of the Secretary-General of the UN, mentioned "persistent reports of acts of intimidation by Israeli armed forces and of Israeli attempts to suggest to the population, by loud-speakers mounted on cars, that they might be better off on the East Bank. There have also been reports that in several localities buses and trucks were put at the disposal of the population for travel purposes."[31]

Over 410,000 Palestinians were displaced in 1967, some of them for the second time. As it had done in 1948, the UN again called upon Israel to permit the return of the refugees. The Security Council in its resolution 237 of 14 June 1967 and the General Assembly in its resolution 2252 (ES-V) of 4 July 1967 called upon Israel to facilitate the return of those inhabitants who had fled since the outbreak of hostilities. The combined efforts of the International Red Cross, UNRWA and the Great Powers succeeded in securing the repatriation of only 14,000 of the Palestinian refugees displaced in June 1967. However, at the same

---

30 From a speech delivered under the auspices of the American Council of Judaism at New York on 2 November 1967. Regarding the causes of the Palestine exodus, see also Walid Khalidi, *Why Did The Palestinians Leave?*, Arab League Office, London, 1963.
31 UN Document A/6797, p. 13, 15 September 1967.

time as this token repatriation, Israel forced 17,000 Palestinians to leave the occupied territories and to seek refuge on the East Bank of the Jordan.[32]

The Israelis have attempted to mitigate the impact on world opinion of the Palestine refugee tragedy by pointing to the existence of other refugee problems in the world today. Such an attempt, however, cannot distort nor submerge the issue. The Palestine refugee tragedy is unique in the annals of modern civilization. It cannot be equated with other refugee problems, whether as regards its underlying cause or its relative dimensions.[33] At no time in history – at least in modern history – has a majority of the population of a country been deliberately and forcibly uprooted by a minority of foreign origin with the object of taking over its lands, its homes, its towns and cities. This unique character of the Palestine refugee problem is emphasized by Sir John Glubb, who said:

> "It is quite essential vividly to grasp the unique conditions of the struggle in Palestine. We have witnessed many wars in this century, in which one country seeks to impose its power on others. But in no war, I think, for many centuries past, has the objective been to remove a nation from its country and to introduce another and entirely different race to occupy its lands, houses and cities and live there. This peculiarity lends to the Palestine struggle a desperate quality which bears no resemblance to any other war in modern history."[34]

In 1971 twelve million refugees left Bangladesh. But when the India-Pakistan war came to an end, they all returned to their homes. Not so in the case of the Palestinians, who were deliberately displaced to make room for Jewish immigrants and to ensure that the new State of Israel would not be diluted by Gentiles.

The uprooting of the Palestinians from their homeland can have no excuse or justification. Not only is it a breach of international law and of the principles of the United Nations Charter, but it also constitutes an unparalleled violation of elementary principles of humanity and civilization.

---

32 For details of Israel's attitude on the question of repatriation of the refugees of the 1967 war, see the report of the Commissioner-General of UNRWA, UN Document A/6713, 15 September 1967, and Henry Cattan, *Palestine, the Arabs and Israel*, pp. 113–114, Longman, 1969.
33 The number of refugees in 1948 represented more than two-thirds of the Palestine Arab population.
34 Sir John Glubb, *The Middle East Crisis*, p. 41, Hodder and Stoughton, London, 1967.

Section 2
Seizure of
territories in excess
of the partition resolution

The areas seized by Israel in 1948 and 1949 in excess of the boundaries of the Jewish State as fixed by the resolution of 29 November 1947 have been described earlier.[35] The partition resolution had allocated to the Jewish State 57 per cent of the area of Palestine: in 1948 and 1949 the Jews enlarged this to 80 per cent.

Having seized by force these additional territories, Israel refused to abandon them, even to gain peace with its neighbours. This refusal was one of the causes of the failure of the conciliation efforts attempted by the Conciliation Commission for Palestine. One of the first acts of the Conciliation Commission in 1949 was to secure the agreement of the Arab States and Israel at Lausanne on what has since been described as the Lausanne Protocol. This Protocol was signed on 12 May 1949 and was worded as follows:

> "The United Nations Conciliation Commission for Palestine, anxious to achieve as quickly as possible the objectives of the General Assembly's resolution of 11 December 1948 regarding refugees, the respect for their rights and the preservation of their property, as well as territorial and other questions, has proposed to the Delegation of Israel and to the Delegations of the Arab States that the working documents attached thereto be taken as a basis for discussion with the Commission.
>
> The interested Delegations have accepted this proposal with the understanding that the exchanges of views which will be carried on by the Commission with the two parties will bear upon the territorial adjustments necessary to the above indicated objectives."

To the Protocol was annexed a map on which were indicated

"the boundaries defined in General Assembly resolution 181 (II) of 29 November

---

35 See Section 4 of Chapter IV.

1947, which has thus been taken as the basis of discussion with the Commission."[36]

In its Third Progress Report, the Conciliation Commission gave an account of the results of its discussions with the parties on the basis of the Lausanne Protocol. This Progress Report is illuminating because it sets out the position taken by Israel from the outset on some of the basic issues involved in the Palestine Question, a position which prevented the success of the Commission's efforts at meditation.

On the territorial issue, Israel's attitude was in no way conducive to a settlement. Israel went back on its acceptance in the Lausanne Protocol of the partition resolution as a basis for discussion, and insisted on taking instead the armistice lines as a basis, even demanding more Arab territories, namely Western Galilee and the Gaza Strip. This is clear from the Third Progress Report of the Conciliation Commission, which mentions that on the territorial question Israel proposed that its frontiers with Egypt and Lebanon should be the frontiers of Palestine while under the British mandate. This proposal, if accepted, would have meant Israel's annexation of Western Galilee and the Gaza Strip, both of which were wholly Arab areas that had been reserved for the Palestine Arabs under General Assembly resolution 181 (II) of 29 November 1947. As regards its frontier with Jordan, Israel proposed a boundary corresponding to the armistice lines. The proposal again implied the annexation by Israel of several Arab territories which it had seized in 1948 and 1949 but which were reserved for the Palestine Arabs under the General Assembly resolution. In effect, Israel's territorial proposals at the Lausanne discussions in 1949 meant that the Palestine Arabs would be left with about 15 per cent of the area of their own country.

Israeli apologists usually accuse the Arabs of having rejected the partition of Palestine and claim that this rejection, coupled with the armed intervention by the Arab States in 1948, had caused the partition resolution to lapse, and therefore justified Israel's occupation of areas in excess of the resolution. This argument is specious and is devoid of any basis either in fact or in law.

On the one hand, this argument conveniently overlooks the facts of history, for it is clear that the Israelis had planned to expand the area of the Jewish State beyond the boundaries envisaged by the United Nations resolution even before the date on which the partition was to take effect. It is established that before the end of the mandate on 15 May 1948 and, therefore, before any possible intervention by the Arab States, the Jews, taking advantage of their superior military preparation and organization, had occupied a number of Arab cities and seized a considerable part of the territory of Palestine, including areas allocated by the partition resolution to the Arab State. The chronology of events in Palestine during the six months preceding the end of the mandate shows that Jewish forces had seized and occupied most of the Arab cities of Palestine:

---

36 Third Progress Report of the United Nations Conciliation Commission for Palestine, UN Document A/927, 21 June 1949.

Tiberias was occupied on 19 April 1948, Haifa on 22 April, Jaffa on 28 April, the Arab quarters in the New City of Jerusalem on 30 April, Beisan on 8 May, Safad on 10 May and Acre on 14 May 1948.[37]

Moreover, as previously mentioned in Section 2 of Chapter V, the plan to seize areas in excess of the partition resolution was deliberate and was formed by the Jews before the outbreak of the war with the Arab States. Such a plan can be inferred from the intentional omission of any reference to boundaries of the new State in the Proclamation of the State of Israel on 14 May 1948.

On the other hand, the argument has no basis in law. The Palestinians had a perfect legal right to oppose the dismemberment of their country and to defend the territorial integrity of their homeland. The Arab refusal to accept partition and the ensuing strife between Arabs and Jews could in no way confer upon Israel the right to aggravate the wrong and to usurp the little of the country that had been left to its original inhabitants. In other words, the Arab-Israeli conflict of 1948 could not take away the rights of the Palestine Arabs nor enlarge the rights of the Jews.

As regards the intervention of the Arab States, it was proclaimed at the time that the object of their intervention was to go to the help of the Palestinians who were the victims of Zionist terrorism and were threatened by the superior military force of the Jews. Lieutenant-General Burns has remarked that the Arabs outside Palestine had as much right to come to the assistance of Arabs in Palestine as Jews outside Palestine to come to the assistance of Jews within.[38]

Israel's seizure in 1948 and 1949 of territories outside the geographical limits of the Jewish State as fixed by the partition resolution was a patent usurpation committed in violation of the General Assembly resolution. It is important to observe that the UN did not consider that the conflict of 1948 affected the partition resolution, for, as explained in Chapter VIII, *post*, the General Assembly accepted Israel into the fold of the UN only after "recalling its resolutions of 29 November 1947 and 11 December 1948 and taking note of the declarations and explanations made by the representative of the Government of Israel before the *Ad Hoc* Committee in respect of the implementation of the said resolutions." This took place on 11 May 1949, long after the end of the 1948 conflict. Hence Israel cannot, in order to justify its seizure of territories in excess of the partition resolution, claim that the resolution had lapsed as a result of the armed conflict of 1948.

The seizure by Israel of four-fifths of Palestine not only constituted a grave violation of the resolution, but it destroyed its territorial basis. True, the Arabs objected to the partition plan; but the Israelis completely wrecked it in order to seize a larger area of land than that allocated to the Jewish State by the resolution.

---

37 See *Middle East Journal*, Washington, D.C., 1948, Vol. 2, pp. 215–221, and 329–332. See also G. Kirk, *op. cit.*, pp. 262–266.
38 E. L. M. Burns, *Between Arab and Israeli*, p. 127, George G. Harrap & Co., London, 1962.

Section 3
Plunder, confiscation and expropriation of Arab property

All the property, movable and immovable, of a million Palestine refugees was seized and taken over by Israel in 1948. This plunder is one of the greatest mass robberies in the history of Palestine, in respect of which little was said, and much less was done. Since only 10 per cent of the Arab population remained in Israeli-occupied territory, the property seized represented 90 per cent of what the Arabs owned in Palestine.

The magnitude of the spoliation is realized if one considers that Arab property seized and taken over by Israel in 1948 comprised the following main items:

(i) A large number of cities, towns and villages complete with their contents. The wholly Arab cities and towns of Jaffa, Acre, Nazareth, Lydda, Ramleh, Beersheba, Beisan, Majdal, Isdud, Beit Jibrin and Shafa Amr, the Arab quarters of the New City of Jerusalem, Haifa, Tiberias, Safad and over eight hundred villages[39] were seized and taken over by Israel. As their Arab inhabitants were terrorized or expelled, or fled in conditions of chaos and confusion, all these cities, towns and villages were taken over, in almost all cases, complete with their contents.

(ii) Land outside urban areas. According to official figures already mentioned, the Arabs owned the bulk of the land of Palestine. This included cultivable land covering an area of 6,705,568 dunoms, land planted with citrus having an area of 135,368 dunoms, land planted with olive-trees, bananas and other trees having an area of 1,054,065 dunoms, and large tracts of grazing land.

(iii) Commercial and industrial property. This includes the rights, assets, goods and equipment of tens of thousands of individuals, companies, partnerships,

---

39 The number of Arab villages which existed in 1945 in the territories occupied by Israel was 863: A. Granott, *Agrarian Reform and the Record of Israel*, p. 89, London, 1956.

industrial and commercial establishments, factories, flour-mills and workshops. Don Peretz mentions that 7,800 shops, offices, workshops and storehouses were taken over by the Israelis.[40]

(iv) Movables, possessions and personal effects. This item represents the movable property and personal possessions of a million persons. The loot included furniture, household effects, and, in many cases, money, silver, rugs, tapestries, paintings and works of art.

In the case of movables, there was an orgy of looting which is reminiscent of days before the advent of civilization. The testimony about this large-scale looting is unanimous. In his Progress Report, Count Bernadotte observed that most of the refugees left practically all their possessions behind.[41] He then added:

> "Moreover, while those who had fled in the early days of the conflict had been able to take with them some personal effects and assets, many of the latecomers were deprived of everything except the clothes in which they stood, and apart from their homes (many of which were destroyed) lost all furniture and assets, and even their tools of trade."[42]

Writing later, Ralph Bunche, the Acting Mediator on Palestine, stated in his Progress Report that "the bulk of the refugees left their homes on foot at short notice taking little or nothing with them."[43] Similarly, the Director of Field Operations for the UN's Disaster Relief Project observed: "While a few were able to carry personal effects and some money, flight was generally disorderly and with almost no possessions."[44] Referring to the exodus of the Palestine refugees, Edwin Samuel stated: "The next stage in this tragedy was widespread Jewish looting of Arab property."[45] George Kirk wrote:

> "It was apparently at Jaffa that Jewish troops first succumbed to the temptation to indulge in wholesale looting . . . and within a few days Jewish troops were looting the newly captured Arab suburbs of Jerusalem (see Kimche, *Seven Fallen Pillars*, p. 224; Levin, *Jerusalem Embattled*, pp. 116, 135–136, 226). Ben Gurion himself afterwards admitted that the extent to which respectable Jews of all classes became involved was a shameful and distressful spectacle (Israel, *Government Handbook*, 5712, London, Seymour Press, 1951/52)."[46]

S. G. Thicknesse wrote in 1949:

---

40 Don Peretz, *Israel and the Palestine Arabs*, p. 165, note (8), The Middle East Institute, Washington, D.C., 1958.
41 UN Document A/648, p. 14.
42 Ibid, p. 47.
43 UN Document A/689, p. 1.
44 W. de St. Aubin, "Peace and Refugees in the Middle East", *Middle East Journal*, 1949, p. 252.
45 *Middle East Journal*, 1949, p. 14.
46 George Kirk, *The Middle East 1945–1950*, p. 263, Oxford University Press, London, 1954.

"While it is comparatively simple to describe, or investigate, the present state of Arab immovable property, it is quite impossible to give any documented account of the fate of Arab movable property. It is very unlikely that the Government of Israel has assessed the value and extent of the immense amount of Arab property destroyed and looted (systematically as well as unsystematically) by Jewish groups and individuals both during and since the Palestine war."[47]

Don Peretz has cited the Israeli Custodian of Absentee property as follows:

"In a statement describing the early period, the Custodian of Absentee Property reported to the Knesset's Finance Committee early in 1949 that, during the violent transition from mandatory to Israeli control, before a firm authority was established, the Arabs abandoned great quantities of property in hundreds of thousands of dwellings, shops, storehouses and workshops. They also left produce in fields and fruit in orchards, groves and vineyards, placing 'the fighting and victorious community before serious material temptation'. (Extract from Custodian's report to the Knesset Finance Committee given on 18 April 1949.)"[48]

"Temptation" is often an excuse pleaded as a mitigating circumstance by common thieves in criminal prosecutions, but this is the first time that it has been put forward by a Government as an excuse for the massive plunder of a nation on such a large scale.

In the case of immovables, their misappropriation was the subject of more methodic planning. This operation was done in two phases.

In a first phase between 1948 and 1950 Israel physically laid its hands upon all lands and buildings that belonged to the Palestinian refugees and enacted legislation which aimed at their formal seizure. The first legislation in this regard was the Abandoned Areas Ordinance (1948). According to this Ordinance, the Government could declare any occupied area as "abandoned" and in such event regulations could be made concerning "the expropriation and confiscation" of the property. There can be no doubt that property which its owners had to leave behind in circumstances of coercion, terrorism or expulsion cannot properly be described as "abandoned" property. The refugees never intended to abandon their homes and their lands. Such a description was deceptive and was a distortion of the true situation.

The Abandoned Areas Ordinance was followed by the Cultivation of Waste Lands Regulations (1948). "Waste land" was defined as land which was not cultivated or, in the opinion of the Minister of Agriculture, was not "efficiently" cultivated. Such land could be seized by the Minister of Agriculture. It is obvious that, since the Palestine refugees were not allowed to return to their lands and could not cultivate them, this regulation was a device to seize all Arab land owned by the refugees in Israeli-held territory.

Then came the Absentee Property Regulations (1948), which extended the

47 S. G. Thicknesse, *Arab Refugees*, pp. 27–28, Royal Institute of International Affairs, London, 1949.   48 Don Peretz, *op. cit.*, p. 148.

scope of the seizure to all Arab refugee property of any nature. In accordance with these regulations, "absentee property" was vested in the Custodian of Absentee Property. The Custodian was entitled to administer the property, but not to sell it nor to lease it for a period exceeding five years. "Absentee property" was defined as property owned or possessed by an "absentee". The term "absentee" meant any person who on 29 November 1947 was a citizen or resident of the Arab States or was a Palestinian citizen who had left his place of residence, even though to take refuge in another part of Palestine. This meant, in effect, that all property, including land, buildings, movables and moneys owned by Arabs who did not remain at their habitual place of residence in Israeli-held territory was vested in the Israeli Custodian. These regulations consummated the seizure of all property belonging to the Palestinian refugees.

Encouraged by the inaction of the UN and its inability to implement its resolutions, even those concerning the repatriation of the refugees and the protection of their property, Israel took the next step, namely the confiscation of Arab refugee property. This was done in the following manner. First, the Absentee Property Law (1950) was enacted on 14 March 1950. This law again vested "absentee property" in the Israeli Custodian but its basic feature was that it authorized the Custodian to sell vested property, not generally, but to "a Development Authority which shall be established by the Knesset" at a price not less than the "official value" (Article 19). As regards urban property the expression "official value" was defined to mean a sum $16\frac{2}{3}$ times the "net annual value" of the property as fixed for tax purposes in the year 1947/1948.[49] Such "official value", being derived from a valuation made for tax purposes, bore no relation to its real or market value. The derivation of the value of property from a tax valuation in accordance with the "official value" formula, coupled with its expression in devalued Israeli pounds, produces a value which varies between 5 and 10 per cent of the real value of the property. The "official value" set by the Israeli authorities upon immovable property owned by the refugees was thus a thin disguise for a confiscation at a nominal consideration.[50]

Then on 31 July 1950 the Development Authority (Transfer of Property) Law was enacted. The Development Authority was a governmental entity which was set up in order to buy, rent, lease or otherwise acquire property. It was also empowered to sell or otherwise dispose of property, but only to the State, the Jewish National Fund, Government institutions, or local authorities. All land that belonged to the Palestine refugees outside urban areas was "sold"

---

49 In accordance with the Urban Property Tax Ordinance, 1928, the "net annual value" was assessed once every five years for tax purposes. Such net annual value was arrived at by deducting 20 to $33\frac{1}{3}$ per cent for repairs and other charges from the estimated gross annual value of built-up property. In the case of land the "net annual value" was six per cent of the estimated capital value. In the case of rural property, the tax was based upon the estimated productivity of the soil.

50 For a criticism of the "official value" criterion adopted by Israel, see Sami Hadawi, *Palestine: Loss of a Heritage*, pp. 62–66, Naylor Company, 1963.

by the Custodian of Absentee Property to the Development Authority which in turn "sold" it to the Jewish National Fund or leased it to co-operative agricultural settlements. The greater part of urban and built-up property that belonged to the Palestine refugees was also "sold" by the Custodian to Israeli lessees or squatters. The interposition of the Development Authority as the buyer of Arab refugee property was a means for concealing the confiscation. The device of interposing the Development Authority was explained as follows:

> "The Development Authority was based upon a sort of legal fiction. It was not desired to transfer abandoned land to Government ownership, as this would be interpreted as confiscation of the abandoned property. The Government was disinclined to take such a step, which would have been unfavourably regarded abroad, and no doubt opposed."[51]

Even the Arabs who remained in Israeli-held territory were not spared.[52] They were deprived of their lands by several confiscatory measures, some administrative and others legislative. Among confiscatory measures disguised in the form of legislation, mention may be made of the extension of the Absentee Property Law to Arab residents who had changed their place of residence before 1 August 1948; the Regulations of 1949 enabling the Minister of Defence to declare certain areas "security zones" and evict all their Arab inhabitants; the Law Concerning Uncultivated Lands, 1949; the Expropriation Law, 1950; the Land Acquisition Law, 1953, and the Law of Limitation, 1958. The effect of some of these laws is briefly mentioned hereafter. By the Absentee Property Law of 1950 the term "absentee" was extended to include Arabs who, though they remained in Israeli-occupied territory in 1948, had the misfortune of leaving temporarily their ordinary place of residence. The effect of this law was that if an Arab left his village in 1948 and sought refuge in a city or a neighbouring village so as to avoid a possible fate such as that of the villagers of Deir Yassin, he was classified as an "absentee" and his property was seized and given away to the Development Authority. By this means nearly half the Arab lands belonging to owners who had remained in Israeli-controlled territory was taken and confiscated. The Land Acquisition Law (1953) validated the seizure made prior to its date of land belonging to resident Arabs which had been allegedly taken for "security reasons or development purposes" and vested title to such land in the Development Authority. The owners were offered in exchange either some other land which was to be allotted by the authorities or some nominal compensation in cash.[53] Another means which was adopted by Israel to dispossess the Arab

---

51 A. Granott, *op. cit.*, pp. 100–101.
52 For an account of the confiscation of Arab property and generally for the treatment of the Arab minority in Israel, see Sabri Jiryis, *The Arabs in Israel*, pp. 55–90, The Institute for Palestine Studies, Beirut, 1968.
53 As to the fictitious nature of the compensation offered for the expropriation of the lands of the Arab minority in Israeli-held territory, see the memorandum of Al Ard Company, submitted in 1964 by a group of Arabs in Israel to the Secretary-General of the UN: French version in *Les Temps Modernes*, 1967, No. 253 bis, Paris, p. 792.

minority of its lands was the Law of Limitation (1958). This law required the claimant to unregistered land to prove continuous undisputed possession for a period of fifteen years. Failing such proof, the land would be forfeited to the Israeli Government. Since most of the land of Palestine was unregistered and claims thereto rested upon a possessory title, and since the required proof was in many cases almost impossible to adduce by reason of the prevailing circumstances, the Law of Limitation meant, in effect, the confiscation of all unregistered Arab-owned land. It is reliably estimated that the Palestine Arabs who remained in Israel were dispossessed of 80 per cent of their land holdings. The total area of land possessed by Arabs living in Israeli-held territory on 4 June 1967 amounted to some 200,000 dunoms (about 50,000 acres), that is, less than 1 per cent of the area of the country.

It is clear from this review of Israel's confiscatory land legislation that its policy not only was to create an exclusively Jewish State by displacing the non-Jewish inhabitants, but also aimed at the dispossession of the Arabs, both refugees and residents, of all their lands, houses and buildings.

Notwithstanding their considerable financial means and all kinds of economic pressures and inducements, it took the Jews about seventy years from 1880, when Zionist colonization efforts started in Palestine, until 1948 to acquire 1,491,699 dunoms, representing less than 6 per cent of the land of Palestine. In less than two years from the date of the establishment of the State of Israel, they were able to usurp and confiscate almost the totality of Arab-owned lands of Palestine which came under their occupation.

The efforts of the UN to protect Arab refugee property and to save it from confiscation were defeated by Israel's intransigence. The Conciliation Commission for Palestine mentioned in its Third Progress Report that it had presented to the Israeli Government a list of preliminary measures which it considered fair and just for the protection of Arab refugee property.[54] Israel ignored the request. Another request made by the Conciliation Commission for the appointment of a mixed committee to deal with the question of the preservation of Arab orange groves was rejected.[55] The Conciliation Commission also asked Israel to abrogate the Absentee Property Law and to suspend all measures of requisition and occupation of Arab houses and lands. Again, this effort bore no fruit. The Conciliation Commission reported that "the Israeli delegation informed the Committee that its Government was unable to abrogate the Absentee Act or to suspend measures of requisition of Arab immovable property."[56]

In its resolution 394 (V) of 14 December 1950 the General Assembly directed the UN Conciliation Commission for Palestine, *inter alia*, to "continue negotiations with the parties concerned regarding measures for the protection of the rights, property and interests of the refugees." In its Tenth Progress Report

---

54 Third Progress Report, Document A/927, 21 June 1949.
55 Fourth Progress Report, Document A/992, 22 September 1949.
56 *Ibid.*

(1951) the Conciliation Commission stated that it had asked for an assurance from Israel that no steps had been taken or would be taken by that Government which might be likely to impair the task with which the Refugee Office had been entrusted. The outcome of the Commission's efforts was summarized in its statement that: "No reply was received to that request."[57] The Conciliation Commission could not be more completely ignored by Israel.

It seems that the Conciliation Commission was not entirely discouraged by Israel's attitude, for it continued its efforts, largely academic, for the protection of Arab refugee property. In its Fifteenth Progress Report, the Commission reported as follows:

> "In its letter dated 28 September 1956 to the Government of Israel, the Commission went on to recall that, apart from the overall question of compensation, it had a responsibility in connection with the protection of the property rights of the refugees. In this respect, the Commission noted that it had not yet received a reply to its inquiries as to the administration of Arab property. The Commission also stated that it had before it a request from the Governments of the Arab States for information with regard to Arab refugee property in Israel. For these reasons the Commission requested the Government of Israel to provide it with concrete information as to the way in which refugee property was being administered, what measures were being taken to protect that property and safeguard its identity and what measures might have been taken with regard to the restitution to the refugee owners of rents or other income from their property which might have accrued since the property was taken over by the Israeli Custodian."[58]

This request of the Conciliation Commission was also ignored by Israel.

The UN's concern over Arab refugee property and its protection cooled down with the passage of time. This became manifest when the Arab States, in the face of the Conciliation Commission's failure to secure any protection of refugee property, sought the appointment by the UN of an independent Custodian for the protection and administration of such property. Between 1961 and 1967 several attempts were made to secure the appointment of such a Custodian, but all these attempts were defeated by the failure to secure the required majority at the General Assembly.[59]

Israel's violations of Arab property rights in Palestine constitute clear breaches of international law and of United Nations resolutions. Moreover, these breaches carry their own sanctions: all seizures, confiscations and expropriations of Arab property are null and void under both international law and UN resolutions.

It is settled under international law that private enemy property, whether movable or immovable, cannot be seized, looted, confiscated or sold by the occupying Power. The rule is stated by Oppenheim in these terms:

---

57 Document A/1985, 15 July 1951.   58 UN Document A/3199, 4 October 1956.
59 As regards efforts at the UN for protection of Arab refugee property, see Henry Cattan, *Palestine, the Arabs and Israel*, pp. 86 and 169–171, Longman, 1969.

> "Immovable private enemy property may under no circumstances or conditions be appropriated by an invading belligerent. Should he confiscate and sell private land or buildings, the buyer would acquire no right whatever to the property."[60]

Private personal property which does not consist of war material cannot even be seized. Articles 46 and 48 of the Hague Regulations stipulate that private enemy property may not be confiscated, and pillage is formally prohibited.[61] Nazi acts of plunder of private property in occupied territory during the Second World War were condemned as war crimes by the International Military Tribunal at Nuremberg.[62]

Oppenheim observes that if the occupier has appropriated and sold private or public property which may not legitimately be appropriated by a military occupant, such property may afterwards be claimed from the purchaser without payment of compensation.[63]

The protection of private property laid down by international law was reaffirmed by Article 17 (2) of the Universal Declaration of Human Rights of 10 December 1948, which stated that "no one shall be arbitrarily deprived of his property."

The appropriation, or more precisely, the misappropriation by Israel of Arab property is also void under UN resolutions. A specific protection of Arab property in the Jewish State (and of Jewish property in the Arab State) was envisaged by resolution 181 (II) of the General Assembly of 29 November 1947. This resolution embodied a prohibition against expropriation of such property, except for public purposes and subject to prior payment of compensation. Article 8 of Chapter 2 of the Declaration[64] required from the Arab and Jewish States under the resolution stated:

> "8. No expropriation of land owned by an Arab in the Jewish State (or by a Jew in the Arab State) shall be allowed except for public purposes. In all cases of expropriation full compensation as fixed by the Supreme Court shall be paid previous to dispossession."

This prohibition was one of the stipulations which were recognized by the resolution as constituting fundamental laws that could not be defeated by any "law, regulation or official action", and which were placed "under the guarantee of the United Nations". The effect of resolution 181 (II) in this regard was, therefore, to put it beyond Israel's power validly to seize, confiscate, or expropriate Arab property.

---

60 Oppenheim, *International Law*, 7th ed., Vol. II, p. 403, Longman, London, 1952.
61 *Ibid.*, p. 405.
62 *Ibid.*, p. 406.
63 Oppenheim, *op. cit.*, p. 619. Title founded on violation of law is void. See the application of this rule to unlawful requisitions and enactments of authorities in military occupation: D. P. O'Connell, *International Law*, Vol. I, pp. 496–497, 1965.
64 In 1948 Israel gave "a formal undertaking to accept the provisions" of this Declaration: see Appendix V and Section 3 of Chapter VIII, *post*.

In the preceding discussion no distinction has been made in regard to the location of the property. If, as we have seen, Israel's power to expropriate property in the proposed Jewish State was prohibited by the UN, except for public purposes, and then only subject to severe restrictions, its power to expropriate Arab property within the territory of the proposed Arab State or within the area of the City of Jerusalem was simply non-existent. Such considerations, however, have not been a subject of concern to Israel. Following its occupation of the Old City of Jerusalem in June 1967, it proceeded to expropriate Arab properties in the City and its surroundings. Both the General Assembly and the Security Council condemned these expropriations and declared them to be invalid.[65]

---

65 See Section 6, *post*, as well as Appendices XI, XII, XIV, XVII, XVIII, XXIV and XXX.

Section 4
Attacks and acts
of aggression in breach
of the Armistice Agreements

The War of 1948 was concluded by four Armistice Agreements signed by Israel with Egypt on 24 February 1949, with Lebanon on 23 March 1949, with Jordan on 3 April 1949, and with Syria on 20 July 1949. The Armistice Agreements provided that no party should commit any warlike or hostile act against the military forces or against civilians in territory under the control of the other party. The Armistice Agreements further provided that they should remain in force until a peaceful settlement was achieved between the parties.

The history of the Armistice Agreements was marked by numerous flagrant breaches committed by Israeli armed forces.[66] In contrast, the Arab States did not undertake any warlike operations against Israel. Not one of them was ever condemned by the Security Council for an attack upon Israel in breach of the Armistice Agreements.

Broadly, Israel's breaches of the Armistice Agreements aimed at two objectives: either to terrorize the Arabs and the Arab States, or to expand and annex more territory.

Since 1949 Israel has been condemned for more than forty acts of armed aggression against the Arab States, almost all causing heavy loss of life. Thirty-four of these condemnations were pronounced by the Security Council to be "flagrant violations" of the Armistice Agreements. Among these condemnations mention may be made of Israel's attacks on Huleh (1953), Qibya (1953),

---

66 Incidents under the Armistice Agreements are described in the records of the Mixed Armistice Commissions as well as in the reports of the Chiefs of Staff of the UN Truce Supervision Organization in Palestine to the Secretary-General of the UN and to the Security Council: Lt. General William Riley, Major-General Vagn Bennike, General Carl von Horn and Lt. General E. L. M. Burns. See also E. H. Hutchison, *Violent Truce*, Devin Adair, New York, 1956; Carl von Horn, *Soldiering for Peace*, Cassell, London, 1966; E. L. M. Burns, *Between Arab and Israeli*, Harrap, London, 1962, and Institute for Palestine Studies, Beirut, 1969.

Nahalin (1954), Gaza (1955), the Syrian outpost on Lake Tiberias (1955), the Syrian villages in the Lake Tiberias area (1960 and 1962), the villages of Samou' (1966), Karameh (1968), Salt (1968) in Jordan, the international airport of Beirut (1968), and on South Lebanon in 1969, 1970 and 1972.

All these Israeli attacks were in the nature of terrorist raids intended "to punish" the Arabs or "to give the Arabs a lesson" or simply to kill Palestinian guerillas. Israel has sought to justify its raids and attacks against its neighbours on the basis of a so-called right of reprisal. In most cases the excuse of reprisal was merely a pretext for aggression. But apart from any such considerations the Security Council denied the existence of any right of reprisal and re-peatedly condemned Israel for its unlawful recourse to it. After Israel's first assertion of a right of reprisal, the Security Council in its resolution No. 56 of 19 August 1948 laid down the principle that "no party is permitted to violate the truce on the ground that it is undertaking reprisals or retaliations against the other party." Israel defied this clear directive and was again con-demned on 24 November 1953 for its attack on Qibya in Jordan. On this occasion the Security Council found that the "retaliatory action at Qibya taken by the armed forces of Israel on 14–15 October 1953 and all such actions con-stitute a violation of the cease-fire provisions of the Security Council resolution No. 54 (1948) and are inconsistent with the parties' obligations under the General Armistice Agreement between Israel and Jordan and the Charter of the United Nations."[67] Two years later, in condemning Israel for its attack on Syrian military forces in the area of Lake Tiberias on 11 December 1955, "in flagrant violation of the cease-fire provisions, the terms of the Armistice Agree-ment and its obligations under the Charter," the Security Council further reminded this State that "the Council had already condemned military action in breach of the General Armistice Agreement, whether or not undertaken by way of retaliation, and has called upon Israel to take effective measures to prevent such action."[68] In its resolution 111 of 19 January 1956 condemning Israel for its attack on Syria in the Lake Tiberias area, the Security Council called upon it to comply with its obligations, "in default of which the Council will have to consider what further measures under the Charter are required to maintain or restore the peace." In 1962 the Security Council reaffirmed its resolution No. 111 of 19 January 1956, which had condemned Israeli military action in breach of the General Armistice Agreement, whether or not undertaken by way of retaliation, and held that the Israeli attack of 16–17 March 1962 on Syria con-stituted a flagrant violation of that resolution.[69] Again, in its resolution of 25 November 1966 condemning Israel's attack on Samou' village in Jordan, the Security Council emphasized "to Israel that actions of military reprisal cannot be tolerated and that if they are repeated, the Security Council will have to consider further and more effective steps as envisaged in the Charter to ensure

---

67 Resolution No. 101, 24 November 1953.
68 Resolution No. 111, 19 January 1956. 69 Resolution No. 171, 9 April 1962.

against the repetition of such acts." And again, in its resolution 248 of 24 March 1968 condemning Israel's military action against Karameh in Jordan, the Security Council declared that "actions of military reprisal and other grave violations of the cease-fire cannot be tolerated and that it would have to consider further and more effective steps to ensure against repetition of such acts." So also in condemning Israel on 16 August 1968 for its "massive and carefully planned" air attack on 4 August 1968 upon the Jordanian town of Salt "in flagrant violation of the UN Charter and resolution 248 (1968)," the Security Council again warned Israel "that if such attacks were to be repeated the Council would duly take account of the failure to comply with the present resolution." The same principle was upheld by the Security Council in subsequent condemnations of Israel.

The consistent attitude of the Security Council since 1948 of condemning Israel's unlawful reprisals was jolted by the US Government's use of its veto in September 1972 to prevent Israel's condemnation for attacks on Lebanon and Syria. The complaint before the Security Council concerned the air raids which Israel launched on a number of villages and Palestinian refugee camps in Lebanon and Syria on 8 September. These raids followed the abduction by the "Black September" group, a Palestinian Resistance organization, three days before at Munich, of Israeli Olympic athletes. The object of the assailants was to exchange the abducted Israeli athletes for a number of Palestinian guerillas detained in Israeli prisons. Israel, however, refused the exchange, and persuaded the German authorities to use force to free those who had been abducted. The result was that the abduction ended tragically, for captors and victims alike, when the German police attempted to ambush the Palestinian guerillas.

In retaliation for Munich Israel launched several air raids on villages and Palestinian refugee camps in Lebanon and Syria, and caused the death of many people, including a number of women and children. There can be no doubt that those who lost their lives, both in the abduction at Munich and in the retaliatory raids, were innocent victims. The fact, however, that the original victims were innocent could in no way justify Israel's retaliatory raids on other innocent people. These raids were nothing but unlawful acts of war committed on the territories of two neighbouring States against innocent people, in violation of international law and of the prohibition of reprisals contained in several United Nations resolutions. However, Israel's condemnation for these illegal reprisals was defeated by a US veto at the Security Council on 10 September 1972. The official explanation of the change in the American position, which hitherto had condemned Israeli reprisals, was that the resolution before the Council deploring military operations by Israel against Lebanon and Syria made no reference to the killings in Munich. But the real explanation seemed to be the US Government's fear of alienating Jewish voters in the then impending presidential elections by concurring with a resolution that deplored the Israeli reprisals. In view of the use of the US veto to prevent the condemnation of Israeli reprisals, Lebanon did not even attempt to seek Israel's condemnation by the Security

Council for the most serious act of aggression of which Lebanon had been the victim since June 1967: this took place on 16 and 17 September 1972, when Israeli forces, in air and land attacks on South Lebanon, killed and injured some two hundred persons, including women and children, and destroyed a large number of houses, in retaliation for the shooting of two Israeli soldiers. Thus, the United Nations, unable until now to prevent violence, is now unable even to deplore it.

In mid-October 1972 an ominous development occurred. Israel abandoned the attempt which it had hitherto made to justify its attacks on its neighbours under the pretence of exercising a right of reprisal – a claim repeatedly condemned, as we have seen, by the United Nations. On 15 October, without any apparent cause or reason, Israeli Phantoms bombed Palestinian centres and installations in Lebanon and Syria, causing the usual loss of innocent lives. This action was explained on the following day by Israel's Prime Minister, who declared at the Knesset that Israel had now adopted a new policy: "to strike at the terrorist organizations wherever we can reach them". In accordance with Israeli official terminology the expression "terrorist organizations" means Palestinian resistance. Two weeks later, on 30 October, Israeli planes bombed four refugee camps around Damascus, killing one hundred men, women and children, and wounding a similar number. This policy, which, in view of the long list of Israel's acts of aggression, can hardly be described as a new one, means an intensification of Israeli aggression against Palestinian resistance fighters, refugee camps and neighbouring Arab countries. There can be no question that such a policy was encouraged by the inability of the Security Council effectively to restrain Israeli aggression, as well as by the exercise of the US veto at the Security Council on 10 September which had the effect of condoning Israeli attacks on Palestinian refugee camps and on neighbouring Arab countries. This policy promises to open a new chapter of terror and violence in the Middle East in violation of the Armistice Agreements and of international law.

One of the pages of this new chapter of terror and violence was written on 21 February 1973 when the Israeli armed forces distinguished themselves by two feats of terrorism that violated international law and shocked world opinion: one was the massacre of Palestine refugees under the pretence of fighting Palestinian guerillas; the other was the shooting down of an Arab civilian airliner. In the early hours of that day, using helicopters and some of the gunboats stolen in Cherbourg in 1969, the Israelis landed commandos on the coast of Lebanon, north of Tripoli, where they attacked two Palestine refugee camps. The attackers dynamited several houses and buildings, some over the heads of their occupants, killed thirty-one of the refugees, and wounded a similar number, more than half of the victims being women and children. Later on the same day Israeli fighters coolly shot down a Libyan Boeing that had strayed off course over Sinai by reason of a failure of its navigation instruments; more than a hundred passengers were killed. Far from terrorizing the Palestinians and other Arabs, all these acts of violence serve only to add oil to the fire.

Israel's other breaches of the Armistice Agreements were intended to achieve its plans for expansion and annexation of more territory. The first of the series was committed hardly a fortnight after the conclusion of the Armistice Agreement with Egypt. On 10 March 1949, in breach of its Armistice Agreement with Egypt dated 24 February 1949, Israel launched an offensive across the armistice lines which brought its forces to the Gulf of Aqaba. During this offensive the Israelis occupied the Palestine Police Post of Umm Rashrash which they afterwards named Eilat.[70]

After this first breach, and presumably encouraged by its result, the Israelis undertook a methodical encroachment on the demilitarized zones established under the Armistic Agreements with Egypt and Syria. Their first act was to seize the El Auja demilitarized zone, which had been set up under the Egyptian-Israeli Armistice Agreement. They began by expelling in 1950 its 6,000 Arab inhabitants.[71] Then, notwithstanding the Security Council's injunctions, they occupied the whole zone, in the words of Lieutenant-General Burns, the UN Chief of Staff, "in flagrant violation of Article VII of the General Armistice Agreement."[72]

The same process was followed by the Israelis in regard to the demilitarized zone set up by the Syrian-Israeli Armistice Agreement. To cite one example mentioned by Lieutenant-General Burns: "the Israelis evacuated the Arab inhabitants of Baqqara and other Arab villages in the zone, and sent them to Sha'ab, near Acre, following this up by razing their houses to the ground with bulldozers."[73] General Carl von Horn, another United Nations Chief of Staff, has thrown much light upon Israel's encroachments on the demilitarized zone bordering Syria.[74] General von Horn has related in detail Israel's encroachment upon the lands of the Syrian village of Tawafik and the destruction by Israeli armed forces in 1962 of the houses of the village for no reason other than the villagers' opposition to such encroachment. He described Israel's cultivation of Arab land as:

> "part of a premeditated Israeli policy to edge east through the Demilitarized Zone towards the old Palestine border (as shown on their maps) and to get all Arabs out of the way by fair means or foul . . ."[75]

But the gravest of all the Israeli breaches of the Armistice Agreements were the two acts of aggression in 1956 and 1967, which assumed the proportions of fully fledged wars. In both cases Israel's underlying objective was expansion.

The Suez War of 1956 was an act of aggression committed in clear violation

---

70 G. Kirk, *The Middle East 1945–1950*, pp. 4, 194, 195, Oxford University Press, London, 1954.
71 See Report of UN Chief of Staff, Major-General Bennike, UN Document S/PV 635.
72 E. L. M. Burns, *op. cit.*, p. 134.
73 *Ibid.*, p. 114.
74 See Carl von Horn, *op. cit.*, pp. 61–124, 250–260.
75 *Ibid.*, pp. 115–116.

of international law and of the Egyptian-Israeli Armistice Agreement.[76] Taking advantage of the situation created by Egypt's nationalization of the Suez Canal and having secured the military support of the United Kingdom and France, both of whom had grudges of their own against Egypt, Israel could not resist the temptation of destroying the Egyptian Army, occupying the Gaza Strip and the Sinai Peninsula, and opening the Gulf of Aqaba for its shipping. In furtherance of this plan, Israeli forces launched on 29 October 1956 their attack against Egypt, occupied the Gaza Strip and the Sinai Peninsula, and seized Sharm El Sheikh, which guarded the Strait of Tiran and the entrance to the Gulf of Aqaba. At the same time, Anglo-French forces landed at Port Said in order to seize the Suez Canal. World opinion was shocked by this aggression. The General Assembly of the UN denounced the invasion of Egypt and the Gaza Strip and called upon Israel immediately to withdraw behind the armistice lines of 1949, and upon the United Kingdom and France immediately to withdraw from Egyptian territory.[77]

Israel withdrew reluctantly under the combined pressure of the UN, the USA and Soviet Russia.

Unfortunately, no similar unanimous opposition to aggression materialized in the case of Israel's attack on the Arab States in 1967. In view of its extreme gravity and its continuance until the present day, this last act of aggression will be discussed in greater detail in the next section.

---

76 For an account of the Suez War, see Kennett Love, *Suez*, Longman, London, 1969, and for the manoeuvres behind the scenes in connection with the Suez War, see Anthony Nutting, *No End of a Lesson, The Story of Suez*, Constable, London, 1967.

77 General Assembly resolutions of 2 November 1956, 4 November 1956, 5 November 1956, 7 November 1956, 19 January 1957, and 2 February 1957.

Section 5
The War of 5 June 1967

The War of 5 June 1967 started with Israel's surprise attack upon Egyptian airfields. This lightning attack was followed by Israel's invasion and occupation of the Gaza Strip, the Sinai Peninsula, the Old City of Jerusalem, the West Bank of Jordan and the Golan region of Syria. Despite the issuing of four cease-fire orders by the Security Council, the invasion of Arab territories stopped only after Israel had substantially achieved its territorial objectives. More than six years have elapsed and Israel still occupies these territories, without the war having been brought to an end. The war is at present merely suspended by a cease-fire voluntarily observed by Egypt and Israel since 7 August 1970.

The main legal issue that arises under international law with regard to this war is whether it constituted an act of aggression on the part of Israel, or whether it was a defensive war justified by Article 51 of the UN Charter.

Israel and Egypt have mutually accused each other of initiating armed hostilities. What are the facts?

The facts are well established. On the morning of 5 June 1967, at 0745 hours, and at ten minute intervals thereafter, wave after wave of Israeli bombers began to attack Egyptian airfields, destroying aircraft on the ground and putting runways out of action. In less than three hours, over 300 out of 340 Egyptian aircraft – representing almost the totality of the Egyptian air force – were destroyed, mostly on the ground. Nineteen Egyptian airfields were hit and rendered unserviceable on the first day of the attack.

Then, within half an hour of the beginning of the Israeli air-strikes, Israeli ground forces launched an offensive against Egyptian positions in the Gaza Strip and the Sinai Peninsula. Deprived of all air cover, Egyptian ground troops fought a rear-guard and hopeless action. In less than four days, the Israeli army overran the Gaza Strip and the Sinai Peninsula and reached the eastern bank of the Suez Canal.

The Israeli air-strike on 5 June 1967 was not confined to Egypt. After destroying the Egyptian air force in a matter of hours, the Israelis attacked before noon on the same day Syrian and Jordanian airfields and destroyed a number of aircraft on the ground.[78]

Concurrently with its attack on Egypt and in plain disregard of the truth, Israel fabricated a charge of aggression against its victim and presented it in a dramatic manner to the Security Council. At the very moment that Israel was making its devastating air-strikes against Egyptian airfields and was throwing its armour into an irresistible offensive against Egyptian ground forces, its Permanent Representative at the UN awoke the President of the Security Council (Hans R. Tabor of Denmark) from his sleep at 0310 New York time on the morning of 5 June to inform him that he had just received reports "that Egyptian land and air forces have moved against Israel and Israeli forces are now engaged in repelling the Egyptian forces."[79] The Israeli Representative asked that the Security Council be convened to hear an urgent communication which he wished to make to that body.

Twenty minutes later, the President of the Security Council was informed by the Egyptian Permanent Representative to the UN that "Israel has committed a treacherous premeditated aggression against the United Arab Republic this morning. The Israelis launched attacks against the Gaza Strip, Sinai, airports in Cairo, in the area of the Suez Canal and at several other airports within the United Arab Republic."[80]

The Security Council convened on the morning of 5 June. The Israeli representative again repeated the charge that Israeli defence forces "are now repelling the Egyptian Army and Air Force." And in order to appear convincing he furnished to the Council the following false details:

> "In the early hours of this morning Egyptian armoured columns moved in an offensive thrust against Israel's borders. At the same time Egyptian planes took off from airfields in Sinai and struck out towards Israel. Egyptian artillery in the Gaza Strip shelled the Israel villages of Kissufim, Nahal-Oz and Ein Hashelosha. Netania and Kefar Javetz have also been bombed. Israeli forces engaged the Egyptians in the air and on land and fighting is still going on . . .
>
> In accordance with Article 51 of the Charter, I bring this development to the immediate attention of the Security Council."[81]

---

78 For an account of military operations during the Israeli-Arab War of 5 June 1967, see Randolph and Winston Churchill, *The Six-Day War*, Heinemann, 1967; Yves Cuau, *Israël Attaque*, Laffont, 1968; E. Rouleau, J. F. Held, J. and S. Lacouture, *Israël et les Arabes*, Seuil, 1967.

79 UN Document S/PV 1347, 5 June 1967, p. 1.   80 *Ibid.*, p. 1.

81 UN Document S/PV 1347, 5 June 1967, p. 4. Foreign correspondents who were allowed to visit one of the places mentioned, Nahal-Oz, were surprised to discover that there were neither dead nor wounded and that the inhabitants were made to go into shelters several hours before the outbreak of hostilities: Yves Cuau, *op. cit.*, p. 147. Since Israel's representative at the UN was addressing the Security Council several hours after Israel's offensive had begun, the shelling by Egyptian artillery of the places mentioned by him, if it did at all occur, must have taken place *after* Israel's attack on the Gaza Strip had commenced.

Most radio stations and newspapers spread the fabricated story of an Egyptian aggression against Israel and the whole world sympathized with the supposed victim.

On the following day, Abba Eban, Israel's Foreign Minister, did not hesitate to repeat this fabricated story to the Security Council. Addressing the Council on 6 June, the Israeli Minister declared:

> "*When the approaching Egyptian aircraft appeared on our radar screens*, soon to be followed by artillery attacks on our villages near the Gaza Strip, I instructed Ambassador Rafael to inform the Security Council, in accordance with Article 51 of the Charter. I know that that involved arousing you, Mr President, at a most uncongenial hour of the night, but we felt that the Security Council should be most urgently seized."[82]

The great deception practised by Israel on the UN and the whole world could not last very long. The story that it was Egypt that commenced the war by an attack against Israel is now completely discredited. Even the Israelis themselves have abandoned the pretence.[83] Obviously, they could not continue to invoke an imaginary Egyptian attack in order to justify their action as constituting a defensive measure under Article 51 of the Charter. They therefore changed their tactics. Nowadays the Israelis rely instead on the argument that, although not attacked by Egypt, they were in danger of being attacked, and hence they resorted to a pre-emptive strike.

The argument of a pre-emptive strike is neither warranted by the facts, nor justified by the Charter of the United Nations.

Let us first examine the facts. A careful appraisal of the chain of events that preceded the War of 5 June 1967 leads to the conclusion that it was Israel, not Egypt, which harboured aggressive intentions. This chain of events started with the grave incident which occurred between Israel and Syria on 7 April 1967 and which was described as "the curtain-raiser to the six-day war".[84] This incident arose from the provocative cultivation by an Israeli armoured tractor, backed by regular armed forces, of two parcels of land in the Syrian-Israeli demilitarized zone. These two parcels belonged to Arab farmers. Their cultivation was decided in a ruling of the Israeli Cabinet on 3 April 1967 and advertised in advance in the press.[85] The cultivation by Israel of Arab-owned land in the demilitarized zone was part of the Israeli programme for dispossession of Arab farmers and for seizure of the demilitarized zone, contrary to the Syrian-

---

82 UN Document S/PV 1348, 6 June 1967.
83 The pretence was officially abandoned for the first time by Israel on 4 June 1972 when it published the Israeli Government's decision adopted on 4 June 1967 to attack Egypt, Syria and Jordan. The further pretence that Israel was threatened with extermination in June 1967 was shown to be false by three Israeli generals and was described as an exaggeration designed to justify the further annexation of Arab territory: see *Le Monde*, 3 June 1972.
84 Charles W. Yost, "The Arab-Israeli War: How It Began", *Foreign Affairs*, Vol. 46, No. 2, January 1968, p. 310.
85 See the Syrian complaint to the Security Council, S/7845, 9 April 1967.

Israeli Armistice Agreement.[86] The Israeli armoured tractor was met by Syrian small-arms fire. This was answered by a massive Israeli military action which included the use of artillery, tanks and aircraft. Several Syrian villages were bombarded and Israeli jet fighters reached the Damascus area. Six Syrian aircraft were shot down. In reporting this incident to the Security Council, Syria stated:

> "Several times during the past two weeks the Israelis continued to cultivate the disputed areas in the Demilitarized Zone for the sole purpose of instigating hostilities. This they did by armoured tractors protected by tanks and every armament, illegally placed in the Demilitarized Zone, in violation of the General Armistice Agreement. This demonstrates beyond any doubt a clear criminal intent to provoke a large-scale war with Syria."[87]

Israel followed the incident of 7 April by overt and public threats of military action against Syria. On 10 May 1967, General Rabin, the Israeli Chief of Staff, said that Israeli forces might "attack Damascus and change its Government." On 11 May, Israel's Prime Minister Eshkol declared in a public speech that in view of past incidents, "we may have to adopt measures no less drastic than those of 7 April." On 13 May, in a radio interview, Israel's Prime Minister spoke of drastic measures to be taken against Syria "at the place, the time, and in the manner we choose." It is significant that these threats were also whispered by the Israelis in the ears of "journalists and foreign diplomats including the Soviets."[88] On 15 May 1967 Syria drew the attention of the Security Council to the threatening statements made by Israeli leaders which evidenced an intent to launch military action against it.[89]

Israeli threats of military action against Syria were followed by troop movements and concentrations. On 15 May, Israel organized a military parade in Jerusalem in breach of the Armistice Agreement with Jordan and in defiance of UN resolutions relating to the status of Jerusalem. Syria, Egypt and Soviet Russia received reports of Israeli troop concentrations along Syria's border. Although such troop concentrations were denied by Israel, there is no doubt that there was some noisy sabre-rattling by Israel at the time.

The threats made by responsible Israeli military and political leaders during the second week of May 1967 were of great significance and carried serious consequences. These threats were the direct cause of the tension which started to mount in the Middle East until the explosion of 5 June 1967. What could have been the purpose behind Israel's threats against Syria and behind its troop concentrations, real or simulated? One can only presume that Israel's aim was to exert such pressure on Syria as to bring Egypt into the fray. The invasion of Syria would not realize Israel's basic objectives, both military and territorial.

---

86 As to the Syrian-Israeli demilitarized zone, see the preceding Section.
87 UN Document S/7845, 9 April 1967, p. 5.
88 Charles W. Yost, "The Arab-Israeli War: How It Began", *Foreign Affairs*, Vol. 46, No. 2, January 1968, p. 310.
89 UN Document S/7885, 15 May 1967, p. 1.

Israel was more interested in engaging Egypt, which possessed the only Arab army that stood in the way of its territorial and expansionist ambitions. If, as is likely, this was Israel's plan, it succeeded perfectly.

Faced with Israel's threats of military action, Syria sought Egypt's assistance under the Mutual Defence Pact concluded between them in November 1966. Egypt responded by moving troops to Alexandria and Ismailia. At the same time, Egypt requested on 16 May the withdrawal of UNEF from Egyptian territory, and after the withdrawal ordered on 22 May the closure of the Gulf of Aqaba to Israeli shipping and strategic war material destined for Israel.

Although the purpose of the measures taken by Egypt immediately preceding the war was misunderstood and even deliberately misconstrued, reliable evidence shows that they were essentially defensive in character and were meant to deter Israel from attacking Syria. In several public declarations President Nasser declared that Egypt would not unleash the war, though it would resist Israeli aggression against any Arab country. His purpose was clearly "to deter Israel rather than provoke it to a fight."[90] In his famous speech of 22 May 1967 in which he announced the closing of the Gulf of Aqaba to Israel, President Nasser explained what he meant when he said Egypt was "ready for battle". This "meant that we would indeed fight if Syria or any other Arab State was subjected to aggression."[91]

The defensive objective behind Egyptian troop movements prior to the outbreak of war is now becoming obvious to world opinion:

> "By May of 1967 limited mobilizations had occurred on both sides of the armistice lines, and the United Arab Republic, believing with considerable justification that Israel was about to make a major military move against Syria, began a substantial build-up of forces in the Sinai Peninsula."[92]

The same defensive consideration explains Egypt's request for the withdrawal of UNEF from the Egyptian side of the armistice lines. This move has been tendentiously presented as an indication of Egypt's aggressive intentions against Israel. Yet such action was necessary to meet the situation that would arise if Israel carried out its threat to invade Syria, and Egypt were compelled to extend effective assistance to the victim of aggression. It is significant that prior to ordering the withdrawal of UNEF at Egypt's request, the Secretary-General of the UN suggested to Israel that the force be stationed on the Israeli side of the armistice lines. But Israel's representative quickly turned down the suggestion as being "entirely unacceptable to his government."[93] It is clear that the retention of the UN Emergency Force along the armistice lines with Egypt

---

90 *The Observer*, 4 June 1967.   91 See *New York Times*, 26 May 1967.

92 "The Arab-Israeli Conflict and International Law", *Harvard International Law Journal*, Vol. 9, 1968, p. 242.

93 Charles W. Yost, *op. cit.* p. 313. As to the circumstances of UNEF's withdrawal and Israel's rejection of the Secretary-General's offer to move the UN Force to the Israeli side of the armistice line, see U Thant's address in UN publication OPI/429–01419, January, 1971.

did not suit Israel's plans. In any event, "if Israel merely wanted to defend itself, it should have allowed the United Nations Force to come to its side of the boundary, as suggested by U Thant. There is a great deal of evidence that Israel desired more territory."[94]

The evidence shows that it was not Egypt, but Israel, which had a firm intention to attack the other. In his memoirs, President Lyndon Johnson mentions the findings of Secretary of Defence Robert McNamara concerning the situation: "Three separate intelligence groups had looked carefully into the matter, McNamara said, and it was our best judgment that a UAR attack was not imminent."[95]

As to the Israelis, the situation was different: "The Israeli service chiefs, for their part, became increasingly insistent on attack, and accused the pacifists of treason for their shillyshallying."[96] President Johnson mentions that in May 1967 Israel asked the US Government to send an international naval escort to open the Strait of Tiran and fixed "a deadline" of a week or two before it took military action.[97]

It must be evident to an impartial observer that the crisis which developed in May 1967 and eventually erupted in the War of 5 June was of Israel's own making. Israel created and magnified the crisis as part of its war plan. In such circumstances Israel can hardly invoke the argument of a preventive strike in order to deal with a situation which it created itself.

The argument of a preventive strike also fails on legal grounds. Israel cannot invoke Article 51 of the Charter to justify a pre-emptive strike. The Charter recognizes the right of self-defence against an armed attack, but not of a pre-emptive strike in advance of any attack. Article 51 of the Charter provides:

"51. Nothing in the present Charter shall impair the inherent right of individual or collective self-defence if an armed attack occurs against a member of the United Nations, until the Security Council has taken the measures necessary to maintain international peace and security . . ."

The condition then for the application of Article 51 is the occurrence of an armed attack. Philip Jessup observes:

"Article 51 of the Charter suggests a further limitation on the right of self-defence: it may be exercised only 'if an armed attack occurs' . . . This restriction in Article 51 very definitely narrows the freedom of action which states had under traditional law. A case could be made out for self-defence under the traditional law where the injury was threatened but no attack had yet taken place. Under the Charter, alarming military preparations by a neighbouring state would justify a

---

94 Quincy Wright, *AJIL*, Vol. 64, No. 4, 1970, p. 80.
95 Lyndon Johnson, *The Vantage Point*, p. 293, Holt, Rinehart and Winston, New York, 1971.
96 Maxime Rodinson, *Israel and the Arabs*, p. 199, Penguin Books, 1968.
97 Lyndon Johnson, *op. cit.*, pp. 293–295.

resort to the Security Council, but would not justify resort to anticipatory force by the state which believed itself threatened."[98]

The invasion of a neighbouring country's territory is not an exercise of the right of self-defence.[99] The right of self-defence is not preventive. "Self-defence," observes G. Schwarzenberger, "does not cover preventive measures against remote future contingencies."[100] John Hargrove rejects Israel's claim of having acted in self-defence "since it is not altogether clear what were the injuries being inflicted upon Israel that we would be willing to say would in all cases give rise to a right of armed invasion in self-defence."[101] The same writer observes:

> "Many words have been uttered, at both public and private expense, in arguing the correctness of Israel's claim to have been acting in self-defence notwithstanding the explicit qualification in Article 51 of the United Nations Charter, which recognizes the right to use force in self-defence 'if an armed attack occurs.' I will not re-argue the question here, but will simply state the personal view that, in our primordial international community, an exception to the prohibition of violence that legitimizes such a first strike would make the world a substantially more dangerous place in which to live, and that this is not the sort of world envisaged in the United Nations Charter.[102] So far as I am aware, Israel stands alone among governments in espousing her position on this point."[103]

Although reliance on Article 51 of the Charter is ruled out, both on the facts and on the law, some have found for Israel a *casus belli* in Egypt's closure of the Strait of Tiran. It is therefore necessary to examine this contention.

The closure of the Strait of Tiran to Israeli shipping and to strategic war material destined for Israel was part of Egypt's response to the threats made by Israel against Syria. This action was defensive in its object and in its nature. However, two questions have been raised as to the legality of the Egyptian action: first, whether Egypt was justified in exercising a right of blockade in this case, and secondly, whether Israel possessed a right of innocent passage through Egyptian territorial waters.

---

98 Philip C. Jessup, *A Modern Law of Nations*, pp. 165–166.
99 D. P. O'Connell, *International Law*, Vol. I, p. 342, Stevens and Oceana, 1965.
100 G. Schwarzenberger, "Principles of International Law", *Hague Recueil*, 1955, Vol. 87, p. 333.
101 John Lawrence Hargrove, "Abating the Middle East Crisis through the United Nations", *Kansas Law Review*, Vol. 19, No. 3, 1971, p. 367.
102 The author adds in a footnote: "Two United Nations legal bodies have given rise in recent years to a good deal of discussion on this point. These are the Special Committee on Principles of International Law Concerning Friendly Relations and Co-operation Among States in Accordance with the Charter, and the Special Committee on the Question of Defining Aggression. The overwhelming majority of Member States that have addressed the point in these two bodies have taken the position that a genuine 'armed attack' must indeed occur before defensive force can legitimately be used. *I know of no Member that has expressly argued that Article 51 could justify a 'pre-emptive' attack."*
103 *Kansas Law Review, op. cit.*, p. 367.

Two basic facts provide the answer to those two questions. On the one hand, the Strait of Tiran lies within Egypt's territorial waters and its navigable channel is situated less than a mile from the Egyptian coast. On the other hand, the relationship between Egypt and Israel in 1967 was still based on the Armistice Agreement of 24 February 1949 and was technically a latent state of war. In these circumstances, the Egyptian action was a legal exercise by Egypt of its right of sovereignty over its territorial sea and an assertion of a right of belligerence recognized by international law.

The Armistice Agreement between Egypt and Israel did not terminate the state of war legally existing between them. It "did not even create a *de facto* termination of the war between those States."[104] Howard S. Levie observes:

> "It may be stated as a positive rule that an armistice agreement does not terminate the state of war between the belligerents, either *de jure* or *de facto*, and that the state of war continues to exist and to control the actions of neutrals as well as belligerents."[105]

The right to exercise a blockade is not affected by the armistice.[106] In fact, the passage of Israeli warships through the Strait of Tiran was prohibited by Article II of the Armistice Agreement between Egypt and Israel. Article II provided that no element of the forces of one party shall enter or pass through waters within three miles of the coastline of the other party.

Turning to the question as to whether Israel possessed a right of innocent passage through the Strait of Tiran which was violated by Egypt's action, it is evident that the right of innocent passage exists only in time of peace.[107] Even on the assumption that the Strait of Tiran could be considered an international waterway, "there would seem to be no question but that the right of passage through an international waterway which lies within the territorial sea is affected by a state of war."[108] Maxime Rodinson has observed in this regard: "In the absence of any specific international convention, was any state obliged to grant passage, through coastal waters extending less than two miles from its shores, to strategic material intended for another state with which it is legally at war? Besides, all that had been effected was a return to the situation operating from 1949 to 1956."[109]

The Convention on the Territorial Sea of 1958, which deals with the right of innocent passage of foreign ships through straits used for international navigation, did not bind Egypt since it was not a party to it. But even if this Convention had been applicable to Egypt, it can be argued "that under Article 14 (4), which

---

104 Howard S. Levie, "The Nature and Scope of the Armistice Agreement", *AJIL*, 1956, p. 886.
105 *Ibid.*, p. 884.
106 Oppenheim, *International Law*, Vol. 2, 7th ed., p. 547.
107 *Ibid.*, Vol. 1, 8th ed., p. 493.
108 Charles B. Selak, "The Legal Status of the Gulf of Aqaba", *AJIL*, 1958, p. 684.
109 Maxime Rodinson, *op. cit.*, p. 196.

defines innocent passage as 'not prejudicial to peace, good order, or security of the coastal state', the UAR might act to exclude Israeli shipping, especially in the light of Israel's major retaliatory raid on Syria in April 1967."[110]

Israel possessed no right of innocent passage either through Egypt's territorial waters or through the Strait of Tiran. Professor Roger Fisher of Harvard University has observed that

> "it is debatable whether international law confers any right of innocent passage through such a waterway. Despite an Israeli request the International Law Commission in 1956 found no rule which would govern the Strait of Tiran. Although the 1958 Convention on the Territorial Sea does provide for innocent passage through such Straits, the United States representative, Arthur Dean, called this 'a new rule' and the UAR has not signed the treaty."[111]

Professor Fisher further questioned whether Israel could in view of its raids and threats against Syria claim a right of innocent passage through Egyptian territorial waters:

> "In April Israel conducted a major retaliatory raid on Syria and threatened raids of still greater size. In this situation, was Egypt required by international law to continue to allow Israel to bring in oil and other strategic supplies through Egyptian territory – supplies which Israel could use to conduct further military raids? That was the critical question of law."[112]

When the crisis over the closure of the Strait of Tiran arose in May 1967 the attitude of some of the Great Powers was prompted more by political than by legal considerations. The US Government was influenced by Israel's claim that it had been given in 1957 a "commitment" by President Eisenhower regarding a right of passage through the Gulf of Aqaba.[113] But even if any such "commitment" were, in fact, given, it could in no way bind Egypt or affect its sovereign rights over its territory.

It is unfortunate that in the face of Egypt's action two of the Great Powers, the USA and the UK, thought of setting up a naval task force "to break Nasser's blockade and open the Strait of Tiran,"[114] instead of taking steps to have this pre-eminently legal question referred by the Security Council to the International Court of Justice. A rare opportunity was then missed to test the validity of Egypt's action by means of an advisory opinion of the International Court and possibly to settle an international dispute by peaceful and juridical means.

---

110 "The Arab-Israeli War and International Law", *Harvard International Law Journal*, Vol. 9, 1968, p. 247.
111 Professor Roger Fisher, Letter to the *Sunday New York Times*, 11 June 1967.
112 Professor Roger Fisher, *ibid.*
113 On 20 February 1957, President Eisenhower expressed the view that the Gulf of Aqaba constituted international waters and that no nation had the right to prevent free and innocent passage in the Gulf.
114 Lyndon Johnson, *op. cit.*, p. 292.

But whether or not under international law Egypt's closure of the Strait of Tiran was a legitimate act, Israel had no justification for its attack on Egypt. Even on a most favourable assumption that Israel possessed a right of passage through the Strait of Tiran, it was still not entitled to resort to war in order to establish its right. Under no possible construction could the closure of the Strait of Tiran be considered to constitute an "armed attack" by Egypt against Israel within the meaning of Article 51 of the Charter. If Israel really intended to question the validity of Egypt's action, it had other means at its disposal. But Israel's conduct since the end of hostilities, its refusal to withdraw from the occupied territories, its annexation of the City of Jerusalem and its determination to retain some of the occupied territories, are all indicative of an intention other than that of establishing a right of navigation through the Gulf of Aqaba.

All the arguments advanced by Israel to justify its attack on Egypt, Syria and Jordan on 5 June 1967 collapse upon a critical examination of the facts and the law. There exists ample evidence to establish that the war which Israel then launched was a war of aggression undertaken in breach of its Armistice Agreements with Egypt, Syria and Jordan, and in violation of the UN Charter and of international law.

Section 6
Annexation of Jerusalem

Jerusalem, unique among the cities of the world, holy for one thousand million Christians, five hundred million Moslems and fourteen million Jews, is the spiritual centre for one half of humanity.

Founded by the Canaanites, Jerusalem was captured by David in 1000 B.C. and became the political and religious capital of the new Jewish Kingdom. Its "indigenous population remained and was absorbed."[115] The Jewish occupation of Jerusalem lasted some four and a half centuries. In 587 B.C. the Babylonians destroyed the city and carried the Jews into captivity. The Babylonians ruled Jerusalem for fifty years. After them Jerusalem was held in succession by the Persians, the Greeks, the Romans, the Christians, the Arabs and the Turks. Turkish rule ended in 1917. Since then the fate of Jerusalem has been linked with the vicissitudes of the Arab-Israeli conflict.

Jews, Christians and Moslems have all in turn ruled Jerusalem. The longest rule was by the Moslems. Rev. Charles T. Bridgeman observes that "the Israelites and the Jews have governed the city for only about 600 years, even including the years when Herod ruled as a vassal of Rome."[116] The Christians ruled Jerusalem from A.D. 323 until A.D. 614 (Byzantine period), A.D. 628 to A.D. 637 (Byzantine reconquest), A.D. 1100 to A.D. 1187 (Latin Kingdom of Jerusalem), A.D. 1229 to A.D. 1239 (cession to Frederick II), and from 1922 until 1948 (British mandate), in all, for a period of 423 years. The Moslems (Arabs and Turks) ruled Jerusalem for almost thirteen centuries.

---

115 Michel Join-Lambert, *Jerusalem*, London, Elek Books, 1958, p. 36: "The prophets were not to forget this composite original character of Jerusalem; in the days of her faithlessness they were to remind her of it in harsh terms. 'Thy birth and thy nativity is of the land of Canaan; thy father was an Amorite, and thy mother an Hittite.' (*Ezek.* 16:3)": *Ibid.*, p. 36

116 Rev. Charles T. Bridgeman's letter to the President of the Trusteeship Council, 16 January 1950, UN Document A/1286, p. 13.

Jerusalem is of religious importance to three faiths.

Jerusalem is the birthplace of Christianity. Almost all the sacred shrines and sanctuaries connected with the birth, life and death of Christ are found in Jerusalem and in nearby Bethlehem: the Holy Sepulchre, the Via Dolorosa, the Church of the Nativity, the Cenacle, Gethsemane, and thirty-eight other churches.[117]

Jerusalem is also holy for Islam:

"All Islamic traditions and sacred writings point to the unmistakable fact that Jerusalem is holy for all Muslims, second only in holiness to Mecca and Medina. It is the first *qibla* (direction for prayer) and the third of the sacred cities. The only sanctuaries precedent to Al-Haram in Jerusalem are the Ka'ba in Mecca and the Haram (sanctuary) of Medina."[118]

To Judaism, Jerusalem has been a holy city since it became the site of Solomon's Temple. This temple, built in 950 B.C., destroyed by the Babylonians in 515 B.C., partly rebuilt on the return of the Jews from captivity and reconstructed in Herod's time, was again destroyed by the Romans, following the Jewish insurrection in A.D. 70. After the dispersal of the Jews by the Romans in A.D. 70 and A.D. 135, Jerusalem became a magnet for Jewish religious aspirations, and since the birth of political Zionism at the end of the 19th century, it has also become a target for Jewish nationalistic ambitions.

These nationalistic ambitions found their expression in the Balfour Declaration and received a practical implementation under the British mandate over Palestine. It was under this mandate that more than half a million Jews came to Palestine.

In 1947 the General Assembly of the UN recommended the internationalization of Jerusalem as part of its plan for the partition of Palestine. The partition resolution provided that the City of Jerusalem should be established as a *corpus separatum* under a special international régime and should be administered by the UN. The Trusteeship Council was designated as the Administering Authority on behalf of the UN and was required, within five months, to elaborate and approve a detailed Statute of the City. The resolution also provided that the City should be demilitarized, its neutrality should be declared and preserved, and no para-military formations, exercises or activities should be permitted within its borders. The resolution further envisaged that the Statute elaborated by the Trusteeship Council should remain in force for ten years, unless the Trusteeship Council found it necessary to undertake a re-examination of its provisions at an earlier date. After the expiration of ten years the whole scheme should be subject to re-examination by the Trusteeship Council in the light of the experience acquired with its functioning. The residents of the City

---

117 For a list of Christian churches and institutions in Israeli-held areas outside the Old City of Jerusalem, see Rev. Charles T. Bridgeman, *op. cit.*, pp. 12–17.

118 H. S. Karmi, "How Holy is Palestine to the Muslims?", *The Islamic Quarterly Magazine*, Vol. 14, No. 2, April-June 1970, p. 69.

should then be free to express by means of a referendum their wishes as to possible modifications of the régime of the City.[119]

The resolution for the internationalization of Jerusalem remained a dead letter. At the end of the British mandate Israeli forces seized four-fifths of the area designated by the resolution as the *corpus separatum* for the City of Jerusalem, and Jordanian forces seized the remainder, including the Old City.

However, the occupation of Jerusalem by Israeli and Jordanian military forces did not end UN efforts in favour of the internationalization of the City. In his Progress Report dated 16 September 1948 Count Folke Bernadotte, UN Mediator for Palestine, recommended that the City of Jerusalem should be placed under effective UN control with maximum feasible local autonomy for its Arab and Jewish communities.[120] At its third regular session the General Assembly accepted the Mediator's recommendation and instructed the Conciliation Commission for Palestine to present to the next session of the Assembly detailed proposals for a permanent international régime for the Jerusalem area.[121] The Conciliation Commission held discussions with representatives of the Arab States and of Israel. While the Arab delegations showed themselves, in general, prepared to accept the principle of an international régime for Jerusalem, Israel declared itself unable to accept such a régime; it did, however, accept an international régime of the Holy Places in the Old City.[122] These Holy Places were then under Jordanian control. The Conciliation Commission presented to the General Assembly a plan for the internationalization of Jerusalem. However, the new plan deviated from the General Assembly's instructions and was consequently ignored.

On 9 December 1949, in resolution 303, the General Assembly restated its intention that Jerusalem should be placed under a permanent international régime and confirmed the basic provisions of its resolution of 29 November 1947. The General Assembly also requested the Trusteeship Council to complete the preparation of the Statute of Jerusalem and to proceed immediately with its implementation.

On 4 April 1950 the Trusteeship Council approved a Statute for the City of Jerusalem, but soon came to the conclusion that neither Jordan nor Israel was prepared to collaborate in its implementation.[123] In fact, Israel had moved its ministerial offices to Jerusalem and on 23 January 1950 had proclaimed the City its capital. Since then no further action was taken by the UN to implement the internationalization of Jerusalem, and the *de facto* military situation created in 1948 continued until 1967.

---

119 Thus the international régime envisaged for Jerusalem did not possess any character of permanency, since it was open to the residents of the City, after a period of ten years, to modify it, if they wished.   120 UN Document A/648, p. 18.
121 Resolution 194(III) of 11 December 1948 (Appendix VI).
122 See the Report of the Conciliation Commission for Palestine dated 2 September 1950, UN Document A/1367/Rev. 1, pp. 10–11.
123 See Special Report of the Trusteeship Council, UN Document A/1286.

At the very outset of the War of 5 June 1967 Israel occupied the Arab-controlled sector of Jerusalem and immediately proceeded to "unify" the city. This unification was nothing but an annexation. On 28 June 1967 Israel extended its "law, jurisdiction and administration" to an enlarged municipal area of Jerusalem which included the Old City.

In addition to the annexation of Jerusalem, Israel took several other measures in the city which were contrary to international law, to the Geneva Conventions of 1949 and to UN resolutions. These measures included the deportation of persons, the dynamiting and razing of Arab homes, and the confiscation and expropriation of Arab property.[124]

The UN was deeply concerned by the measures taken by Israel to change the status of Jerusalem. Both the General Assembly and the Security Council condemned these measures. In its resolution 2253 (ES-V) of 4 July 1967 the General Assembly declared these measures invalid. It further called upon Israel to rescind all measures taken, and to desist from taking any action which would alter the status of Jerusalem. Ten days later, by its resolution 2254 (ES-V) of 14 July 1967, the General Assembly deplored the failure of Israel to implement its previous resolution, and reiterated its terms.

The Security Council also adopted four resolutions that condemned Israel's actions in Jerusalem. These were: resolution 252 of 21 May 1968, resolution 267 of 3 July 1969, resolution 271 of 15 September 1969, and resolution 298 of 25 September 1971. In these resolutions, the Security Council deplored the failure of Israel to show any regard for General Assembly and Security Council resolutions. It proclaimed the invalidity of the measures taken to change the status of Jerusalem, and called upon Israel to rescind them and to desist from taking any further steps which attempt to change the status of the City. In its resolution of 25 September 1971 the Security Council declared that it:

> "3. Confirms in the clearest possible terms that all legislative and administrative actions taken by Israel to change the status of the City of Jerusalem, including the expropriation of land and properties, the transfer of populations, and legislation aimed at the incorporation of the occupied section are totally invalid and cannot change that status."

The nullity of all measures taken by Israel to settle the occupied territories, including occupied Jerusalem, was again reaffirmed by the General Assembly in its resolution 3005 of 15 December 1972 (Appendix XXXII).

Israel, however, did not heed these UN resolutions: it neither rescinded any measures, nor desisted from taking any new ones. Israel's attitude is that Jerusalem was at the time of David and Solomon a Jewish city and on that ground it claims the right to restore its Jewish character after thirty centuries.

---

124 For details about the illegal measures taken by Israel in Jerusalem after its occupation, see UN Documents A/6793, A/6797, S/8146, S/8158, Statement of Rouhi Al-Khatib, deported Arab Mayor of Jerusalem, to the Security Council of 3 May 1968, and his monograph, *The Judaization of Jerusalem*, P.L.O. Research Centre, Beirut, 1970.

The measures which Israel has taken, and is still taking despite UN condemnations, aim, on the one hand, at the displacement of the original inhabitants of Jerusalem, both Christian and Moslem, and at the dispossession of their lands and properties, and aim, on the other hand, at packing the Holy City with the greatest possible number of Jews.

This forcible transformation by a military occupier of the character of the Holy City for political and religious motives does violence to law and to history.

During the last two thousand years and until the unnatural demographic changes that resulted from Jewish immigration under the British mandate and subsequent Israeli rule, Jerusalem was inhabited mainly by pagans for a while, and then almost exclusively by Christians and Moslems. For almost nineteen centuries, beginning with the dispersal of the Jews by the Romans in the 1st century, almost no Jews lived in Jerusalem. M. Franco, who made a special study of the position of the Jews in the Ottoman Empire, mentions that the famous Spanish traveller Benjamin of Tudela found 200 Jews in Jerusalem in the year A.D. 1173.[125] M. Franco observes that, apparently, the Jews who lived at the time that Benjamin of Tudela visited the city were expelled, for in 1180 another traveller, Petahia of Ratisbon, found in Jerusalem one coreligionist only.[126] In A.D. 1267 a Spanish rabbi, Moïse Ben Nahman, found two Jews in Jerusalem.[127] In 1875, according to a report submitted to the Anglo-Jewish Association, the number of Jews in Jerusalem was about 13,000.[128] In 1922, according to the census of the Government of Palestine, the Jewish population of Jerusalem numbered 33,971 out of a total population of 62,578 for the urban area of Jerusalem.[129] The 1931 census shows an increase of the Jewish population to 51,222 out of a total population of 90,503 for the urban area of Jerusalem.[130] In 1946, according to an estimate of population made for the UN, the Jewish population in the City of Jerusalem, envisaged as a *corpus separatum*, was 99,690 out of a total population of 205,230.[131]

The percentages of population in the sub-district of Jerusalem in 1946 were 62 per cent Arabs and others, and 38 per cent Jews.[132] As a result of the forcible demographic changes brought about by Israel since 1948, and in particular since 1967, these proportions are now reversed. According to present Israeli figures,

---

125 M. Franco, *Histoire des Israélites de l'Empire Ottoman*, p. 4, Durlacher, Paris, 1897.
126 *Ibid.*, p. 4.
127 *Ibid.*, p. 5. See also Rev. Charles T. Bridgeman, *op. cit.*, p. 13.
128 *Ibid.*, p. 195.
129 *Statistical Abstract of Palestine*, 1941, p. 12.
130 *Ibid.*, p. 12.
131 See UN Document A/AC 14/32, 11 November 1947, Official Records of the 2nd Session of the General Assembly, *Ad Hoc* Committee, 1947, p. 304. The above figures disprove the statement of Abba Eban in his letter of 15 November 1971 to the Secretary-General of the UN, in which he opposed the Security Council's resolution of 25 September 1971 and declared that: "For the past 200 years the Jews have been the largest community" in Jerusalem. For the text of this statement, see UN Document S/10392, 19 November 1971.
132 UN Document A/AC 14/32, *op. cit.*, p. 292.

the population of Jerusalem is now 300,000, three-quarters of whom are Jews and one-quarter Moslems (61,000) and Christians (11,000).[133]

The alteration of the demographic composition of Jerusalem has been accompanied by a forcible and illegal dispossession of the Arab inhabitants.

While the Jews owned before the end of the mandate about one-third of the built-up property in the City, their land ownership in the sub-district of Jerusalem did not exceed 2 per cent.[134] Since 1948, and especially after their occupation and annexation of Jerusalem in 1967, the Israeli authorities have systematically expropriated Arab property so as to make the City Jewish, both in terms of population and in terms of land ownership.

Israel's attempt forcibly to restore the Jewish character of Jerusalem to what it was, or may have been, at the time of David and Solomon seeks to obliterate three thousand years of history. Since those distant times the most momentous events have occurred in Jerusalem which have charted a new course for humanity and have left a profound impact on the world. History cannot be unwritten or obliterated, even by force.

The annexation of Jerusalem violates international law, UN resolutions and Israel's own undertakings prior to its admission to UN membership.[135] Such annexation, moreover, violates the established historic and religious status of the City, and constitutes a sacrilegious usurpation of a City holy to one half of mankind.

---

133 In 1946 the number of Christians in Jerusalem was 31,350 (Rev. Charles T. Bridgeman, *op. cit.*, p. 14) and in Bethlehem was over 11,000. It thus appears that 75 per cent of the Christian population of Jerusalem and Bethlehem have been displaced since the creation of Israel.

134 See UN Document A/AC 14/32, *op. cit.*, p. 293, and Appendix VI thereto.

135 These undertakings are referred to in Section 3 of Chapter VIII, *post*.

Section 7
Violations of human rights

Respect for human rights has now become a definite legal obligation recognized by international law. Although in the past international law has shown more concern for the rights of States than for the rights of individuals, three international instruments, adopted shortly after the Second World War, have consecrated the principle of respect and protection of human rights. These instruments were: the Charter of the UN (1945), the Universal Declaration of Human Rights (1948), and the Geneva Conventions (1949).

Respect for human rights and fundamental freedoms is one of the basic principles emphasized by the Charter.[136] Oppenheim remarks:

> "Though imperfect from the point of view of enforcement, the relevant provisions of the Charter constitute legal obligations of the members of the United Nations and of the Organisation as a whole. The fundamental human rights and freedoms acknowledged by the Charter must henceforth be regarded as legal rights recognized by International Law."[137]

The Charter, however, did not define or specifically enumerate human rights.

The Universal Declaration of Human Rights enumerated some human rights, such as the right to life, liberty, security, property and others.

The four Geneva Conventions of 1949, in particular the Convention Relative to the Protection of Civilian Persons in Time of War, of 12 August 1949, embodied the principle of protection of civilians in time of war and the prohibition of violations of certain human rights. Article 27 provided that civilians, described as "protected" persons, are entitled, in all circumstances, to respect for their persons, their honour, their family rights, their religious convictions,

---

136 See the Preamble and Articles 1(3), 13, 55 and 62(2) of the Charter.
137 Oppenheim, *International Law*, Vol. I, 8th ed., pp. 740, 742.

their manners and customs. Acts which were specifically forbidden were: murder, torture, infliction of corporal punishment (Article 32); punishment for an offence not committed by the person punished or infliction of collective penalties; intimidation, terrorism and pillage; reprisals against persons and property (Article 33); individual or mass forcible transfers or deportation of persons (Article 49); and destruction of real or personal property, except where such destruction is absolutely necessary for military operations (Article 53). Israel and the Arab States became parties to this Convention.

In addition to its obligations under the UN Charter, the Universal Declaration of Human Rights and the Geneva Conventions, Israel assumed, in accordance with the partition resolution of 29 November 1947, a specific obligation to respect and protect the "human rights and fundamental freedoms" of the Palestinian Arabs who were to be citizens of the proposed Jewish State. The partition resolution stated that the constitutions of the Arab and Jewish States to be established in accordance with its terms should include, *inter alia*, provisions for "guaranteeing to all persons ... the enjoyment of human rights and fundamental freedoms ..." Israel accepted the obligations imposed by the partition resolution in its cable to the Secretary-General of the United Nations dated 15 May 1948 (see Appendix V).

Did Israel respect the human rights of the Palestinian Arabs?

Of all human rights, the most natural is the right of a person to live, work and die in his own country. This right was denied, and continues to be denied, by Israel to two million Palestinians in a most brutal and inhuman way. The objective of Israel's uprooting of the Palestinians, and its refusal to allow their return to their homes were explained in the first section of this chapter. In this light, Israel's violations of the human rights of the Palestinians become doubly heinous.

The Palestinians who remained under Israeli occupation did not fare better. They were reduced to the status of second-class citizens and were subjected to various forms of oppression: arrest, detention, restriction on their liberty of movement, expropriation of their properties, and, in a number of cases, destruction of their homes and villages.[138]

Israel's violations of the human rights of the Palestinians increased and were intensified after the War of 5 June 1967. Following the occupation of the remaining parts of Palestine – the West Bank and the Gaza Strip – Israel was faced with a large Arab population in the territory under its control[139] as well as a more active Palestinian resistance. Israel felt no compunction in resorting to illegal and brutal means to spread terror, reduce opposition and force the submission of the civilian Arab population, even though such means constituted grave violations of human rights. These violations included the uprooting and

---

138 See Sections 3 and 7 of this chapter.
139 More than one million Palestinians came under Israel's occupation as a result of its invasion of the West Bank and the Gaza Strip in June 1967.

expulsion of the Palestinians,[140] mass destruction of homes and villages,[141] torture, imprisonment, deportation, prolonged curfews and collective punishments, particularly in the Gaza Strip.[142]

Prior to June 1967, the attitude of the UN towards Israel's violations of human rights was one which, apart from the adoption each year of stereotyped resolutions deploring Israel's refusal to allow the return of the Palestine refugees, could be characterized as one of passiveness and almost of indifference. In contrast, after June 1967, the UN displayed a greater concern over the violations of human rights committed by Israel in the occupied territories. On 14 June 1967 the Security Council by its resolution 237 called upon Israel to ensure the safety, welfare and security of the inhabitants of the occupied areas and recommended to the Governments concerned scrupulous respect for the humanitarian principles governing the treatment of prisoners of war and the protection of civilians in time of war contained in the Geneva Conventions of 12 August 1949. The Council further asked the Secretary-General to report on the effective implementation of this resolution. But Israel ignored this resolution and even refused to receive the Special Representative appointed by the Secretary-General in order to visit the occupied territories and to report on the implementation of the resolution. Israel's flimsy pretext was that the Special Representative should also perform a function which had not been ordered by the Security Council: to inquire into the conditions of the Jews in the Arab countries. On 27 September 1968 the Security Council deplored in its resolution 259 the delay in the implementation of its resolution of 14 June 1967 and again requested the Secretary-General to despatch a Special Representative "to the Arab territories under military occupation by Israel following the hostilities of 5 June 1967" in order to report on the implementation of its previous resolution. The Security Council also requested Israel to receive the Special Representative of the Secretary-General, to co-operate with him and to facilitate his work. Israel again refused to receive the Secretary-General's Representative, thus preventing any international inquiry on the spot into its treatment of the civilian population and into complaints regarding its violations of human rights in the occupied territories.

---

140 About 180,000 new refugees were displaced in June 1967, and some 200,000 were displaced for a second time.

141 See Henry Cattan, *Palestine, the Arabs and Israel*, pp. 109–111, Longman, 1969. For demolition of refugee shelters and forcible transfer of Palestinian refugees in the Gaza Strip in the summer of 1971, see the Report of the Secretary-General, A/8383 of 17 September 1971, A/8383 Add. 1 of 23 November 1971 and the Report of the Commissioner-General of UNRWA, A/8713, 9 September 1972, pp. 7–8.

142 For reports on Israeli violations of human rights in the occupied territories, see UN Documents A/6701, A/6723, A/6793, A/6797, A/8089, A/8389, S/8146, S/8158, as well as newspaper accounts in *The Sunday Times*, 19 November 1967; *The Economist*, 9 December 1967; *The Guardian*, 26 January 1968, 19 February 1968; *The Observer*, 18 January and 18 February 1968, and 1 August 1971; *The Times*, 28 October 1969, 22 July 1971, 31 July 1971, 16 August 1971, 3 September 1971.

On 19 December 1968, the General Assembly decided to establish a Special Committee to investigate Israeli practices affecting the human rights of the civilian population in the occupied territories. This committee was not permitted by Israel to visit the occupied territories. However, notwithstanding Israel's refusal to co-operate, the Special Committee conducted its investigations and reported to the General Assembly that Israel was pursuing in the occupied territories "policies and practices which are in violation of the human rights of the population of those territories."[143] The Special Committee referred to the establishment of Israeli settlements in the occupied territories and declared that "the occupying Power is pursuing a conscious and deliberate policy calculated to depopulate the area."[144] On 15 December 1970 the General Assembly called upon Israel immediately to implement the recommendations of the Special Committee, and to comply with its obligations under the Geneva Convention relative to the Protection of Civilian Persons in Time of War, of 12 August 1949, the Universal Declaration of Human Rights, and the relevant resolutions adopted by various international organizations. The General Assembly further requested the Special Committee to continue its work in order to ensure the safeguarding of the human rights of the population of the occupied territories.[145] Israel, however, again paid no heed to this resolution.

In October 1971, the Special Committee charged with the investigation of Israeli practices affecting human rights submitted a second report in which it declared that Israel was continuing its practices and policies which constituted fundamental violations of human rights. The report also stated that Israel was carrying out a policy of "progressive and systematic elimination of every vestige of Palestinian presence" in occupied areas. This policy, the Special Committee observed, "would have the effect of obliterating Arab culture and the Arab way of life in the area, and, contrary to international law, of transforming it into a Jewish State."[146] Following this report, the General Assembly adopted on 20 December 1971 a resolution in which it proclaimed its grave concern about violations of human rights in the occupied territories. It further

"strongly called upon Israel to rescind forthwith all measures and to desist from all policies and practices such as:

(a) The annexation of any part of the occupied Arab territories;
(b) The establishment of Israeli settlements on those territories and the transfer of parts of its civilian population into the occupied territories;
(c) The destruction and demolition of villages, quarters and houses and the confiscation and expropriation of property;
(d) The evacuation, transfer, deportation and expulsion of the inhabitants of the occupied Arab territories;

---

143 See A/8089, 26 October 1970.
144 *Ibid.*, p. 34.
145 Resolution 2727 (XXV), 15 December 1970 (Appendix XXIII).
146 See A/8389, p. 55, 5 October 1971.

(e) The denial of the right of the refugees and displaced persons to return to their homes;

(f) The ill-treatment and torture of prisoners and detainees;

(g) Collective punishment."[147]

Needless to say, Israel has shown no more regard for this resolution than it did for other UN resolutions.

In October 1972 the same Special Committee reported to the General Assembly that Israel was annexing and settling Arab territories occupied in 1967, in violation of the human rights of the population. The report said that deportations, the demolition of houses and the establishment of Israeli settlements were on the increase since the preceding year, and again urged some form of international supervision of the occupied areas to protect the Arab population. On 15 December 1972 the General Assembly, acting on the Special Committee's report, adopted resolution 3005 (Appendix XXXII) in which it called again upon Israel to rescind and desist from its policies and practices in the occupied territories.

Concurrently with the General Assembly, the UN Commission on Human Rights[148] and other international organizations have also condemned Israel for its violations of human rights in the occupied territories. But all these resolutions have not curbed Israel's determination to pursue its practices and policies, even though they have been repeatedly condemned as violations of the human rights of the Palestinians under international law.

---

147 Resolution 2851 (XXVI), 20 December 1971 (Appendix XXVII).

148 See resolutions of Commission on Human Rights of 27 February 1968, 4 March 1969, 23 March 1970 and 15 March 1971. In a resolution adopted on 22 March 1972 (Appendix XXVIII), the Commission on Human Rights accused Israel of "war crimes" in the occupied territories. In a resolution adopted on 14 March 1973 (Appendix XXXIII) the Commission on Human Rights asked Israel to stop establishing settlements in occupied Arab territories, and to cancel all measures changing the physical character and demographic composition of those lands. The Commission said that Israel's deliberate policy of annexation and of settlement in the occupied territories was in contravention of the Charter of the United Nations, the international humanitarian law, and with the basic human rights and fundamental freedoms.

CHAPTER VII

THE SECURITY COUNCIL RESOLUTION 242 OF 22 NOVEMBER 1967

Section 1
Basic provisions of
the resolution

Israel's violations of UN resolutions and of international law mentioned in the preceding chapter considerably aggravated the injustice that resulted from the emergence of Israel in the land of Palestine and from the displacement of the Palestinians from their homeland. The UN condemned, as we have seen, a number of these violations, particularly those that involved acts of war, breaches of human rights, or measures tending to change the status of Jerusalem; it deplored some of them and remained completely silent over many others. However, the UN did not go beyond condemning, censuring and deploring; at no time did it take any corrective action or envisage any rectification of the situation. This fact encouraged Israel to continue in its defiance of UN resolutions with the result that the unjust and unnatural situation created in Palestine in 1948 has remained without redress.

It was only after the world commotion caused by the War of 5 June 1967 that the UN began thinking in terms of an overall solution to the Arab-Israeli conflict and felt the need to establish a just and lasting peace. Following the outbreak of this last war an emergency special session of the General Assembly of the UN was convened at the request of Soviet Russia. Its object was to consider the situation and to bring about the immediate withdrawal of Israel's forces behind the armistice lines. From 19 to 30 June the General Assembly debated the situation. During the debate two attitudes emerged.

On the one hand, Soviet Russia requested the condemnation of Israel as an aggressor and demanded its immediate withdrawal from the territories which it had occupied.

On the other hand, the US Government opposed Israel's condemnation as an aggressor and the adoption of a resolution calling for withdrawal of its forces from the territories which it had occupied. Instead, it submitted a resolution which would have had the Assembly consider that the objective of a stable and durable peace in the Middle East should be achieved through negotiated arrangements to be based on five principles: mutual recognition of the political independence and territorial integrity of all countries in the area, encompassing recognized boundaries, and including disengagement and withdrawal; freedom of innocent maritime passage; a just and equitable solution of the refugee problem; limitation of arms shipments to the area; and recognition of the right of all sovereign nations to exist in peace and security. The American resolution thus enlarged the issues and sought to secure not only the withdrawal of Israeli forces but, primarily, a political settlement between the Arab States and Israel.

In consequence of the division between the USA and Soviet Russia on the question of Israel's withdrawal from the occupied territories, the Soviet resolution calling for an immediate withdrawal of Israeli forces and the American resolution calling for negotiations between the parties, as well as all other resolutions and amendments backing one or other of these two conflicting positions, failed to gain the two-thirds majority required for their adoption by the General Assembly.

Nothing concrete happened until 9 November 1967, when the Security Council convened at Egypt's request in order to examine the situation again. The conflict between the positions of Soviet Russia and of the USA, which had prevented the adoption of any resolution by the General Assembly, was again reflected in the deliberations of the Security Council. However, on 22 November 1967, agreement was reached on resolution 242, which laid down a formula for what was described as "a just and lasting peace in the Middle East". (See Appendix XIII.)

This resolution emphasized the inadmissibility of the acquisition of territory by war and affirmed that the fulfilment of the principles of the Charter requires the establishment of a just and lasting peace in the Middle East which should include the application of both the following principles:

(i) Withdrawal of Israeli armed forces from territories occupied in the recent conflict.

(ii) Termination of all claims or states of belligerency and respect for and acknowledgement of the sovereignty, territorial integrity and political independence of every State in the area and their right to live in peace within secure and recognized boundaries free from threats or acts of force.

The resolution further affirmed the necessity:

(i) For guaranteeing freedom of navigation through international waterways in the area;

(ii) For achieving a just settlement of the refugee problem;

(iii) For guaranteeing the territorial inviolability and political independence of every State in the area, through measures including the establishment of demilitarized zones.

Finally, the resolution requested the Secretary-General to designate a Special Representative to proceed to the Middle East to establish and maintain contact with the States concerned, in order to promote agreement and assist efforts to achieve a peaceful and accepted settlement in accordance with the provisions and principles of the resolution.

Under the pressure of military occupation of their territories, Egypt and Jordan agreed to implement the resolution. Syria and the Palestinians rejected it. Although the resolution was in its favour, Israel refused to implement its provision concerning withdrawal of its armed forces from the occupied territories. Although its attitude on this matter had been apparent since June 1967, Israel's refusal to withdraw from the occupied territories was formally notified to Ambassador Gunnar Jarring, the Special Representative appointed by the Secretary-General under the terms of the resolution, several years later in a communication dated 26 February 1971.[1]

Although it seems that the Security Council's resolution has now foundered on Israel's refusal to implement its provision concerning withdrawal from the occupied territories, it is still considered by most Powers, including the Great Powers, as embodying an appropriate formula for a solution of the Arab-Israeli conflict. For this reason it is necessary to examine whether the resolution conforms to the UN Charter and international law and whether, in fact, it offers a suitable means for the restoration of peace in the area. This enquiry will be undertaken in the following section.

---

1   The Israeli communication stated: "Israel would not withdraw to the pre-5 June 1967 lines" (A/8541, S/10403, 30 November 1971). Israel claimed that it would withdraw only to safe and secure boundaries to be determined by negotiations between the parties. This meant, in effect, that under the pretext of obtaining safe and secure boundaries Israel planned to retain and annex some of the territories which it had occupied in a war of aggression which it had itself initiated.

Section 2
Incompatibility
with the Charter
and with international law

Although the Security Council is a political body, the Charter clearly intended that it should exercise its functions within the confines of law and justice.[2] Article 24 of the Charter provides that in discharging its duties for the maintenance of international peace and security "the Security Council shall act in accordance with the Purposes and Principles of the United Nations." The Purposes and Principles of the UN are set forth in Articles 1 and 2 of the Charter. They include, *inter alia*, the duty of the UN to act "in conformity with the principles of justice and international law," to develop friendly relations among nations based on "respect for the principle of equal rights and self-determination of peoples," to promote and encourage "respect for human rights and for fundamental freedoms for all without distinction as to race, sex, language, or religion."

In its resolution of 22 November 1967 the Security Council affirmed that the "fulfilment of Charter principles requires the establishment of a just and lasting peace in the Middle East . . ." But what did the resolution, in fact, propose for the establishment of a just peace? In effect, what the resolution essentially proposed was the restoration of the territorial status that existed prior to 5 June 1967 in consideration of Arab recognition of the State of Israel. In other words, the resolution sought to settle the 1967 conflict, but left the basic Palestine situation unresolved and without redress. Viewed in the light of its concrete proposals for the establishment of peace, the resolution is open to four grave objections.

(1) The resolution fails to redress the wrongs done in Palestine and even purports to legitimate the Palestine injustice.

The number of wrongs done in Palestine is simply appalling: the Balfour

---

2   See Section 2 of Chapter III, *supra*.

Declaration, which promised a home for the Jews in an Arab country; a mass Jewish immigration forced upon the original inhabitants; the iniquity of partition; the emergence of the State of Israel; the usurpation of four-fifths of the territory of Palestine by an alien minority; the uprooting and the forcible displacement of its indigenous population; the plunder of their possessions, and the confiscation of their lands and homes.

What does the resolution offer for redress of this succession of injustices? All that it offers is the affirmation of the necessity for achieving "a just settlement of the refugee problem", as if such a recommendation would solve, or maybe shelve, the basic Palestine Question. In limiting the proposed redress to the refugee problem, the Security Council has overlooked the fact that this problem is merely one of several issues involved. The Question of Palestine is not simply a refugee problem; it has wider dimensions and involves the restoration of the fundamental and legitimate rights of the Palestinians.

Moreover, instead of seeking to redress the wrongs done to the Palestinians, the resolution even seeks to reward the wrongdoer. Overlooking the illegitimacy of Israel, the resolution prescribes as one of its two basic principles "respect for and acknowledgement of the sovereignty, territorial integrity and political independence of every State in the area." Since the sovereignty, territorial integrity and political independence of the Arab States were never in doubt or dispute, this provision aims in effect at securing Arab recognition of Israel, of its sovereignty and of its territorial conquests prior to 5 June 1967.

(2) The resolution implies ratification of the conquest by Israel in 1948 and 1949 of territories in excess of the partition resolution.

The Security Council resolution prescribes the withdrawal of Israeli armed forces from territories occupied "in the recent conflict". There is no mention of any withdrawal from territories occupied by Israel in 1948 and 1949 in excess of the partition resolution.[3] By implication, therefore, the resolution legitimates Israel's previous conquests, although such conquests were made in violation of the resolution of the General Assembly of 29 November 1947. At the same time, and in the same breath, the resolution emphasizes "the inadmissibility of the acquisition of territory by war." This is a patent contradiction. If such acquisition was inadmissible in 1967, it was equally inadmissible in 1948 and 1949. Thus the Security Council appears to be condoning the territorial conquests of Israel made in violation of both international law and the resolution of the General Assembly, and in so doing it can hardly be said to be faithful to the principles of the Charter.

(3) The resolution wrongly assumes that recognition of Israel by the Arab States puts an end to the conflict.

---

3 Quincy Wright observes: "The resolution of November 22nd is advantageous to Israel in requiring withdrawal only from territory occupied in 1967. The territory occupied by Israel under the 1949 Armistice beyond the UN partition line of 1947 might have been added." *AJIL*, Vol. 64, No. 4, p. 78, September 1970.

It is clear that the Security Council is seeking to settle the Arab-Israeli conflict over the heads of the Palestinians as if such a conflict were a matter of concern only between Israel and the Arab States. The main victims are left out in the cold. Such an attitude shows either ignorance of, or indifference to, the real issues involved. Cherif Bassiouni and Eugene Fisher have emphasized the true nature of the problem in these terms:

> "Exclusive concern for Israel confuses the judgment of those who look upon the struggle merely as between Israel and the neighbouring Arab States, thus misunderstanding the true nature of Middle East problems and failing even to recognize the basic character of the Palestine issue itself. Indeed, the observer can clearly see, if he will, the fact that every guerilla infiltration, every commando raid, every act of sabotage has been the work, not of Israel's neighbouring States, but of Palestinians determined to regain their homeland."[4]

As pointed out in Section 3 of Chapter V the Arab States cannot dispose of Palestine, nor impair the rights of the Palestinians. Recognition of Israel by the Arab States neither puts an end to the conflict, nor confers legitimacy on Israel. The inalienable rights of the Palestinians to their country cannot be by-passed or nullified by means of a deal between Israel and the neighbouring Arab States.

(4) The last objection is that, if the resolution is construed as it has been, namely that Israel's withdrawal is contingent on a settlement, then it would in this respect also run counter to the Charter and to international law.

The resolution has been construed in certain quarters to mean that its provision for Israel's withdrawal from the occupied territories is contingent upon the conclusion of peace between the Arab States and Israel. Although there is nothing in the tenor of the resolution that bears out such a construction, William P. Rogers, US Secretary of State, declared:

> "To call for Israeli withdrawal as envisaged in the UN resolution without achieving agreement on peace would be partisan toward the Arabs. To call on the Arabs to accept peace without Israeli withdrawal would be partisan toward Israel. Therefore, our policy is to encourage the Arabs to accept a permanent peace based on a binding agreement and to urge the Israelis to withdraw from occupied territory when their territorial integrity is assured as envisaged by the Security Council resolution."[5]

If this is the true meaning of the resolution, then Israel is enabled under the pressure of the occupation of Arab territories to exact Arab recognition of its legitimacy and of its conquests, and thus to reap benefits from its aggression. This would constitute a clear violation of international law and of the Charter. The occupation of Arab territories by Israel in 1967 was an international wrong and a violation of the Charter. To allow Israel to maintain its occupation until it exacts a price for its withdrawal is an aggravation of the wrong. It has been

---

4   "The Arab-Israeli Conflict", *St John's Law Review*, p. 460, January 1970.
5   Address by William P. Rogers before the Galaxy Conference, Washington, 9 December 1969.

observed that "by making Israel's obligation to relinquish militarily occupied territory conditional upon Arab agreement to a comprehensive settlement, the United Nations . . . gave its endorsement to the achievement of a settlement by Israeli force."[6]

To call for Israel's withdrawal would not be partisan toward the Arabs: it would simply mean putting an end to a wrong. It is now a recognized principle of international law that a treaty secured by force or under the pressure of military occupation is null and void. A peace treaty, says Oppenheim, imposed by the victorious aggressor has no legal validity.[7] Lauterpacht, in his Report of 1953 on the law of treaties to the International Law Commission stated:

> ". . . a treaty imposed by or as the result of force or threats of force . . . is invalid by virtue of the operation of the general principle of law which postulates freedom of consent as an essential condition of the validity of consensual undertakings . . . Moreover, in so far as war or force or threats of force constitute an internationally illegal act, the results of that illegality – namely, a treaty imposed in connexion with or in consequence thereof – are governed by the principle that an illegal act cannot produce legal rights for the benefit of the law-breaker." (*Yearbook of the International Law Commission*, Vol. 2, p. 148, 1953.)

The principle that a treaty is void if its conclusion has been procured by the threat or the use of force was adopted by the International Law Commission at Vienna in 1969 (Article 52 of the Vienna Convention on the Law of Treaties, 1969). Jennings observes that "a cession imposed by illegal force is void . . . The general principles of law that consensual obligations cannot be founded in force, and that *ex injuria jus non oritur* lead to the same conclusion."[8] Similarly, Brownlie states: "The modern law prohibits conquest and regards the treaty of cession as a nullity."[9] Quincy Wright has condemned Israel's claim to remain in occupation of Arab territories until it secures a peace treaty. "One cannot say," he observed, "that negotiations over territory are fair where one or the other party occupies most of it. . . . Modern international law, affirmed by the Stimson Doctrine, holds that a treaty made by duress against the state is invalid."[10]

Any condition attached to the aggressor's withdrawal is contrary to international law. This view was upheld by President Eisenhower, who insisted upon Israel's unconditional withdrawal from the territories which it seized in 1956. President Eisenhower then said that if a nation which attacked and occupied foreign territory in the face of UN disapproval were allowed to impose

---

6 John Lawrence Hargrove, "Abating the Middle East Crisis through the United Nations", *Kansas Law Review*, p. 369, 1971.
7 *International Law*, Vol. 2, 7th ed., p. 219.
8 R. Y. Jennings, *The Acquisition of Territory in International Law*, p. 67, Manchester University Press and Oceana.
9 Ian Brownlie, *Public International Law*, p. 159, Clarendon Press, 1966.
10 *AJIL*, Vol. 64, pp. 74 and 78, 1970.

conditions on its withdrawal, this would be tantamount to turning back the clock of international order.[11]

In adopting its resolution of 22 November 1967, the Security Council was influenced much more by considerations relating to the maintenance of a *fait accompli* established by force than by the Purposes and Principles of the UN. Its formula for peace is incompatible with the Charter, with international law and with General Assembly resolutions. In effect, this formula seeks to establish peace, without restoring justice. The result appears certain: that the implementation of the resolution will lead neither to peace, nor to justice.

In recent years, the General Assembly of the United Nations has sought to remedy some of the fatal flaws in the Security Council's resolution. It has adopted certain resolutions that have laid stress upon the inalienable rights of the Palestinians and have emphasized the fact that respect for their rights is an indispensable element of any just peace in the Middle East. In its resolution 2535 (XXIV) B of 10 December 1969 (Appendix XIX), the General Assembly declared that "the problem of the Palestine refugees has arisen from the denial of their inalienable rights under the Charter of the United Nations and the Universal Declaration of Human Rights," and it reaffirmed "the inalienable rights of the people of Palestine". Then, in its resolution 2628 (XXV) of 4 November 1970 (Appendix XXI), it stated that "respect for the rights of the Palestinians is an indispensable element in the establishment of a just and lasting peace in the Middle East." Again, in its resolution 2672 (XXV) C of 8 December 1970 (Appendix XXII), the General Assembly reaffirmed its resolution of 4 November and declared that "the people of Palestine are entitled to equal rights and self-determination, in accordance with the Charter of the United Nations." In its resolution 2787 (XXVI) of 6 December 1971 (Appendix XXV), the General Assembly reaffirmed the inalienable rights of the Palestinian people, among other peoples, to freedom, equality and self-determination. It should be remarked that in all these resolutions the General Assembly spoke of the rights of "the people of Palestine" or "the Palestinians", as distinct from the rights of "the refugees".

Then in its resolution 2949 (XXVII) of 8 December 1972 (Appendix XXX) the General Assembly trod new ground. After reaffirming certain principles already laid down in previous resolutions concerning the inadmissibility of acquisition of territories by force and the respect for the rights of the Palestinians, the resolution introduced two new and important guiding principles.

First, the General Assembly declared that changes carried out by Israel in the occupied territories in contravention of the Geneva Conventions of 1949 are null and void. It called upon Israel to rescind them forthwith and to desist from all policies and practices affecting the physical character or demographic composition of the occupied territories. It also called upon all States not to recognize

---

11 Dwight D. Eisenhower, *Waging Peace 1956–1961*, p. 188, Doubleday, 1965.

such changes and measures carried out by Israel in the occupied territories, and invited them to avoid actions, including actions in the field of aid, that could constitute recognition of that occupation. This new provision is of far-reaching significance, both politically and juridically. In 1967 the General Assembly had, as mentioned in Section 6 of Chapter VI, declared invalid the measures taken by Israel to change the status of Jerusalem. In 1972 the General Assembly extended this invalidity to changes and measures taken by Israel in all the occupied territories. Thus, the General Assembly emphatically asserted the principle that an illegal *fait accompli* creates no rights in international law.

Secondly, and this also constitutes a significant move, the General Assembly requested the Security Council, in consultation with the Secretary-General and his Special Representative, to take all appropriate steps with a view to the full and speedy implementation of Security Council resolution 242 of 22 November 1967, "taking into account all the relevant resolutions and documents of the United Nations in this connection." The implementation of this provision could be of capital importance. If this provision is to be given its natural meaning, presumably the relevant resolutions to be taken into account include the resolution on partition, the implementation of which would entail the geographical contraction of Israel to the limits of the Jewish State as envisaged by the United Nations in 1947. Presumably also the relevant resolutions to be taken into account include the resolutions that provide for the return of the Palestine refugees to their homes, the implementation of which would de-Judaize the present racist State of Israel. Presumably the relevant resolutions to be taken into account also include the resolutions that require respect for the inalienable rights of the Palestinians and respect for the status of Jerusalem. Again, of the "documents of the United Nations" to which the resolution refers, it seems that the most important is the Charter itself of the United Nations.

Finally, on 13 December 1972 the General Assembly adopted seven resolutions, numbered 2963 A to F, concerning various aspects of the problem (Appendix XXXI). Of particular interest are resolutions C, D and E. These three resolutions:

— "Strongly deplored" measures taken by Israel "involving the physical and demographic structure in the Gaza Strip including the destruction of refugee shelters and the forcible transfer of population," and called upon Israel to "desist forthwith" from such measures (resolution C).

— Called once more upon Israel to take immediate steps for the return of the displaced inhabitants of the Israeli-occupied territories to their homes and camps and to "desist forthwith from all measures affecting the physical, geographic and demographic structure of the occupied territories" (resolution D).

— Affirmed that "the people of Palestine are entitled to equal rights and self-determination, in accordance with the Charter of the United Nations"; expressed once more "its grave concern that the people of Palestine have not been permitted to enjoy their inalienable rights and to exercise their right to self-determination"; and declared "that full respect for and realization of the inalienable rights of the people of Palestine are indispensable for the establishment of a just and lasting peace in the Middle East" (resolution E).

However, the promising features contained in the various resolutions adopted by the General Assembly since 1969 are not likely to fulfil the expectation of restoring justice or the rights of the Palestinians. This pessimistic view is based on two considerations.

First, Israel has scornfully rejected all these resolutions. What is also regrettable is that even Ambassador Gunnar Jarring, the Secretary-General's Special Representative charged with securing a settlement of the Arab-Israeli conflict, has taken no account of the General Assembly's resolutions and has shown little enthusiasm for them. In fact, when Israel showed concern over the adoption by the General Assembly of its resolution 2628 (XXV) of 4 November 1970, which affirmed that respect for the rights of the Palestinians is an indispensable element in the establishment of a just and lasting peace in the Middle East (Appendix XXI), Ambassador Jarring hurried to assure Israel's Foreign Minister that he was proceeding on the basis that there was no change in his mandate, which he continued to regard as having been defined in Security Council resolution 242 of 22 November 1967.[12] Ambassador Jarring's attitude raises the question whether, in his capacity as the Secretary-General's Representative, he can properly ignore General Assembly resolutions. Meanwhile, however, such an attitude suggests that General Assembly resolutions proclaiming and emphasizing the rights of the Palestinians might be ignored in trying to work out a settlement.

Secondly, even if more respect were to be shown by the parties concerned towards General Assembly resolutions, nevertheless the implementation of these resolutions is not likely to bring peace or to resolve the conflict, for the simple reason that the General Assembly has preserved the basic features of the Security Council's resolution of 22 November 1967. In fact, the General Assembly's resolution of 8 December 1972 specifically declares that the establishment of peace in the Middle East should include the application of the two principles envisaged by the Security Council's resolution, namely, Israel's withdrawal from the occupied territories, and Arab recognition of the State of Israel and of its territorial integrity. As already explained, the Security Council's resolution of 1967 falls short of providing a suitable framework for a just and lasting peace. Therefore, in reaffirming quite justifiably the rights of the Palestinians but upholding at the same time the principles underlying the Security Council's resolution, the General Assembly is pursuing, in fact, two mutually defeating objectives: it is seeking to restore some semblance of right and justice while preserving at the same time the basic injustice.

In conclusion, it is evident that neither the Security Council's resolution of 1967, nor the General Assembly resolutions that have sought to correct its deficiencies succeed in restoring right and justice in Palestine. The need for a new formula for peace is obvious.

---

12 UN Document S/10070, Annex II, 4 January 1971.

CHAPTER VIII

THE RESTORATION
OF RIGHT AND
JUSTICE IN PALESTINE

Section 1
The need for
a new formula for peace

The history of Palestine from the Balfour Declaration until the present has been one of avoidance of law and justice. The number of wrongs, illegalities and injustices committed in this country is shocking. No one can reasonably question the need, one would say the obligation, to restore right and justice. When the majority of the inhabitants of a country are forcibly displaced, and their lands and homes are taken over by others, a grave wrong is done. Unless the law of the jungle is to prevail, this wrong must be redressed. As Dr John H. Davis, former Commissioner-General of UNRWA, has observed:

> "The world is bound to regard the acts committed against the Palestine Arabs, at the time of the creation of Israel and subsequently, as constituting grave injustices which must be rectified in the name of humanity and in the interest of peace."[1]

How can right and justice be restored in Palestine by means other than war? By negotiation between the parties? By mediation, conciliation and arbitration? By a settlement imposed by the Great Powers? Let us review the conceivable alternatives.

The method which first occurs to one's mind is a settlement to be reached by negotiation and agreement between the Arabs and Israel. This, however, seems illusory and unrealistic for the following reasons, amongst others.

The first reason is that Israel has no intention of negotiating a settlement, but intends to impose one. Despite its display of readiness to negotiate a settlement, there is no secret about its real intentions and demands. Israel wants Arab recognition of its legitimacy and of the legitimacy of its territorial conquests of 1948, 1949 and of some, at least, of its conquests of 1967. The latter include the Gaza Strip, Sharm El Sheikh and the Golan Heights of Syria. Israel claims these territories and others on the allegation that it wishes to ensure its "security".

---

1 John H. Davis, *The Evasive Peace*, p. 97, John Murray, London, 1968.

This argument would be laughable, if it were not tragic, especially when it is remembered that it is Israel that has been responsible since 1948 for all aggressions, culminating in the War of 5 June 1967. But the argument concerning "security" serves to conceal Israel's real intentions and its appetite for territory. As to Jerusalem, Israel has declared that its annexation in 1967 of this City is "irreversible" and "not negotiable".

Furthermore, Israel does not propose in any peace settlement to implement UN resolutions on Palestine, or to repatriate the Palestine refugees, or to restore their human rights, their fundamental freedoms, and their lands and homes. Generally speaking, Israel's terms do not contemplate the redress of the great injustice done in Palestine. Its aim is merely to consolidate its gains and to satisfy further ambitions, both political and territorial. It is obvious that Israel is not seeking peace, but only a reward for its aggressions and a ratification of its usurpations and spoliations. In the face of Israel's intransigence and demands, the conclusion of peace by agreement between the parties seems to lie in the realm of fantasy.

Secondly, the rectification of the situation requires the undoing of acts done in Palestine in violation of law and justice, and in breach of the legitimate rights of the Palestinians. At no time has Israel shown any disposition to redress the wrongs done or to recognize the elementary rights of the Palestinians. On the contrary, it has acted and continues to act so as to make the ousting of the Palestinians from their country a permanent and irreversible fact. In these circumstances, is it reasonable to expect that Israel would agree to undo what it has done: in fact, to undo itself as a politico-religious State? Is any agreement conceivable so long as the Israelis want Palestine without the Palestinians?

Thirdly, the support – whether military, political or financial – which Israel receives from the US Government, and the pressure which it exerts on the Arab States by its military occupation of their territories are two factors that encourage it to hold on to its conquests. Indeed, these two factors harden its intransigence and increase its appetite for more territory.

In the light of the preceding considerations it seems inconceivable, even naïve, to think that a solution of the Arab-Israeli conflict could be reached by negotiation, whether in the form of direct or "proximity" talks, with the present Israeli leadership. This conclusion is borne out by the fact that despite five years of efforts by Ambassador Gunnar Jarring to secure the implementation of the Security Council's resolution of 22 November 1967 – a resolution which, as we have seen, is clearly to Israel's advantage – he was unable to obtain Israel's agreement to the withdrawal of its armed forces from the territories occupied in June 1967.

The preceding considerations also rule out other means of settlement such as mediation, conciliation, arbitration and the like. The experience of Count Bernadotte, of the Conciliation Commission for Palestine, and now of Ambassador Jarring, all bear witness to the illusory value of mediation and conciliation as a means for settling the Palestine conflict.

Conceivably, one might be tempted to think that the conflict could be resolved by means of a settlement imposed by the Great Powers. This eventuality, however, is also unrealistic and illusory by reason of the attitude of the two superpowers and their involvement in the conflict. The USA and Soviet Russia are not interested in a settlement that would restore right and justice in Palestine, but in a settlement that is tailored to their interests and ambitions. For the US Government, the primary considerations seem to be the Jewish vote and its influence on presidential elections, the control of the Mediterranean, and the general strategy against Communism. For Soviet Russia, the primary consideration is the extension of its influence in the Arab World. It is strange to observe that the extension of Soviet influence in the Arab World was achieved and promoted principally by means of and as a result of American support for Israel, which the Arabs sought to counterbalance by turning to Soviet Russia for aid and assistance. The USA and Soviet Russia have complicated the Palestine problem by their support of partition in 1947 and have aggravated it by exploiting the resulting situation for their own ends, and against each other. As a result, a polarization of the conflict has occurred, with the US Government supporting Israel and Soviet Russia supporting the Arab States. But this polarization is more apparent than real, because these two superpowers each have their own political stake in the continued existence of Israel, despite its illegitimacy and its illegitimate actions. This explains why even though there exist many differences between them, both the USA and Soviet Russia support the Security Council's resolution of 22 November 1967, which, as we have seen, seeks to preserve and legitimate Israel, but in fact restores neither right nor justice.

Moreover, in so far as the relationship between Soviet Russia and Egypt is concerned, even this apparent polarization was shattered in July 1972 when President Sadat requested the withdrawal of Soviet military experts. This gesture brought into focus the divergent objectives of Soviet Russia and of Egypt in relation to the Arab-Israeli conflict and to the means and manner of its solution.

The obstacles that stand in the way of a settlement of the Arab-Israeli conflict, either by agreement between the parties or through the efforts of the Great Powers, might appear so formidable and discouraging as to lead to the conclusion that the best course to follow would be one of inaction, instead of action. This is what actually happened after the Arab-Israeli War of 1948, when the situation remained one of no war, no peace. Such a situation is clearly to the advantage of the aggressor, since the result has been a deeper implantation of Israel in Palestine, the establishment of more Israeli settlements on Arab land, and the creation of more *faits accomplis*, with the expectation that the present truce lines will, with time, become permanent frontiers. A situation of no war, no peace will only aggravate existing conditions and will inevitably lead to another war. This has been the experience in the past. The Arab-Israeli war of 1948 was left unsettled and the basic conflict left unresolved. The consequence was that two wars erupted, in 1956 and 1967, both of which almost led to a confrontation between the two superpowers.

The violation of the human rights and fundamental freedoms of the Palestinians has led to an accelerating sequence of violence, attacks and reprisals. This escalation of violence prompted the Secretary-General of the United Nations to place on the agenda of the international organization at its twenty-seventh session the question of "measures to prevent terrorism and other forms of violence which endanger or take innocent lives or jeopardize fundamental freedoms." It would perhaps have been more helpful if the Secretary-General had placed on the agenda of the United Nations the question of the reasons for violence, and in the case of the Palestinians, the measures that would remedy the injustice of which they are the victims. It seems evident that not all forms of violence can be placed in the same category. Violence flowing from a national injustice should not be confused with criminal violence committed for material gain or merely for the sake of anarchy. It is important not to concentrate on the effect and overlook the cause. However much one deplores violence, one must deplore more the injustice which is its cause. In the case of the Palestinians, the cause of their violence is the revolting injustice of which they are the victims. So long as this injustice subsists, violence is bound to continue.

The conclusion is unavoidable that the only way to restore right and justice in Palestine by means other than war is for the UN, with the assistance of the International Court of Justice if necessary, to reappraise the situation and, regardless of conditions created by force, to lay down a new formula for peace.

Such a peace formula should have as its aim not merely the restoration of the position prior to 5 June 1967, as is the case with the resolution of the Security Council of 22 November 1967, but the restoration of peace *and justice*. Without justice, one would be building on sand. In broad terms, justice requires the dismantling of the Zionist racist political structure set up in Palestine, the return of the Palestine refugees to their homes, and the restoration of the human rights and fundamental freedoms of the Palestinians. Peace in the Middle East cannot be indefinitely maintained by Phantoms, tanks and bombs, if the legitimate rights of the Palestinians are, as at present, ignored and trampled to the ground. In its resolution 377(V) of 3 November 1950, in which it defined its powers with respect to world tensions, the General Assembly of the UN declared:

"... enduring peace will not be secured solely by collective security arrangements against breaches of international peace and acts of aggression, but that a genuine and lasting peace depends also upon the observance of all the Principles and Purposes established in the Charter of the United Nations, upon the implementation of the resolutions of the Security Council, the General Assembly, and other principal organs of the United Nations intended to achieve the maintenance of peace and security, and especially upon respect for and observance of human rights and fundamental freedoms for all and on the establishment and maintenance of conditions of economic and social well-being in all countries."

Section 2
The need for
effective UN intervention

It is not enough, however, to lay down a new formula for peace. It is equally important to secure its implementation.

The UN Mediator for Palestine, Count Folke Bernadotte, strongly favoured UN supervision and control of the Palestine situation in 1948. He suggested UN control and supervision for the implementation of some of his recommendations to the General Assembly. Thus, he recommended that the City of Jerusalem should be placed under "effective United Nations control," that the repatriation of the refugees should be "supervised and assisted by the United Nations Conciliation Commission", that this last body should supervise the observance of the UN guarantee of the rights of all Arabs in the Jewish State and of all Jews in the Arab State.[2] Again, Count Bernadotte suggested that the Conciliation Commission should supervise the observance of such arrangements as might be decided by the UN concerning boundaries, roads, railroads, minority rights, and other matters.[3]

However, at the point where things are at present, something more than UN supervision is required: actual and effective intervention is needed. Since 1948 some two hundred resolutions have been adopted by the UN in respect of Palestine and the Arab-Israeli conflict. But all these resolutions have been flouted by Israel and no action has been taken to secure their observance and implementation. Unfortunately, since its establishment, the record of the UN has been one of helplessness and impotence in the face of international conflicts. But there is still a chance for the UN to react and to uphold the ideals of the Charter, and the principles of justice and international law. However, this cannot be done merely by the passing of resolutions. It is equally necessary, if not more important, to implement these resolutions, if not voluntarily executed,

---

2   UN Document A/648, p. 18.   3   *Ibid.*, p. 19.

by coercive action under the Charter. Dr John H. Davis has remarked that "in the end, one must even be prepared to impose corrective measures on Israel against her will."[4] On several occasions the Security Council has warned Israel that it would take steps to give effect to its decisions,[5] but it has never carried out its threats.

It is evident that, without international pressure and coercion, Israel will not comply with UN resolutions or abandon the fruits of its military conquests or undo any of its acts that have caused the Palestine tragedy. This is, therefore, the crux of the matter: without coercion, there can be no solution, no restoration of right and justice, no peace in Palestine.

Naturally, coercion by the UN is easier to envisage than to bring about. The veto of the Great Powers could hamper effective UN action, particularly against Israel, which by means of its pressure groups can influence one superpower, at least, in its favour. But though the Great Power veto might hamper effective UN action, it can no longer defeat or paralyse such action since the General Assembly adopted its famous resolution 377(V) of 3 November 1950. In this resolution the General Assembly declared that if the Security Council, because of lack of unanimity of the permanent members, fails to exercise its primary responsibility for the maintenance of international peace and security, the General Assembly shall consider the matter with a view to making appropriate recommendations to members for collective measures, including the use of armed force. In other words, the General Assembly can, in case of need, substitute itself for the Security Council. It is clear, therefore, that the UN can act, either through the Security Council or through the General Assembly, to settle the Arab-Israeli conflict on a basis compatible with the Principles and Purposes of the Charter. Hence, in regard to this conflict, the UN faces a choice: either to uphold the Charter and use the coercive means that it has envisaged, or to bow to the rule of force. The intervention of the UN is, therefore, a political necessity. Much more, such intervention is an international legal obligation.

---

4   John H. Davis, *The Evasive Peace*, p. 107, John Murray, London, 1968.
5   A reference to some of these warnings is found in Section 4 of Chapter VI, *ante*.

Section 3
UN intervention is an international legal obligation

UN intervention to rectify the Palestine situation is an international legal obligation. This obligation arises in the first place under the Charter.

Article 1 of the Charter states:

> "The Purposes of the United Nations are:
> 1. To maintain international peace and security, and to that end: to take effective collective measures for the prevention and removal of threats to the peace, and for the suppression of acts of aggression or other breaches of the peace, and to bring about by peaceful means, and in conformity with the principles of justice and international law, adjustment or settlement of international disputes or situations which might lead to a breach of the peace."

Article 14 of the Charter provides:

> "Subject to the provisions of Article 12, the General Assembly may recommend measures for the peaceful adjustment of any situation, regardless of origin, which it deems likely to impair the general welfare or friendly relations among nations, including situations resulting from a violation of the provisions of the present Charter setting forth the Purposes and Principles of the United Nations."

Articles 33, 36 and 37 of the Charter vest the Security Council with wide powers for the maintenance of international peace and security. Article 33(2) provides that the Council shall, when it deems necessary, call upon the parties to settle their dispute by negotiation, enquiry, mediation, conciliation, arbitration and judicial settlement. However, the Council's powers are not restricted to seeking a settlement through these means. It can itself recommend the methods or procedures of settlement. Article 36(1) states:

> "The Security Council may, at any stage of a dispute of the nature referred to in Article 33 or of a situation of like nature, recommend appropriate procedures or methods of adjustment."

Article 37(2) goes even farther. It empowers the Security Council to recommend the terms of settlement:

> "If the Security Council deems that the continuance of the dispute is in fact likely to endanger the maintenance of international peace and security, it shall decide whether to take action under Article 36 or to recommend such terms of settlement as it may consider appropriate."

Thus, in taking action to redress the situation in Palestine, the UN would be merely implementing its first purpose, and discharging its duty under the Charter.

Moreover, and quite apart from its duty under the Charter, the obligation of the UN to intervene in order to secure a fair and equitable settlement is even more impelling in the case of the Palestine Question by reason of two other considerations.

First, the UN bears a special responsibility in respect of the situation that now exists in Palestine. By adopting its resolution on partition, the UN has helped to put in motion certain political forces which it could neither control nor contain. This has led to disastrous consequences for the people of Palestine. The UN is bound to repair the damage that has resulted from the partition resolution, particularly since the resolution was inherently wrong and contained the germs of trouble.

Second, the UN is under an obligation to intervene by reason of specific undertakings assumed both by the General Assembly and by Israel.

In 1947, the General Assembly gave a clear and unequivocal guarantee to the Palestinians who were to live in the proposed Jewish State in respect of their human rights and fundamental freedoms. The resolution of the General Assembly of 29 November 1947 stated in Article 1 of Chapter 4 of the Declaration required from the Jewish and Arab States as follows:

> "1. The provisions of Chapters 1 and 2 of the Declaration shall be under the guarantee of the United Nations and no modification shall be made in them without the assent of the General Assembly of the United Nations. Any member of the United Nations shall have the right to bring to the attention of the General Assembly any infraction or danger of infraction of any of these stipulations, and the General Assembly may thereupon make such recommendations as it may deem proper in the circumstances."

Chapter 1 of the Declaration concerned Holy Places, religious buildings and sites, while Chapter 2 concerned religious and minority rights.

The effect of this provision of the resolution was to place the rights of the Arabs in the Jewish State (and of the Jews in the Arab State) – whether such rights are political or human or proprietary – under the guarantee of the UN. What happened since then is a matter of common knowledge. Nine-tenths of the Palestinian Arabs, who for centuries had lived in territories now occupied by Israel, were driven out and expelled from their homes, dispossessed of their properties and deprived of their human and fundamental rights. Apart from the voting of resolutions, what has the UN done to remedy the breach by Israel of its obligation to respect the rights of the original inhabitants of Palestine? What has the UN done to honour its guarantee? What is the value of the guarantee given to the Palestine Arabs by the UN if it is not implemented? The UN is, therefore, under a duty to take concrete and effective action in order to honour its guarantee to the people of Palestine.

Moreover, Israel was admitted to membership of the UN only after it gave certain undertakings and assurances concerning its observance of General Assembly resolutions, and in particular, concerning the implementation of the resolutions of 29 November 1947 and 11 December 1948. These two resolutions embody, *inter alia*, Israel's obligations concerning boundaries, respect for the human rights and fundamental freedoms of the Palestine Arabs, the return of the refugees to their homes, and the status of Jerusalem. It will be recalled that Israel's first application for admission to the UN was rejected by the Security Council on 17 December 1948. When Israel renewed its application for admission on 24 February 1949, the General Assembly invited it to clarify its attitude concerning the execution of its resolutions. Several meetings of the *Ad Hoc* Political Committee were held, during which Israel's representative was questioned in detail and at length about Israel's intentions regarding the execution of General Assembly resolution 181(II), the repatriation of the Palestine refugees, and the international status of Jerusalem.[6] Among the questions that were directed to Israel's representative was a specific inquiry as to whether Israel had made the required Declaration to the UN for the guarantee of the Holy Places, human rights, fundamental freedoms and minority rights, as required by the resolution of 29 November 1947.[7] Israel's representative replied that "only the State of Israel gave the requested formal undertaking to accept its provisions", and he referred to Security Council document S/747, which embodied the cablegram addressed by Israel's Foreign Minister to the Secretary-General of the UN on 15 May 1948 in this regard.[8]

Israel's representative was also specifically asked the question "whether, if Israel were admitted to membership in the UN, it would agree to co-operate subsequently with the General Assembly in settling the question of Jerusalem and the refugee problem or whether, on the contrary, it would invoke Article 2, paragraph 7 of the Charter which deals with the domestic jurisdiction of States?" Abba Eban, who was then Israel's representative, was most co-operative and spoke a language which was essentially different from the one he speaks now as Israel's Foreign Minister. This is what he then said in reply:

---

6 See the report of these meetings in Official Records of the General Assembly, *Ad Hoc* Political Committee, Part II, pp. 179–360, 1949.
7 Official Records of the 3rd Session of the General Assembly, *op. cit.*, Part II, p. 302, 1949.
8 *Ibid.*, pp. 348–349. For the text of Security Council document S/747, see Appendix V, *post*.

"The Government of Israel will co-operate with the Assembly in seeking a solution to those problems . . . I do not think that Article 2, paragraph 7, of the Charter, which relates to domestic jurisdiction, could possibly affect the Jerusalem problem, since the legal status of Jerusalem is different from that of the territory in which Israel is sovereign . . . My own feeling is that it would be a mistake for any of the Governments concerned to take refuge, with regard to the refugee problem, in their legal right to exclude people from their territories . . ."[9]

Israel's representative then added:

"Moreover, as a general theory – and as I explained yesterday – during the past year we arrived, in connexion with resolutions of the General Assembly, at the view that we must be very careful not to make an extreme application of Article 2, paragraph 7, if such an application would deprive Assembly decisions of all compelling force. The admission of Israel to the United Nations would obviously result in making applicable to it Article 10 of the Charter, and the General Assembly would then be able to make recommendations directly to the Government of Israel, which would, I think, attribute to those resolutions extremely wide validity."[10]

The Cuban representative summed up the debate on Israel's admission in the following terms:

"Certain happenings which had shocked public opinion had perforce been investigated on different lines than would have been the case had Israel been a Member of the United Nations. The representative of Israel had given an assurance that, if that country were admitted as a Member, such matters as the settlement of frontiers, the internationalization of Jerusalem and the Arab refugee problem would not be regarded as within its domestic jurisdiction and protected from intervention under the terms of Article 2, paragraph 7 (of the Charter)."[11]

Those were the formal undertakings and assurances given by Israel to the UN prior to its admission to membership of the international organization. It is reasonable to assume that it was only on the basis of the clarification of its attitude and its declarations and explanations that Israel was admitted on 11 May 1949 to UN membership. This is apparent from the terms of the resolution which admitted Israel to UN membership. The Preamble of the resolution stated:

"*Noting* furthermore the declaration by the State of Israel that it 'unreservedly accepts the obligations of the United Nations Charter and undertakes to honour them from the day when it becomes a Member of the United Nations',

Recalling its resolutions of 29 November 1947 and 11 December 1948 and taking note of the declarations and explanations made by the representative of the

---

9 Official Records of the 3rd Session of the General Assembly, Part II, *Ad Hoc* Political Committee, pp. 286–287, 1949.
10 Official Records of the 3rd Session of the General Assembly, *op. cit.*, Part II, p. 286, 1949.
11 *Ibid.*, p. 351, 1949.

Government of Israel before the *Ad Hoc* Committee in respect of the implementation of the said resolutions."[12]

Israel's "declarations and explanations" involved, therefore, the two following basic undertakings:

First, Israel would implement General Assembly resolution 181(II) of 29 November 1947 (concerning territory, the City of Jerusalem, the Holy Places and minority rights of the Arabs within the Jewish State), and General Assembly resolution 194(III) of 11 December 1948 (concerning the repatriation of the Palestine refugees and payment of compensation for the property of those who did not wish to return).

Secondly, Israel would not invoke, in regard to the implementation of General Assembly resolutions, paragraph 7 of Article 2 of the Charter relating to domestic jurisdiction.

Accordingly, Israel's admission to membership of the UN was neither unqualified, nor unconditional. Israel's admission must be considered to have been conditional upon its undertaking to implement the resolutions of the General Assembly, and in particular, the two resolutions of 29 November 1947 and 11 December 1948.

However, despite its formal declarations and assurances, Israel has violated both of those resolutions and has failed to honour the undertakings which it gave prior to its admission to the UN.

It is therefore evident that an intervention by the UN designed to secure the implementation by Israel of its undertakings and the fulfilment of the conditions of its admission is fully warranted. Such intervention is all the more necessary since Israel has deviated in every material respect from the General Assembly resolution which envisaged the creation of a Jewish State.[13]

An intervention by the UN to settle the Arab-Israeli conflict on a legal and equitable basis cannot be defeated by Israel's invoking the argument of domestic jurisdiction under paragraph 7 of Article 2 of the Charter. Apart from the fact that Israel has undertaken, as we have seen, at the time of its admission to the UN, not to invoke this provision, Israel's international legal status differs fundamentally from the status of any other State. Unlike any other State, Israel was the creation of a resolution of the General Assembly. This resolution fixed its territorial limits, subjected it to definite restrictions and obligations, deprived it of any power to enact any laws or regulations or to take any action that might conflict or interfere with the rights protected by the resolution, and placed the Holy Places and the rights of the Palestine Arabs under the guarantee of the UN.[14] The obligations and restrictions thus imposed upon Israel constitute

---

12 Resolution No. 273(III) of 11 May 1949 (see Appendix VII).
13 As to Israel's deviations from the partition resolution, see Section 2 of Chapter V.
14 It should be observed that international law recognizes the possibility of restrictions upon the liberty of action of a state with regard to its citizens: Oppenheim, *International Law*, Vol. I, 8th ed., p. 296, Longman, London, 1955.

definite limitations of Israel's sovereignty. These limitations are of a permanent character, for they cannot be modified without the assent of the General
Assembly of the UN. The General Assembly specifically reserved to itself the
power to inquire into any infringement of the stipulations embodied in the
resolution and to make such recommendations as it might deem proper. Being
as it were a statutory creation, Israel does not enjoy an unrestricted sovereignty.
It cannot act in breach of the resolution which envisaged its creation and limited
its powers, because any such act on its part would be *ultra vires* and without any
legal effect. Its acts and its legislation remain under the control of the General
Assembly.[15] Hence, Israel is precluded from invoking sovereignty to defeat
any action by the UN designed to restore the legitimate rights of the Palestinians or to protect the City of Jerusalem and the Holy Places of Palestine. "The
modern law of nations," states Hedley Cooke,

> "admits not only of the general, i.e. universally applicable, limitations upon
> sovereignty, but also of special restrictions imposed on one or more nation-states
> due to their special circumstances . . . In the United Nations Palestine Partition
> Resolution of 1947 . . . the Palestine Jews were directed – as a condition precedent
> to full recognition of independent status – to submit a draft national constitution
> for UN approval. So it was clear that the nations still had in mind certain limita-
> tions upon Israel's sovereignty . . . and the community of Nations may still
> demand of her an accounting on this score . . . Israel's sovereignty, as contrasted
> with France's and Switzerland's, is permanently limited by her duties, as em-
> bodied in her charter of existence, towards the Arab residents of the area which
> she controls . . ."[16]

The primary aim of an intervention by the UN must be to remove the
Palestine injustice by its roots. So long as this basic injustice subsists, violence is
bound to continue. Putting a lid on a boiling kettle will not stop it from boiling.
The UN is under a clear and imperative duty to intervene, and intervene
effectively, in order to restore right and justice in Palestine as this is the only
way that the Arab-Israeli conflict can be resolved peacefully. Not only does
peace in the Middle East depend upon the discharge by the UN of its obligation
in this matter, but the UN's very future as an instrument for the preservation of
law and justice among nations is at stake.

---

15 The declaration by the General Assembly, in its resolution dated 4 July 1967, of the
invalidity of the measures taken by Israel to change the status of Jerusalem (Appendix
XI) can be considered to be an exercise by the General Assembly of its powers to nullify
acts done and legislation enacted by Israel in breach of the Assembly's resolution.
Similarly, the Assembly's declaration, in its resolution dated 8 December 1972 (Appendix XXX) of the invalidity of the changes effected by Israel in the occupied territories,
contrary to the Geneva Conventions of 1949, was again an exercise of its power to
nullify Israel's illegal acts and to declare them null and void.
16 Hedley V. Cooke, *Israel – A Blessing and a Curse*, pp. 174, 178–180, Stevens, London,
1960.

APPENDICES

Appendix I

Article 22 of the Covenant of the League of Nations,
28 June 1919

Article 22. To those colonies and territories which as a consequence of the late war have ceased to be under the sovereignty of the States which formerly governed them and which are inhabited by peoples not yet able to stand by themselves under the strenuous conditions of the modern world, there should be applied the principle that the well-being and development of such peoples form a sacred trust of civilization and that securities for the performance of this trust should be embodied in this Covenant.

The best method of giving practical effect to this principle is that the tutelage of such peoples should be entrusted to advanced nations who by reason of their resources, their experience or their geographical position can best undertake this responsibility, and who are willing to accept it, and that this tutelage should be exercised by them as Mandatories on behalf of the League.

The character of the mandate must differ according to the stage of the development of the people, the geographical situation of the territory, its economic conditions and other similar circumstances.

Certain communities formerly belonging to the Turkish Empire have reached a stage of development where their existence as independent nations can be provisionally recognized subject to the rendering of administrative advice and assistance by a Mandatory until such time as they are able to stand alone. The wishes of these communities must be a principal consideration in the selection of the Mandatory.

Other peoples, especially those of Central Africa, are at such a stage that the Mandatory must be responsible for the administration of the territory under conditions which will guarantee freedom of conscience and religion, subject only to the maintenance of public order and morals, the prohibition of abuses such as the slave trade, the arms traffic and the liquor traffic, and the prevention of the establishment of fortifications or military and naval bases and of military training of the natives for other than police purposes and the defence of territory, and will also secure equal opportunities for the trade and commerce of other Members of the League.

There are territories, such as South-West Africa and certain of the South Pacific Islands, which, owing to the sparseness of their population, or their small size, or their remoteness from the centres of civilization, or their geographical contiguity to the territory of the Mandatory, and other circumstances, can be best administered under the laws of the Mandatory as integral portions of its territory, subject to the safeguards above mentioned in the interests of the indigenous population.

In every case of Mandate, the Mandatory shall render to the Council an annual report in reference to the territory committed to its charge.

The degree of authority, control or administration to be exercised by the Mandatory shall, if not previously agreed upon by the Members of the League, be explicitly defined in each case by the Council.

A permanent Commission shall be constituted to receive and examine the annual reports of the Mandatories and to advise the Council on all matters relating to the observance of the mandates.

Appendix II

The Mandate for Palestine, 24 July 1922

"The Council of the League of Nations:

Whereas the Principal Allied Powers have agreed, for the purpose of giving effect to the provisions of Article 22 of the Covenant of the League of Nations, to entrust to a Mandatory selected by the said Powers the administration of the territory of Palestine, which formerly belonged to the Turkish Empire, within such boundaries as may be fixed by them; and

Whereas the Principal Allied Powers have also agreed that the Mandatory should be responsible for putting into effect the declaration originally made on November 2nd, 1917, by the Government of His Britannic Majesty, and adopted by the said Powers, in favour of the establishment in Palestine of a national home for the Jewish people, it being clearly understood that nothing should be done which might prejudice the civil and religious rights of existing non-Jewish communities in Palestine, or the rights and political status enjoyed by Jews in any other country; and

Whereas recognition has thereby been given to the historical connexion of the Jewish people with Palestine and to the grounds for reconstituting their national home in that country; and

Whereas the Principal Allied Powers have selected His Britannic Majesty as the Mandatory for Palestine; and

Whereas the mandate in respect of Palestine has been formulated in the following terms and submitted to the Council of the League for approval; and

Whereas His Britannic Majesty has accepted the mandate in respect of Palestine and undertaken to exercise it on behalf of the League of Nations in conformity with the following provisions: and

Whereas by the aforementioned Article 22 (paragraph 8), it is provided that the degree of authority, control or administration to be exercised by the Mandatory, not having been previously agreed upon by the Members of the League, shall be explicitly defined by the Council of the League of Nations;

Confirming the said Mandate, defines its terms as follows:

ARTICLE 1

The Mandatory shall have full powers of legislation and of administration, save as they may be limited by the terms of this mandate.

ARTICLE 2

The Mandatory shall be responsible for placing the country under such political, administrative and economic conditions as will secure the establishment of the Jewish national home, as laid down in the preamble, and the development of self-governing institutions, and also for safeguarding the civil and religious rights of all the inhabitants of Palestine, irrespective of race and religion.

ARTICLE 3

The Mandatory shall, so far as circumstances permit, encourage local autonomy.

ARTICLE 4

An appropriate Jewish agency shall be recognized as a public body for the purpose of advising and co-operating with the Administration of Palestine in such economic, social and other matters as may affect the establishment of the Jewish national home and the interests of the Jewish population in Palestine, and, subject always to the control of the Administration, to assist and take part in the development of the country.

The Zionist Organization, so long as its organization and constitution are in the opinion of the Mandatory appropriate, shall be recognized as such agency. It shall take steps in consultation with His Britannic Majesty's Government to secure the co-operation of all Jews who are willing to assist in the establishment of the Jewish national home.

ARTICLE 5

The Mandatory shall be responsible for seeing that no Palestine territory shall be ceded or leased to, or in any way placed under the control of, the Government of any foreign Power.

ARTICLE 6

The Administration of Palestine, while ensuring that the rights and position of other sections of the population are not prejudiced, shall facilitate Jewish immigration under suitable conditions and shall encourage, in co-operation with the Jewish agency referred to in Article 4, close settlement by Jews on the land, including State lands and waste lands not required for public purposes.

ARTICLE 7

The Administration of Palestine shall be responsible for enacting a nationality law. There shall be included in this law provisions framed so as to facilitate the acquisition of Palestinian citizenship by Jews who take up their permanent residence in Palestine.

ARTICLE 8

The privileges and immunities of foreigners, including the benefits of consular jurisdiction and protection as formerly enjoyed by Capitulation or usage in the Ottoman Empire, shall not be applicable in Palestine.

Unless the Powers whose nationals enjoyed the aforementioned privileges and immunities on August 1st, 1914, shall have previously renounced the right to their re-establishment, or shall have agreed to their non-application for a specified period, these privileges and immunities shall, at the expiration of the mandate, be immediately re-established in their entirety or with such modifications as may have been agreed upon between the Powers concerned.

ARTICLE 9

The Mandatory shall be responsible for seeing that the judicial system established in Palestine shall assure to foreigners, as well as to natives, a complete guarantee of their rights.

Respect for the personal status of the various peoples and communities and for their religious interests shall be fully guaranteed. In particular, the control and administration of Waqfs shall be exercised in accordance with religious law and the dispositions of the founders.

ARTICLE 10

Pending the making of special extradition agreements relating to Palestine, the extradition treaties in force between the Mandatory and other foreign Powers shall apply to Palestine.

ARTICLE 11

The Administration of Palestine shall take all necessary measures to safeguard the interests of the community in connection with the development of the country, and, subject to any international obligations accepted by the Mandatory, shall have full power to provide for public ownership or control of any of the natural resources of the country or of the public works, services and utilities established or to be established therein. It shall introduce a land system appropriate to the needs of the country having regard, among other things, to the desirability of promoting the close settlement and intensive cultivation of the land.

The Administration may arrange with the Jewish agency mentioned in Article 4 to construct or operate, upon fair and equitable terms, any public works, services and utilities, and to develop any of the natural resources of the country, in so far as these matters are not directly undertaken by the Administration. Any such arrangements shall provide that no profits distributed by such agency, directly or indirectly, shall exceed a reasonable rate of interest on the capital, and any further profits shall be utilized by it for the benefit of the country in a manner approved by the Administration.

ARTICLE 12

The Mandatory shall be entrusted with the control of the foreign relations of Palestine, and the right to issue exequaturs to consuls appointed by foreign Powers. He shall also be entitled to afford diplomatic and consular protection to citizens of Palestine when outside its territorial limits.

ARTICLE 13

All responsibility in connexion with the Holy Places and religious buildings or sites in Palestine, including that of preserving existing rights and of securing free access to the Holy Places, religious buildings and sites and the free exercise of worship, while ensuring the requirements of public order and decorum, is assumed by the Mandatory, who shall be responsible solely to the League of Nations in all matters connected herewith, provided that nothing in this article shall prevent the Mandatory from entering into such arrangements as he may deem reasonable with the Administration for the purpose of carrying the provisions of this article into effect; and provided also that nothing in this Mandate shall be construed as conferring upon the Mandatory authority to interfere with the fabric or the management of purely Moslem sacred shrines, the immunities of which are guaranteed.

ARTICLE 14

A special Commission shall be appointed by the Mandatory to study, define and determine the rights and claims in connection with the Holy Places and the rights and claims relating to the different religious communities in Palestine. The method of nomination, the composition and the functions of this Commission shall be submitted to the Council of the League for its approval, and the Commission shall not be appointed or enter upon its functions without the approval of the Council.

ARTICLE 15

The Mandatory shall see that complete freedom of conscience and the free exercise of all forms of worship, subject only to the maintenance of public order and morals, are ensured to all. No discrimination of any kind shall be made between the inhabitants of Palestine on the ground of race, religion or language. No person shall be excluded from Palestine on the sole ground of his religious belief.

The right of each community to maintain its own schools for the education of its own members in its own language, while conforming to such educational requirements of a general nature as the Administration may impose, shall not be denied or impaired.

ARTICLE 16

The Mandatory shall be responsible for exercising such supervision over religious or eleemosynary bodies of all faiths in Palestine as may be required for the maintenance of public order and good government. Subject to such supervision, no measures shall be taken in Palestine to obstruct or interfere with the enterprise of such bodies or to discriminate against any representative or member of them on the ground of his religion or nationality.

ARTICLE 17

The Administration of Palestine may organize on a voluntary basis the forces necessary for the preservation of peace and order, and also for the defence of the country, subject, however, to the supervision of the Mandatory, but shall not use them for purposes other than those above specified save with the consent of the Mandatory. Except for such purposes, no military, naval or air forces shall be raised or maintained by the Administration of Palestine.

Nothing in this article shall preclude the Administration of Palestine from contributing to the cost of the maintenance of the forces of the Mandatory in Palestine.

The Mandatory shall be entitled at all times to use the roads, railways and ports of Palestine for the movement of armed forces and the carriage of fuel and supplies.

ARTICLE 18

The Mandatory shall see that there is no discrimination in Palestine against the nationals of any State Member of the League of Nations (including companies incorporated under its laws) as compared with those of the Mandatory or of any foreign State in matters concerning taxation, commerce or navigation, the exercise of industries or professions, or in the treatment of merchant vessels or civil aircraft. Similarly, there shall be no discrimination in Palestine against goods originating in or destined for any of the said States, and there shall be freedom of transit under equitable conditions across the mandated area.

Subject as aforesaid and to the other provisions of this mandate, the Administration of Palestine may, on the advice of the Mandatory, impose such taxes and customs duties as it may consider necessary, and take such steps as it may think best to promote the development of the natural resources of the country and to safeguard the interests of the population. It may also, on the advice of the Mandatory, conclude a special customs agreement with any State the territory of which in 1914 was wholly included in Asiatic Turkey or Arabia.

ARTICLE 19

The Mandatory shall adhere on behalf of the Administration of Palestine to any general international conventions already existing, or which may be concluded hereafter with the approval of the League of Nations, respecting the slave traffic, the traffic in arms and ammunition, or the traffic in drugs, or relating to commercial equality, freedom of transit and navigation, aerial navigation and postal, telegraphic and wireless communication or literary, artistic or industrial property.

ARTICLE 20

The Mandatory shall co-operate on behalf of the Administration of Palestine, so far as religious, social and other conditions may permit, in the execution of any common policy adopted by the League of Nations for preventing and combating disease, including diseases of plants and animals.

ARTICLE 21

The Mandatory shall secure the enactment within twelve months from this date, and shall ensure the execution of a Law of Antiquities based on the following rules. This law shall ensure equality of treatment in the matter of excavations and archaeological research to the nationals of all States Members of the League of Nations. . .

ARTICLE 22

English, Arabic and Hebrew shall be the official languages of Palestine. Any statement or inscription in Arabic on stamps or money in Palestine shall be repeated in Hebrew and any statement or inscription in Hebrew shall be repeated in Arabic.

ARTICLE 23

The Administration of Palestine shall recognize the holy days of the respective communities in Palestine as legal days of rest for the members of such communities.

ARTICLE 24

The Mandatory shall make to the Council of the League of Nations an annual report to the satisfaction of the Council as to the measures taken during the year to carry out the provisions of the mandate. Copies of all laws and regulations promulgated or issued during the year shall be communicated with the report.

ARTICLE 25

In the territories lying between the Jordan and the eastern boundary of Palestine as ultimately determined, the Mandatory shall be entitled, with the consent of the Council of the League of Nations, to postpone or withhold application of such provisions of this mandate as he may consider inapplicable to the existing local conditions, and to make such provision for the administration of the territories as he may consider suitable to those conditions, provided that no action shall be taken which is inconsistent with the provisions of Articles 15, 16 and 18.

ARTICLE 26

The Mandatory agrees that if any dispute whatever should arise between the Mandatory and another Member of the League of Nations relating to the interpretation or the application of the provisions of the mandate, such dispute, if it cannot be settled by negotiation, shall be submitted to the Permanent Court of International Justice provided for by Article 14 of the Covenant of the League of Nations.

ARTICLE 27

The consent of the Council of the League of Nations is required for any modification of the terms of this mandate.

ARTICLE 28

In the event of the termination of the mandate hereby conferred upon the Mandatory, the Council of the League of Nations shall make such arrangements as may be deemed necessary for safeguarding in perpetuity, under guarantee of the League, the rights secured by Articles 13 and 14, and shall use its influence for securing, under the guarantee of the League, that the Government of Palestine will fully honour the financial obligations legitimately incurred by the Administration of Palestine during the period of the mandate, including the rights of public servants to pensions or gratuities.

The present instrument shall be deposited in original in the archives of the League of

Nations and certified copies shall be forwarded by the Secretary-General of the League of Nations to all Members of the League.

DONE AT LONDON the twenty-fourth day of July, one thousand nine hundred and twenty-two."[1]

Appendix III

Resolution 181 (II) adopted by the General Assembly on 29 November 1947 concerning the future government of Palestine

A

The General Assembly,

Having met in special session at the request of the mandatory Power to constitute and instruct a special committee to prepare for the consideration of the question of the future government of Palestine at the second regular session;

Having constituted a Special Committee and instructed it to investigate all questions and issues relevant to the problem of Palestine, and to prepare proposals for the solution of the problem, and

Having received and examined the report of the Special Committee (document A/364)[2] including a number of unanimous recommendations and a plan of partition with economic union approved by the majority of the Special Committee,

Considers that the present situation in Palestine is one which is likely to impair the general welfare and friendly relations among nations;

Takes note of the declaration by the mandatory Power that it plans to complete its evacuation of Palestine by 1 August 1948;

Recommends to the United Kingdom, as the mandatory Power for Palestine, and to all other Members of the United Nations the adoption and implementation, with regard to the future government of Palestine, of the Plan of Partition with Economic Union set out below;

Requests that

(*a*) The Security Council take the necessary measures as provided for in the plan for its implementation;

(*b*) The Security Council consider, if circumstances during the transitional period require such consideration, whether the situation in Palestine constitutes a threat to the peace. If it decides that such a threat exists, and in order to maintain international peace and security, the Security Council should supplement the authorization of the General Assembly by taking measures, under Articles 39 and 41 of the Charter, to empower the United Nations Commission, as provided in this resolution, to exercise in Palestine the functions which are assigned to it by this resolution;

(*c*) The Security Council determine as a threat to the peace, breach of the peace or act of

---

1   The Palestine mandate came into force on 29 September 1922.

2   See Official Records of the Second Session of the General Assembly, Supplement No. 11, Volumes I–IV.

aggression, in accordance with Article 39 of the Charter, any attempt to alter by force the settlement envisaged by this resolution;

(*d*) The Trusteeship Council be informed of the responsibilities envisaged for it in this plan;

Calls upon the inhabitants of Palestine to take such steps as may be necessary on their part to put this plan into effect;

Appeals to all Governments and all peoples to refrain from taking any action which might hamper or delay the carrying out of these recommendations, and

Authorizes the Secretary-General to reimburse travel and subsistence expenses of the members of the Commission referred to in Part I, Section B, paragraph 1 below, on such basis and in such form as he may determine most appropriate in the circumstances, and to provide the Commission with the necessary staff to assist in carrying out the functions assigned to the Commission by the General Assembly.

B[3]

The General Assembly,

Authorizes the Secretary-General to draw from the Working Capital Fund a sum not to exceed $2,000,000 for the purposes set forth in the last paragraph of the resolution on the future government of Palestine.

Hundred and twenty-eighth plenary meeting, 29 November 1947.

At its hundred and twenty-eighth plenary meeting on 29 November 1947 the General Assembly, in accordance with the terms of the above resolution, elected the following members of the United Nations Commission on Palestine:

BOLIVIA, CZECHOSLOVAKIA, DENMARK, PANAMA and PHILIPPINES.

PLAN OF PARTITION WITH ECONOMIC UNION

PART I

Future constitution and government of Palestine

A. TERMINATION OF MANDATE, PARTITION AND INDEPENDENCE

1. The Mandate for Palestine shall terminate as soon as possible but in any case not later than 1 August 1948.

2. The armed forces of the mandatory Power shall be progressively withdrawn from Palestine, the withdrawal to be completed as soon as possible but in any case not later than 1 August 1948.

The mandatory Power shall advise the Commission, as far in advance as possible, of its intention to terminate the Mandate and to evacuate each area.

The mandatory Power shall use its best endeavours to ensure that an area situated in the territory of the Jewish State, including a seaport and hinterland adequate to provide facilities for a substantial immigration, shall be evacuated at the earliest possible date and in any event not later than 1 February 1948.

3. Independent Arab and Jewish States and the Special International Regime for the City of Jerusalem, set forth in part III of this plan, shall come into existence in Palestine two months after the evacuation of the armed forces of the mandatory Power has been completed but in any case not later than 1 October 1948. The boundaries of the Arab State, the Jewish State, and the City of Jerusalem shall be as described in parts II and III below.

---

3   This resolution was adopted without reference to a Committee.

4. The period between the adoption by the General Assembly of its recommendation on the question of Palestine and the establishment of the independence of the Arab and Jewish States shall be a transitional period.

B. STEPS PREPARATORY TO INDEPENDENCE

1. A Commission shall be set up consisting of one representative of each of five Member States. The Members represented on the Commission shall be elected by the General Assembly on as broad a basis, geographically and otherwise, as possible.

2. The administration of Palestine shall, as the mandatory Power withdraws its armed forces, be progressively turned over to the Commission; which shall act in conformity with the recommendations of the General Assembly, under the guidance of the Security Council. The mandatory Power shall to the fullest possible extent co-ordinate its plans for withdrawal with the plans of the Commission to take over and administer areas which have been evacuated.

In the discharge of this administrative responsibility the Commission shall have authority to issue necessary regulations and take other measures as required.

The mandatory Power shall not take any action to prevent, obstruct or delay the implementation by the Commission of the measures recommended by the General Assembly.

3. On its arrival in Palestine the Commission shall proceed to carry out measures for the establishment of the frontiers of the Arab and Jewish States and the City of Jerusalem in accordance with the general lines of the recommendations of the General Assembly on the partition of Palestine. Nevertheless, the boundaries as described in part II of this plan are to be modified in such a way that village areas as a rule will not be divided by state boundaries unless pressing reasons make that necessary.

4. The Commission, after consultation with the democratic parties and other public organizations of the Arab and Jewish States, shall select and establish in each State as rapidly as possible a Provisional Council of Government. The activities of both the Arab and Jewish Provisional Councils of Government shall be carried out under the general direction of the Commission.

If by 1 April 1948 a Provisional Council of Government cannot be selected for either of the States, or, if selected, cannot carry out its functions, the Commission shall communicate that fact to the Security Council for such action with respect to that State as the Security Council may deem proper, and to the Secretary-General for communication to the Members of the United Nations.

5. Subject to the provisions of these recommendations, during the transitional period the Provisional Councils of Government, acting under the Commission, shall have full authority in the areas under their control, including authority over matters of immigration and land regulation.

6. The Provisional Council of Government of each State, acting under the Commission, shall progressively receive from the Commission full responsibility for the administration of that State in the period between the termination of the Mandate and the establishment of the State's independence.

7. The Commission shall instruct the Provisional Councils of Government of both the Arab and Jewish States, after their formation, to proceed to the establishment of administrative organs of government, central and local.

8. The Provisional Council of Government of each State shall, within the shortest time possible, recruit an armed militia from the residents of that State, sufficient in number to maintain internal order and to prevent frontier clashes.

This armed militia in each State shall, for operational purposes, be under the command of Jewish or Arab officers resident in that State, but general political and military control, including the choice of the militia's High Command, shall be exercised by the Commission.

9. The Provisional Council of Government of each State shall, not later than two months after the withdrawal of the armed forces of the mandatory Power, hold elections to the Constituent Assembly which shall be conducted on democratic lines.

The election regulations in each State shall be drawn up by the Provisional Council of Government and approved by the Commission. Qualified voters for each State for this election shall be persons over eighteen years of age who are: (a) Palestinian citizens residing in that State and (b) Arabs and Jews residing in the State, although not Palestinian citizens, who, before voting, have signed a notice of intention to become citizens of such State.

Arabs and Jews residing in the City of Jerusalem who have signed a notice of intention to become citizens, the Arabs of the Arab State and the Jews of the Jewish State, shall be entitled to vote in the Arab and Jewish States respectively.

Women may vote and be elected to the Constituent Assemblies.

During the transitional period no Jew shall be permitted to establish residence in the area of the proposed Arab State, and no Arab shall be permitted to establish residence in the area of the proposed Jewish State, except by special leave of the Commission.

10. The Constituent Assembly of each State shall draft a democratic constitution for its State and choose a provisional government to succeed the Provisional Council of Government appointed by the Commission. The constitutions of the States shall embody chapters 1 and 2 of the Declaration provided for in section C below and include *inter alia* provisions for:

(a) Establishing in each State a legislative body elected by universal suffrage and by secret ballot on the basis of proportional representation, and an executive body responsible to the legislature;

(b) Settling all international disputes in which the State may be involved by peaceful means in such a manner that international peace and security, and justice, are not endangered;

(c) Accepting the obligation of the State to refrain in its international relations from the threat or use of force against the territorial integrity or political independence of any State, or in any other manner inconsistent with the purposes of the United Nations;

(d) Guaranteeing to all persons equal and non-discriminatory rights in civil, political, economic and religious matters and the enjoyment of human rights and fundamental freedoms, including freedom of religion, language, speech and publication, education, assembly and association;

(e) Preserving freedom of transit and visit for all residents and citizens of the other State in Palestine and the City of Jerusalem, subject to considerations of national security, provided that each State shall control residence within its borders.

11. The Commission shall appoint a preparatory economic commission of three members to make whatever arrangements are possible for economic co-operation, with a view to establishing, as soon as practicable, the Economic Union and the Joint Economic Board, as provided in section D below.

12. During the period between the adoption of the recommendations on the question of Palestine by the General Assembly and the termination of the Mandate, the mandatory Power in Palestine shall maintain full responsibility for administration in areas from which it has not withdrawn its armed forces. The Commission shall assist the mandatory Power in the carrying out of these functions. Similarly the mandatory Power shall co-operate with the Commission in the execution of its functions.

13. With a view to ensuring that there shall be continuity in the functioning of administrative services and that, on the withdrawal of the armed forces of the mandatory

Power, the whole administration shall be in the charge of the Provisional Councils and the Joint Economic Board, respectively, acting under the Commission, there shall be a progressive transfer, from the mandatory Power to the Commission, of responsibility for all the functions of government, including that of maintaining law and order in the areas from which the forces of the mandatory Power have been withdrawn.

14. The Commission shall be guided in its activities by the recommendations of the General Assembly and by such instructions as the Security Council may consider necessary to issue.

The measures taken by the Commission, within the recommendations of the General Assembly, shall become immediately effective unless the Commission has previously received contrary instructions from the Security Council.

The Commission shall render periodic monthly progress reports, or more frequently if desirable, to the Security Council.

15. The Commission shall make its final report to the next regular session of the Genera Assembly and to the Security Council simultaneously.

C. DECLARATION

A declaration shall be made to the United Nations by the provisional government of each proposed State before independence. It shall contain *inter alia* the following clauses:

GENERAL PROVISION

The stipulations contained in the declaration are recognized as fundamental laws of the State and no law, regulation or official action shall conflict or interfere with these stipulations, nor shall any law, regulation or official action prevail over them.

CHAPTER 1

Holy Places, religious buildings and sites

1. Existing rights in respect of Holy Places and religious buildings or sites shall not be denied or impaired.

2. In so far as Holy Places are concerned, the liberty of access, visit and transit shall be guaranteed, in conformity with existing rights, to all residents and citizens of the other State and of the City of Jerusalem, as well as to aliens, without distinction as to nationality, subject to requirements of national security, public order and decorum.

Similarly, freedom of worship shall be guaranteed in conformity with existing rights, subject to the maintenance of public order and decorum.

3. Holy Places and religious buildings or sites shall be preserved. No act shall be permitted which may in any way impair their sacred character. If at any time it appears to the Government that any particular Holy Place, religious building or site is in need of urgent repair, the Government may call upon the community or communities concerned to carry out such repair. The Government may carry it out itself at the expense of the community or communities concerned if no action is taken within a reasonable time.

4. No taxation shall be levied in respect of any Holy Place, religious building or site which was exempt from taxation on the date of the creation of the State.

No change in the incidence of such taxation shall be made which would either discriminate between the owners or occupiers of Holy Places, religious buildings or sites, or would place such owners or occupiers in a position less favourable in relation to the general incidence of taxation than existed at the time of the adoption of the Assembly's recommendations.

5. The Governor of the City of Jerusalem shall have the right to determine whether the provisions of the Constitution of the State in relation to Holy Places, religious buildings and sites within the borders of the State and the religious rights appertaining thereto, are being properly applied and respected, and to make decisions on the basis of existing rights in cases of disputes which may arise between the different religious communities or the rites of a religious community with respect to such places, buildings and sites. He shall receive full co-operation and such privileges and immunities as are necessary for the exercise of his functions in the State.

CHAPTER 2

Religious and minority rights

1. Freedom of conscience and the free exercise of all forms of worship, subject only to the maintenance of public order and morals, shall be ensured to all.

2. No discrimination of any kind shall be made between the inhabitants on the ground of race, religion, language or sex.

3. All persons within the jurisdiction of the State shall be entitled to equal protection of the laws.

4. The family law and personal status of the various minorities and their religious interests. including endowments, shall be respected.

5. Except as may be required for the maintenance of public order and good government, no measure shall be taken to obstruct or interfere with the enterprise of religious or charitable bodies of all faiths or to discriminate against any representative or member of these bodies on the ground of his religion or nationality.

6. The State shall ensure adequate primary and secondary education for the Arab and Jewish minority, respectively, in its own language and its cultural traditions.
The right of each community to maintain its own schools for the education of its own members in its own language, while conforming to such educational requirements of a general nature as the State may impose, shall not be denied or impaired. Foreign educational establishments shall continue their activity on the basis of their existing rights.

7. No restriction shall be imposed on the free use by any citizen of the State of any language in private intercourse, in commerce, in religion, in the Press or in publications of any kind, or at public meetings.[4]

8. No expropriation of land owned by an Arab in the Jewish State (by a Jew in the Arab State)[5] shall be allowed except for public purposes. In all cases of expropriation full compensation as fixed by the Supreme Court shall be paid previous to dispossession.

CHAPTER 3

Citizenship, international conventions and financial obligations

1. *Citizenship.* Palestinian citizens residing in Palestine outside the City of Jerusalem, as well as Arabs and Jews who, not holding Palestinian citizenship, reside in Palestine outside

---

4 The following stipulation shall be added to the declaration concerning the Jewish State: "In the Jewish State adequate facilities shall be given to Arabic-speaking citizens for the use of their language, either orally or in writing, in the legislature, before the Courts and in the administration."

5 In the declaration concerning the Arab State, the words "by an Arab in the Jewish State" should be replaced by the words "by a Jew in the Arab State".

the City of Jerusalem shall, upon the recognition of independence, become citizens of the State in which they are resident and enjoy full civil and political rights. Persons over the age of eighteen years may opt, within one year from the date of recognition of independence of the State in which they reside, for citizenship of the other State, providing that no Arab residing in the area of the proposed Arab State shall have the right to opt for citizenship in the proposed Jewish State and no Jew residing in the proposed Jewish State shall have the right to opt for citizenship in the proposed Arab State. The exercise of this right of option will be taken to include the wives and children under eighteen years of age of persons so opting.

Arabs residing in the area of the proposed Jewish State and Jews residing in the area of the proposed Arab State who have signed a notice of intention to opt for citizenship of the other State shall be eligible to vote in the elections to the Constituent Assembly of that State, but not in the elections to the Constituent Assembly of the State in which they reside.

2. *International conventions.* (*a*) The State shall be bound by all the international agreements and conventions, both general and special, to which Palestine has become a party. Subject to any right of denunciation provided for therein, such agreements and conventions shall be respected by the State throughout the period for which they were concluded.

(*b*) Any dispute about the applicability and continued validity of international conventions or treaties signed or adhered to by the mandatory Power on behalf of Palestine shall be referred to the International Court of Justice in accordance with the provisions of the Statute of the Court.

3. *Financial obligations.* (*a*) The State shall respect and fulfil all financial obligations of whatever nature assumed on behalf of Palestine by the mandatory Power during the exercise of the Mandate and recognized by the State. This provision includes the right of public servants to pensions, compensation or gratuities.

(*b*) These obligations shall be fulfilled through participation in the Joint Economic Board in respect of those obligations applicable to Palestine as a whole, and individually in respect of those applicable to, and fairly apportionable between, the States.

(*c*) A Court of Claims, affiliated with the Joint Economic Board, and composed of one member appointed by the United Nations, one representative of the United Kingdom and one representative of the State concerned, should be established. Any dispute between the United Kingdom and the State respecting claims not recognized by the latter should be referred to that Court.

(*d*) Commercial concessions granted in respect of any part of Palestine prior to the adoption of the resolution by the General Assembly shall continue to be valid according to their terms, unless modified by agreement between the concession-holder and the State.

CHAPTER 4

Miscellaneous provisions

1. The provisions of chapters 1 and 2 of the declaration shall be under the guarantee of the United Nations, and no modifications shall be made in them without the assent of the General Assembly of the United Nations. Any Member of the United Nations shall have the right to bring to the attention of the General Assembly any infraction or danger of infraction of any of these stipulations, and the General Assembly may thereupon make such recommendations as it may deem proper in the circumstances.

2. Any dispute relating to the application or the interpretation of this declaration shall be referred, at the request of either party, to the International Court of Justice, unless the parties agree to another mode of settlement.

D. ECONOMIC UNION AND TRANSIT

1. The Provisional Council of Government of each State shall enter into an undertaking with respect to Economic Union and Transit. This undertaking shall be drafted by the Commission provided for in section B, paragraph 1, utilizing to the greatest possible extent the advice and co-operation of representative organizations and bodies from each of the proposed States. It shall contain provisions to establish the Economic Union of Palestine and provide for other matters of common interest. If by 1 April 1948 the Provisional Councils of Government have not entered into the undertaking, the undertaking shall be put into force by the Commission.

The Economic Union of Palestine

2. The objectives of the Economic Union of Palestine shall be:
(*a*) A customs union;
(*b*) A joint currency system providing for a single foreign exchange rate;
(*c*) Operation in the common interest on a non-discriminatory basis of railways; inter-State highways; postal, telephone and telegraphic services, and ports and airports involved in international trade and commerce;
(*d*) Joint economic development, especially in respect of irrigation, land reclamation and soil conservation;
(*e*) Access for both States and for the City of Jerusalem on a non-discriminatory basis to water and power facilities.

3. There shall be established a Joint Economic Board, which shall consist of three representatives of each of the two States and three foreign members appointed by the Economic and Social Council of the United Nations. The foreign members shall be appointed in the first instance for a term of three years; they shall serve as individuals and not as representatives of States.

4. The functions of the Joint Economic Board shall be to implement either directly or by delegation the measures necessary to realize the objectives of the Economic Union. It shall have all powers of organization and administration necessary to fulfil its functions.

5. The States shall bind themselves to put into effect the decisions of the Joint Economic Board. The Board's decisions shall be taken by a majority vote.

6. In the event of failure of a State to take the necessary action the Board may, by a vote of six members, decide to withhold an appropriate portion of that part of the customs revenue to which the State in question is entitled under the Economic Union. Should the State persist in its failure to cooperate, the Board may decide by a simple majority vote upon such further sanctions, including disposition of funds which it has withheld, as it may deem appropriate.

7. In relation to economic development, the functions of the Board shall be the planning, investigation and encouragement of joint development projects, but it shall not undertake such projects except with the assent of both States and the City of Jerusalem, in the event that Jerusalem is directly involved in the development project.

8. In regard to the joint currency system the currencies circulating in the two States and the City of Jerusalem shall be issued under the authority of the Joint Economic Board, which shall be the sole issuing authority and which shall determine the reserves to be held against such currencies.

9. So far as is consistent with paragraph 2 (*b*) above, each State may operate its own central bank, control its own fiscal and credit policy, its foreign exchange receipts and

expenditures, the grant of import licenses, and may conduct international financial operations on its own faith and credit. During the first two years after the termination of the
Mandate, the Joint Economic Board shall have the authority to take such measures as may
be necessary to ensure that – to the extent that the total foreign exchange revenues of the
two States from the export of goods and services permit, and provided that each State takes
appropriate measures to conserve its own foreign exchange resources – each State shall have
available, in any twelve months' period, foreign exchange sufficient to assure the supply of
quantities of imported goods and services for consumption in its territory equivalent to the
quantities of such goods and services consumed in that territory in the twelve months'
period ending 31 December 1947.

10. All economic authority not specifically vested in the Joint Economic Board is reserved to each State.

11. There shall be a common customs tariff with complete freedom of trade between the
States, and between the States and the City of Jerusalem.

12. The tariff schedules shall be drawn up by a Tariff Commission, consisting of representatives of each of the States in equal numbers, and shall be submitted to the Joint Economic Board for approval by a majority vote. In case of disagreement in the Tariff Commission, the Joint Economic Board shall arbitrate the points of difference. In the event that
the Tariff Commission fails to draw up any schedule by a date to be fixed, the Joint
Economic Board shall determine the tariff schedule.

13. The following items shall be a first charge on the customs and other common revenue
of the Joint Economic Board:
(a) The expenses of the customs service and of the operation of the joint services;
(b) The administrative expenses of the Joint Economic Board;
(c) The financial obligations of the Administration of Palestine consisting of:
    (i) The service of the outstanding public debt;
    (ii) The cost of superannuation benefits, now being paid or falling due in the future,
        in accordance with the rules and to the extent established by paragraph 3 of
        chapter 3 above.

14. After these obligations have been met in full, the surplus revenue from the customs
and other common services shall be divided in the following manner: not less than 5 per
cent and not more than 10 per cent to the City of Jerusalem; the residue shall be allocated
to each State by the Joint Economic Board equitably, with the objective of maintaining a
sufficient and suitable level of government and social services in each State, except that the
share of either State shall not exceed the amount of that State's contribution to the revenues
of the Economic Union by more than approximately four million pounds in any year. The
amount granted may be adjusted by the Board according to the price level in relation to the
prices prevailing at the time of the establishment of the Union. After five years, the principles of the distribution of the joint revenues may be revised by the Joint Economic Board
on a basis of equity.

15. All international conventions and treaties affecting customs tariff rates, and those
communications services under the jurisdiction of the Joint Economic Board, shall be
entered into by both States. In these matters, the two States shall be bound to act in accordance with the majority vote of the Joint Economic Board.

16. The Joint Economic Board shall endeavour to secure for Palestine's exports fair and
equal access to world markets.

17. All enterprises operated by the Joint Economic Board shall pay fair wages on a
uniform basis.

Freedom of transit and visit

18. The undertaking shall contain provisions preserving freedom of transit and visit for all residents or citizens of both States and of the City of Jerusalem, subject to security considerations; provided that each State and the City shall control residence within its borders.

Termination, modification and interpretation of the undertaking

19. The undertaking and any treaty issuing therefrom shall remain in force for a period of ten years. It shall continue in force until notice of termination, to take effect two years thereafter, is given by either of the parties.

20. During the initial ten-year period, the undertaking and any treaty issuing therefrom may not be modified except by consent of both parties and with the approval of the General Assembly.

21. Any dispute relating to the application or the interpretation of the undertaking and any treaty issuing therefrom shall be referred, at the request of either party, to the International Court of Justice, unless the parties agree to another mode of settlement.

E. ASSETS

1. The movable assets of the Administration of Palestine shall be allocated to the Arab and Jewish States and the City of Jerusalem on an equitable basis. Allocations should be made by the United Nations Commission referred to in section B, paragraph 1, above. Immovable assets shall become the property of the government of the territory in which they are situated.

2. During the period between the appointment of the United Nations Commission and the termination of the Mandate, the mandatory Power shall, except in respect of ordinary operations, consult with the Commission on any measure which it may contemplate involving the liquidation, disposal or encumbering of the assets of the Palestine Government, such as the accumulated treasury surplus, the proceeds of Government bond issues, State lands or any other asset.

F. ADMISSION TO MEMBERSHIP IN THE UNITED NATIONS

When the independence of either the Arab or the Jewish State as envisaged in this plan has become effective and the declaration and undertaking, as envisaged in this plan, have been signed by either of them, sympathetic consideration should be given to its application for admission to membership in the United Nations in accordance with Article 4 of the Charter of the United Nations.

PART II

Boundaries

[omitted]

PART III

City of Jerusalem

A. SPECIAL REGIME

The City of Jerusalem shall be established as a *corpus separatum* under a special international régime and shall be administered by the United Nations. The Trusteeship Council shall be designated to discharge the responsibilities of the Administering Authority on behalf of the United Nations.

B. BOUNDARIES OF THE CITY

The City of Jerusalem shall include the present municipality of Jerusalem plus the surrounding villages and towns, the most eastern of which shall be Abu Dis; the most southern, Bethlehem; the most western, Ein Karim (including also the built-up area of Motsa); and the most northern Shu'fat, as indicated on the attached sketch-map (annex B).

C. STATUTE OF THE CITY

The Trusteeship Council shall, within five months of the approval of the present plan, elaborate and approve a detailed Statute of the City which shall contain *inter alia* the substance of the following provisions:

1. *Government machinery; special objectives.* The Administering Authority in discharging its administrative obligations shall pursue the following special objectives:

(*a*) To protect and to preserve the unique spiritual and religious interests located in the city of the three great monotheistic faiths throughout the world, Christian, Jewish and Moslem; to this end to ensure that order and peace, and especially religious peace, reign in Jerusalem;

(*b*) To foster co-operation among all the inhabitants of the city in their own interests as well as in order to encourage and support the peaceful development of the mutual relations between the two Palestinian peoples throughout the Holy Land; to promote the security, well-being and any constructive measures of development of the residents, having regard to the special circumstances and customs of the various peoples and communities.

2. *Governor and administrative staff.* A Governor of the City of Jerusalem shall be appointed by the Trusteeship Council and shall be responsible to it. He shall be selected on the basis of special qualifications and without regard to nationality. He shall not, however, be a citizen of either State in Palestine.

The Governor shall represent the United Nations in the City and shall exercise on their behalf all powers of administration, including the conduct of external affairs. He shall be assisted by an administrative staff classed as international officers in the meaning of Article 100 of the Charter and chosen whenever practicable from the residents of the city and of the rest of Palestine on a non-discriminatory basis. A detailed plan for the organization of the administration of the city shall be submitted by the Governor to the Trusteeship Council and duly approved by it.

3. *Local autonomy.* (*a*) The existing local autonomous units in the territory of the city (villages, townships and municipalities) shall enjoy wide powers of local government and administration.

(*b*) The Governor shall study and submit for the consideration and decision of the Trusteeship Council a plan for the establishment of special town units consisting, respectively, of the Jewish and Arab sections of new Jerusalem. The new town units shall continue to form part of the present municipality of Jerusalem.

4. *Security measures.* (*a*) The City of Jerusalem shall be demilitarized; its neutrality shall be declared and preserved, and no para-military formations, exercises or activities shall be permitted within its borders.

(*b*) Should the administration of the City of Jerusalem be seriously obstructed or prevented by the non-co-operation or interference of one or more sections of the population, the Governor shall have authority to take such measures as may be necessary to restore the effective functioning of the administration.

(*c*) To assist in the maintenance of internal law and order and especially for the protection of the Holy Places and religious buildings and sites in the city, the Governor shall organize a special police force of adequate strength, the members of which shall be recruited outside of Palestine. The Governor shall be empowered to direct such budgetary provision as may be necessary for the maintenance of this force.

5. *Legislative organization.* A Legislative Council, elected by adult residents of the city irrespective of nationality on the basis of universal and secret suffrage and proportional representation, shall have powers of legislation and taxation. No legislative measures shall, however, conflict or interfere with the provisions which will be set forth in the Statute of the City, nor shall any law, regulation, or official action prevail over them. The Statute shall grant to the Governor a right of vetoing bills inconsistent with the provisions referred to in the preceding sentence. It shall also empower him to promulgate temporary ordinances in case the Council fails to adopt in time a bill deemed essential to the normal functioning of the administration.

6. *Administration of justice.* The Statute shall provide for the establishment of an independent judiciary system, including a court of appeal. All the inhabitants of the City shall be subject to it.

7. *Economic union and economic régime.* The City of Jerusalem shall be included in the Economic Union of Palestine and be bound by all stipulations of the undertaking and of any treaties issued therefrom, as well as by the decisions of the Joint Economic Board. The headquarters of the Economic Board shall be established in the territory of the City.

The Statute shall provide for the regulation of economic matters not falling within the régime of the Economic Union, on the basis of equal treatment and non-discrimination for all Members of the United Nations and their nationals.

8. *Freedom of transit and visit; control of residents.* Subject to considerations of security, and of economic welfare as determined by the Governor under the directions of the Trusteeship Council, freedom of entry into, and residence within, the borders of the City shall be guaranteed for the residents or citizens of the Arab and Jewish States. Immigration into, and residence within, the borders of the city for nationals of other States shall be controlled by the Governor under the directions of the Trusteeship Council.

9. *Relations with the Arab and Jewish States.* Representatives of the Arab and Jewish States shall be accredited to the Governor of the City and charged with the protection of the interests of their States and nationals in connexion with the international administration of the City.

10. *Official languages.* Arabic and Hebrew shall be the official languages of the city. This will not preclude the adoption of one or more additional working languages, as may be required.

11. *Citizenship.* All the residents shall become *ipso facto* citizens of the City of Jerusalem unless they opt for citizenship of the State of which they have been citizens or, if Arabs or Jews, have filed notice of intention to become citizens of the Arab or Jewish State respectively, according to part I, section B, paragraph 9, of this plan.

The Trusteeship Council shall make arrangements for consular protection of the citizens of the City outside its territory.

12. *Freedoms of citizens.* (a) Subject only to the requirements of public order and morals, the inhabitants of the City shall be ensured the enjoyment of human rights and fundamental freedoms, including freedom of conscience, religion and worship, language, education, speech and Press, assembly and association, and petition.

(b) No discrimination of any kind shall be made between the inhabitants on the grounds of race, religion, language or sex.

(c) All persons within the City shall be entitled to equal protection of the laws.

(d) The family law and personal status of the various persons and communities and their religious interests, including endowments, shall be respected.

(*e*) Except as may be required for the maintenance of public order and good government, no measure shall be taken to obstruct or interfere with the enterprise of religious or charitable bodies of all faiths or to discriminate against any representative or member of these bodies on the ground of his religion or nationality.

(*f*) The City shall ensure adequate primary and secondary education for the Arab and Jewish communities respectively, in their own languages and in accordance with their cultural traditions.

The right of each community to maintain its own schools for the education of its own members in its own language, while conforming to such educational requirements of a general nature as the City may impose, shall not be denied or impaired. Foreign educational establishments shall continue their activity on the basis of their existing rights.

(*g*) No restriction shall be imposed on the free use by any inhabitant of the City of any language in private intercourse, in commerce, in religion, in the Press or in publications of any kind, or at public meetings.

13. *Holy Places.* (*a*) Existing rights in respect of Holy Places and religious buildings or sites shall not be denied or impaired.

(*b*) Free access to the Holy Places and religious buildings or sites and the free exercise of worship shall be secured in conformity with existing rights and subject to the requirements of public order and decorum.

(*c*) Holy Places and religious buildings or sites shall be preserved. No act shall be permitted which may in any way impair their sacred character. If at any time it appears to the Governor that any particular Holy Place, religious building or site is in need of urgent repair, the Governor may call upon the community or communities concerned to carry out such repair. The Governor may carry it out himself at the expense of the community or communities concerned if no action is taken within a reasonable time.

(*d*) No taxation shall be levied in respect of any Holy Place, religious building or site which was exempt from taxation on the date of the creation of the City. No change in the incidence of such taxation shall be made which would either discriminate between the owners or occupiers of Holy Places, religious buildings or sites, or would place such owners or occupiers in a position less favourable in relation to the general incidence of taxation than existed at the time of the adoption of the Assembly's recommendations.

14. *Special powers of the Governor in respect of the Holy Places, religious buildings and sites in the City and in any part of Palestine.* (*a*) The protection of the Holy Places, religious buildings and sites located in the City of Jerusalem shall be a special concern of the Governor.

(*b*) With relation to such places, buildings and sites in Palestine outside the city, the Governor shall determine, on the ground of powers granted to him by the Constitutions of both States, whether the provisions of the Constitutions of the Arab and Jewish States in Palestine dealing therewith and the religious rights appertaining thereto are being properly applied and respected.

(*c*) The Governor shall also be empowered to make decisions on the basis of existing rights in cases of disputes which may arise between the different religious communities or the rites of a religious community in respect of the Holy Places, religious buildings and sites in any part of Palestine.

In this task he may be assisted by a consultative council of representatives of different denominations acting in an advisory capacity.

D. DURATION OF THE SPECIAL REGIME

The Statute elaborated by the Trusteeship Council on the aforementioned principles shall come into force not later than 1 October 1948. It shall remain in force in the first instance for a period of ten years, unless the Trusteeship Council finds it necessary to undertake a re-examination of these provisions at an earlier date. After the expiration of this period the whole scheme shall be subject to re-examination by the Trusteeship Council in the light of the experience acquired with its functioning. The residents of the City shall be then free to express by means of a referendum their wishes as to possible modifications of the régime of the City.

PART IV

Capitulations

States whose nationals have in the past enjoyed in Palestine the privileges and immunities of foreigners, including the benefits of consular jurisdiction and protection, as formerly enjoyed by capitulation or usage in the Ottoman Empire, are invited to renounce any right pertaining to them to the re-establishment of such privileges and immunities in the proposed Arab and Jewish States and the City of Jerusalem.

Appendix IV

Resolution 186 (S-2) of the General Assembly dated 14 May 1948 concerning the appointment of a UN Mediator

The General Assembly,
Taking account of the present situation in regard to Palestine,

I

Strongly affirms its support of the efforts of the Security Council to secure a truce in Palestine and calls upon all Governments, organizations and persons to co-operate in making effective such a truce;

II

1. *Empowers* a United Nations Mediator in Palestine, to be chosen by a committee of the General Assembly composed of representatives of China, France, the Union of Soviet Socialist Republics, the United Kingdom and the United States of America, to exercise the following functions:

(*a*) To use his good offices with the local and community authorities in Palestine to:

i. Arrange for the operation of common services necessary to the safety and well-being of the population of Palestine;

ii. Assure the protection of the Holy Places, religious buildings and sites in Palestine;

iii. Promote a peaceful adjustment of the future situation of Palestine.

(*b*) To co-operate with the Truce Commission for Palestine appointed by the Security Council in its resolution of 23 April 1948.

(*c*) To invite, as seems to him advisable, with a view to the promotion of the welfare of the inhabitants of Palestine, the assistance and co-operation of appropriate special agencies of the United Nations, such as the World Health Organization, of the International Red Cross, and of other governmental or non-governmental organizations of a humanitarian and non-political character;

2. *Instructs* the United Nations Mediator to render progress reports monthly, or more frequently as he deems necessary, to the Security Council and to the Secretary-General for transmission to the Members of the United Nations;

3. *Directs* the United Nations Mediator to conform in his activities with the provisions of this resolution, and with such instructions as the General Assembly or the Security Council may issue;

4. *Authorizes* the Secretary-General to pay the United Nations Mediator an emolument equal to that paid to the President of the International Court of Justice, and to provide the Mediator with the necessary staff to assist in carrying out the functions assigned to the Mediator by the General Assembly;

III

Relieves the Palestine Commission from the further exercise of responsibilities under resolution 181 (11) of 29 November 1947.

Appendix V

Cablegram dated 15 May 1948 from the Foreign Secretary of the Provisional Government of Israel to the Secretary-General (UN Document S/747)

[*Original text: English*]
15 May 1948

Have honour inform you that National Council for Jewish State consisting of members of elected representative Jewish bodies Palestine which had applied to United Nations Palestine Commission for recognition as Provisional Council Government under part one B four of resolution of General Assembly on 29 November 1947 met yesterday 14 May and issued proclamation declaring following:

"On 29 November 1947 General Assembly of United Nations adopted resolution for establishment of independent Jewish State in Palestine and called upon inhabitants of country to take such steps as may be necessary on their part to put the plan into effect. This recognition by United Nations of right of Jewish people to establish their independent State may not be revoked. It is moreover self evident right of Jewish people to be a nation as all other nations in its own sovereign State. Accordingly we members of National Council representing Jewish people in Palestine and Zionist movement, met together in solemn assembly today, day of termination of British Mandate for Palestine, by virtue of natural and historic right of Jewish people and of resolution of General Assembly hereby proclaim establishment of Jewish State in Palestine to be called Israel. We hereby declare that as from termination of Mandate this night of 14 to 15 May 1948 and until setting up of duly elected bodies of State in accordance with constitution to be drawn up by constituent assembly not later than 1 October 1948 present National Council shall act as Provisional State Council and its executive organ shall constitute Provisional Government of State of

Israel. State of Israel will be open to immigration of Jews from all countries of dispersion, will promote development of country for benefit of all inhabitants, will be based on precepts of liberty, justice, and peace, will uphold full social and political equality of all citizens without distinction race, creed or sex, will guarantee full freedom of conscience, worship, education, culture and language, will safeguard sanctity and inviolability of shrines and Holy Places of all religions and will dedicate itself to principles of United Nations Charter. State of Israel will be ready to co-operate with organs and representatives of United Nations in implementation of resolution of Assembly of 29 November 1947 and will take steps to bring about economic union over whole of Palestine. We appeal to United Nations to assist Jewish people in building of its State and to admit Israel into family of nations."

Accordingly I beg declare on behalf of Provisional Government of State of Israel its readiness to sign declaration and undertaking provided for respectively in part one C and part one D of resolution of Assembly and beg hereby to apply for admission of State of Israel to membership family of nations.

Behalf Provisional Government of Israel

Moshe SHERTOK
Foreign Secretary

Appendix VI

Resolution 194 (III) of the General Assembly dated
11 December 1948 concerning the Conciliation Commission,
the international régime of Jerusalem, and the return of refugees

The General Assembly,
Having considered further the situation in Palestine,

1. *Expresses* its deep appreciation of the progress achieved through the good offices of the late United Nations Mediator in promoting a peaceful adjustment of the future situation of Palestine, for which cause he sacrificed his life; and

Extends its thanks to the Acting Mediator and his staff for their continued efforts and devotion to duty in Palestine;

2. *Establishes* a Conciliation Commission consisting of three States Members of the United Nations which shall have the following functions:

(*a*) To assume, in so far as it considers necessary in existing circumstances, the functions given to the United Nations Mediator on Palestine by resolution 186 (S-2) of the General Assembly of 14 May 1948;

(*b*) To carry out the specific functions and directives given to it by the present resolution and such additional functions and directives as may be given to it by the General Assembly or by the Security Council;

(*c*) To undertake, upon the request of the Security Council, any of the functions now assigned to the United Nations Mediator on Palestine or to the United Nations Truce Commission by resolutions of the Security Council; upon such request to the Conciliation

Commission by the Security Council with respect to all the remaining functions of the United Nations Mediator on Palestine under Security Council resolutions, the office of the Mediator shall be terminated;

3. *Decides* that a Committee of the Assembly, consisting of China, France, the Union of Soviet Socialist Republics, the United Kingdom and the United States of America, shall present, before the end of the first part of the present session of the General Assembly, for the approval of the Assembly, a proposal concerning the names of the three States which will constitute the Conciliation Commission;

4. *Requests* the Commission to begin its functions at once, with a view to the establishment of contact between the parties themselves and the Commission at the earliest possible date;

5. *Calls upon* the Governments and authorities concerned to extend the scope of the negotiations provided for in the Security Council's resolution of 16 November 1948 and to seek agreement by negotiations conducted either with the Conciliation Commission or directly, with a view to the final settlement of all questions outstanding between them;

6. *Instructs* the Conciliation Commission to take steps to assist the Governments and authorities concerned to achieve a final settlement of all questions outstanding between them;

7. *Resolves* that the Holy Places – including Nazareth – religious buildings and sites in Palestine should be protected and free access to them assured, in accordance with existing rights and historical practice; that arrangements to this end should be under effective United Nations supervision; that the United Nations Conciliation Commission, in presenting to the fourth regular session of the General Assembly its detailed proposals for a permanent international regime for the territory of Jerusalem, should include recommendations concerning the Holy Places in that territory; that with regard to the Holy Places in the rest of Palestine the Commission should call upon the political authorities of the areas concerned to give appropriate formal guarantees as to the protection of the Holy Places and access to them; and that these undertakings should be presented to the General Assembly for approval;

8. *Resolves* that, in view of its association with three world religions, the Jerusalem area, including the present municipality of Jerusalem *plus* the surrounding villages and towns, the most eastern of which shall be Abu Dis; the most southern, Bethlehem; the most western, Ein Karim (including also the built-up area of Motsa); and the most northern Shu'fat, should be accorded special and separate treatment from the rest of Palestine and should be placed under effective United Nations control;

Requests the Security Council to take further steps to ensure the demilitarization of Jerusalem at the earliest possible date;

Instructs the Commission to present to the fourth regular session of the General Assembly detailed proposals for a permanent international regime for the Jerusalem area which will provide for the maximum local autonomy for distinctive groups consistent with the special international status of the Jerusalem area;

The Conciliation Commission is authorized to appoint a United Nations representative, who shall co-operate with the local authorities with respect to the interim administration of the Jerusalem area;

9. *Resolves* that, pending agreement on more detailed arrangements among the Governments and authorities concerned, the freest possible access to Jerusalem by road, rail or air should be accorded to all inhabitants of Palestine;

Instructs the Conciliation Commission to report immediately to the Security Council, for appropriate action by that organ, any attempt by any party to impede such access;

10. *Instructs* the Conciliation Commission to seek arrangements among the Governments and authorities concerned which will facilitate the economic development of the area, including arrangements for access to ports and airfields and the use of transportation and communication facilities;

11. *Resolves* that the refugees wishing to return to their homes and live at peace with their neighbours should be permitted to do so at the earliest practicable date, and that compensation should be paid for the property of those choosing not to return and for loss of or damage to property which, under principles of international law or in equity, should be made good by the Governments or authorities responsible;

Instructs the Conciliation Commission to facilitate the repatriation, resettlement and economic and social rehabilitation of the refugees and the payment of compensation, and to maintain close relations with the Director of the United Nations Relief for Palestine Refugees and, through him, with the appropriate organs and agencies of the United Nations;

12. *Authorizes* the Conciliation Commission to appoint such subsidiary bodies and to employ such technical experts, acting under its authority, as it may find necessary for the effective discharge of its functions and responsibilities under the present resolution;

The Conciliation Commission will have its official headquarters at Jerusalem. The authorities responsible for maintaining order in Jerusalem will be responsible for taking all measures necessary to ensure the security of the Commission. The Secretary-General will provide a limited number of guards for the protection of the staff and premises of the Commission;

13. *Instructs* the Conciliation Commission to render progress reports periodically to the Secretary-General for transmission to the Security Council and to the Members of the United Nations;

14. *Calls upon* all Governments and authorities concerned to cooperate with the Conciliation Commission and to take all possible steps to assist in the implementation of the present resolution;

15. *Requests* the Secretary-General to provide the necessary staff and facilities and to make appropriate arrangements to provide the necessary funds required in carrying out the terms of the present resolution.

Appendix VII

Resolution 273 (III) of the General Assembly dated 11 May 1949
concerning the admission of Israel to UN membership

Having received the report of the Security Council on the application of Israel for membership in the United Nations,[6]

Noting that, in the judgment of the Security Council, Israel is a peace-loving State and is able and willing to carry out the obligations contained in the Charter,

---

6   See document A/818.

Noting that the Security Council has recommended to the General Assembly that it admit Israel to membership in the United Nations,

Noting furthermore the declaration by the State of Israel that it "unreservedly accepts the obligations of the United Nations Charter and undertakes to honour them from the day when it becomes a Member of the United Nations",[7]

Recalling its resolutions of 29 November 1947[8] and 11 December 1948[9] and taking note of the declarations and explanations made by the representative of the Government of Israel[10] before the *ad hoc* Political Committee in respect of the implementation of the said resolutions,

The General Assembly,

Acting in discharge of its functions under Article 4 of the Charter and rule 125 of its rules of procedure,

1. *Decides* that Israel is a peace-loving State which accepts the obligations contained in the Charter and is able and willing to carry out those obligations;

2. *Decides* to admit Israel to membership in the United Nations.

207th plenary meeting,
11 May 1949.

Appendix VIII

Resolution 303 (IV) of the General Assembly dated 9 December 1949 concerning the international régime for Jerusalem

The General Assembly,

Having regard to its resolutions 181 (II) of 29 November 1947 and 194 (III) of 11 December 1948,

Having studied the reports of the United Nations Conciliation Commission for Palestine set up under the latter resolution,

I

Decides, in relation to Jerusalem,

Believing that the principles underlying its previous resolutions concerning this matter, and in particular its resolution of 29 November 1947, represent a just and equitable settlement of the question,

1. To restate, therefore, its intention that Jerusalem should be placed under a permanent international regime, which should envisage appropriate guarantees for the protection of the Holy Places, both within and outside Jerusalem, and to confirm specifically the following provisions of General Assembly Resolution 181 (II). (1) the City of Jerusalem

---

7 See document S/1093.

8 See *Resolutions adopted by the General Assembly* during its second session, pages 131–132.

9 See *Resolutions adopted by the General Assembly* during Part I of its third session, pages 21–25.

10 See documents A/AC.24/SR.45–48, 50 and 51.

shall be established as a *corpus separatum* under a special international regime and shall be administered by the United Nations; (2) The Trusteeship Council shall be designated to discharge the responsibilities of the Administering Authority . . .; and (3) the City of Jerusalem shall include the present municipality of Jerusalem plus the surrounding villages and towns, the most eastern of which shall be Abu Dis; the most southern, Bethlehem; the most western 'Ein Karim (including also the built-up area of Motsa); and the most northern, Shu'fat, as indicated on the attached sketch-map;

2. To request for this purpose that the Trusteeship Council at its next session, whether special or regular, complete the preparation of the Statute of Jerusalem, omitting the new inapplicable provisions, such as articles 32 and 39, and, without prejudice to the fundamental principles of the international regime for Jerusalem set forth in General Assembly resolution 181 (II) introducing therein amendments in the direction of its greater democratization, approve the Statute, and proceed immediately with its implementation. The Trusteeship Council shall not allow any actions taken by any interested Government or Governments to divert it from adopting and implementing the Statute of Jerusalem;

II

Calls upon the States concerned to make formal undertakings, at an early date and in the light of their obligations as Members of the United Nations, that they will approach these matters with good will and be guided by the terms of the present resolution.

Appendix IX

Resolution 237 of the Security Council of 14 June 1967 concerning respect for human rights in the occupied territories

The Security Council,

Considering the urgent need to spare the civil populations and the prisoners of the war in the area of conflict in the Middle East additional sufferings,

Considering that essential and inalienable human rights should be respected even during the vicissitudes of war,

Considering that all the obligations of the Geneva Convention relative to the Treatment of Prisoners of War of 12 August 1949 should be complied with by the parties involved in the conflict,

1. *Calls upon* the Government of Israel to ensure the safety, welfare and security of the inhabitants of the areas where military operations have taken place and to facilitate the return of those inhabitants who have fled the areas since the outbreak of hostilities;

2. *Recommends* to the Governments concerned the scrupulous respect of the humanitarian principles governing the treatment of prisoners of war and the protection of civilian persons in time of war, contained in the Geneva Conventions of 12 August 1949;

3. *Requests* the Secretary-General to follow the effective implementation of this resolution and to report to the Security Council.

Appendix x

Resolution 2252 (ES–V) of the General Assembly dated
4 July 1967 concerning humanitarian assistance

The General Assembly,
Considering the urgent need to alleviate the suffering inflicted on civilians and on prisoners
of war as a result of the recent hostilities in the Middle East,

1. *Welcomes with great satisfaction* Security Council resolution 237 (1967) of 14 June
1967, whereby the Council:
(*a*) Considered the urgent need to spare the civil populations and the prisoners of war in
the area of conflict in the Middle East additional sufferings;
(*b*) Considered that essential and inalienable human rights should be respected even
during the vicissitudes of war;
(*c*) Considered that all the obligations of the Geneva Convention relative to the Treatment of Prisoners of War of 12 August 1949[11] should be complied with by the parties
involved in the conflict;
(*d*) Called upon the Government of Israel to ensure the safety, welfare and security of
the inhabitants of the areas where military operations had taken place and to facilitate the
return of those inhabitants who had fled the areas since the outbreak of hostilities;
(*e*) Recommended to the Governments concerned the scrupulous respect of the humanitarian principles governing the treatment of prisoners of war and the protection of civilian
persons in time of war, contained in the Geneva Conventions of 12 August 1949;[12]
(*f*) Requested the Secretary-General to follow the effective implementation of the
resolution and to report to the Security Council;

2. *Notes with gratitude and satisfaction* and endorses the appeal made by the President of
the General Assembly on 26 June 1967;[13]

3. *Notes with gratification* the work undertaken by the International Committee of the
Red Cross, the League of Red Cross Societies and other voluntary organizations to provide
humanitarian assistance to civilians;

4. *Notes further with gratification* the assistance which the United Nations Children's
Fund is providing to women and children in the area;

5. *Commends* the Commissioner-General of the United Nations Relief and Works
Agency for Palestine Refugees in the Near East for his efforts to continue the activities of
the Agency in the present situation with respect to all persons coming within his mandate;

6. *Endorses,* bearing in mind the objectives of the above-mentioned Security Council
resolution, the efforts of the Commissioner-General of the United Nations Relief and Works
Agency for Palestine Refugees in the Near East to provide humanitarian assistance, as far as
practicable, on an emergency basis and as a temporary measure, to other persons in the area

---

11 United Nations, *Treaty Series*, vol. 75 (1950), No. 972.
12 *Ibid.*, Nos. 970–973.
13 See *Official Records of the General Assembly, Fifth Emergency Special Session, Plenary
Meetings,* 1536th meeting, paras. 29–37.

who are at present displaced and are in serious need of immediate assistance as a result of the recent hostilities;

7. *Welcomes* the close co-operation of the United Nations Relief and Works Agency for Palestine Refugees in the Near East, and of the other organizations concerned, for the purpose of co-ordinating assistance;

8. *Calls upon* all the Member States concerned to facilitate the transport of supplies to all areas in which assistance is being rendered;

9. *Appeals* to all Governments, as well as organizations and individuals, to make special contributions for the above purposes to the United Nations Relief and Works Agency for Palestine Refugees in the Near East and also to the other intergovernmental and non-governmental organizations concerned;

10. Requests the Secretary-General, in consultation with the Commissioner-General of the United Nations Relief and Works Agency for Palestine Refugees in the Near East, to report urgently to the General Assembly on the needs arising under paragraphs 5 and 6 above;

11. *Further requests* the Secretary-General to follow the effective implementation of the present resolution and to report thereon to the General Assembly.

1548th plenary meeting,
4 July 1967.

Appendix XI

Resolution 2253 (ES–V) of the General Assembly dated 4 July 1967 concerning measures taken by Israel to change the status of Jerusalem

The General Assembly,
Deeply concerned at the situation prevailing in Jerusalem as a result of the measures taken by Israel to change the status of the City,

1. *Considers* that these measures are invalid;

2. *Calls upon* Israel to rescind all measures already taken and to desist forthwith from taking any action which would alter the status of Jerusalem;

3. *Requests* the Secretary-General to report to the General Assembly and the Security Council on the situation and on the implementation of the present resolution not later than one week from its adoption.

1548th plenary meeting,
4 July 1967.

Appendix XII

Resolution 2254 (ES–V) of the General Assembly dated
14 July 1967 concerning measures taken by Israel to change
the status of Jerusalem

The General Assembly,
Recalling its resolution 2253 (ES-V) of 4 July 1967,
Having received the report submitted by the Secretary-General,[14]
Taking note with the deepest regret and concern of the non-compliance by Israel with resolution 2253 (ES-V),

1. *Deplores* the failure of Israel to implement General Assembly resolution 2253 (ES-V);

2. *Reiterates* its call to Israel in that resolution to rescind all measures already taken and to desist forthwith from taking any action which would alter the status of Jerusalem;

3. *Requests* the Secretary-General to report to the Security Council and the General Assembly on the situation and on the implementation of the present resolution.

1554th plenary meeting,
14 July 1967.

Appendix XIII

Resolution 242 of the Security Council dated 22 November 1967
concerning the situation in the Middle East

The Security Council,
Expressing its continuing concern with the grave situation in the Middle East,
Emphasizing the inadmissibility of the acquisition of territory by war and the need to work for a just and lasting peace in which every State in the area can live in security,
Emphasizing further that all Member States in their acceptance of the Charter of the United Nations have undertaken a commitment to act in accordance with Article 2 of the Charter,

1. *Affirms* that the fulfilment of Charter principles requires the establishment of a just and lasting peace in the Middle East which should include the application of both the following principles:

---

14 A/6753. For the printed text of this document, see *Official Records of the Security Council, Twenty-second Year, Supplement for July, August and September 1967*, document S/8052.

i. Withdrawal of Israel armed forces from territories occupied in the recent conflict;

ii. Termination of all claims or states of belligerency and respect for and acknowledgement of the sovereignty, territorial integrity and political independence of every State in the area and their right to live in peace within secure and recognized boundaries free from threats or acts of force;

2. *Affirms further* the necessity

(*a*) For guaranteeing freedom of navigation through international waterways in the area;

(*b*) For achieving a just settlement of the refugee problem;

(*c*) For guaranteeing the territorial inviolability and political independence of every State in the area, through measures including the establishment of demilitarized zones;

3. *Requests* the Secretary-General to designate a Special Representative to proceed to the Middle East to establish and maintain contacts with the States concerned in order to promote agreement and assist efforts to achieve a peaceful and accepted settlement in accordance with the provisions and principles in this resolution;

4. *Requests* the Secretary-General to report to the Security Council on the progress of the efforts of the Special Representative as soon as possible.

Adopted unanimously at the 1382nd meeting.

Appendix XIV

Resolution 252 of the Security Council dated 21 May 1968 concerning measures taken by Israel to change the status of Jerusalem

The Security Council,

Recalling General Assembly resolutions 2253 (ES-V) and 2254 (ES-V) of 4 and 14 July 1967,

Having considered the letter (S/8560) of the Permanent Representative of Jordan on the situation in Jerusalem and the report of the Secretary-General (S/8146),

Having heard the statements made before the Council,

Noting that since the adoption of the above-mentioned resolutions, Israel has taken further measures and actions in contravention of those resolutions,

Bearing in mind the need to work for a just and lasting peace,

Reaffirming that acquisition of territory by military conquest is inadmissible,

1. *Deplores* the failure of Israel to comply with the General Assembly resolutions mentioned above;

2. *Considers* that all legislative and administrative measures and actions taken by Israel, including expropriation of land and properties thereon, which tend to change the legal status of Jerusalem are invalid and cannot change that status;

3. *Urgently calls upon* Israel to rescind all such measures already taken and to desist forthwith from taking any further action which tends to change the status of Jerusalem;

4. *Requests* the Secretary-General to report to the Security Council on the implementation of the present resolution.

Appendix XV

Resolution 259 of the Security Council dated 27 September 1968
concerning human rights in the occupied territories

The Security Council,

Concerned with the safety, welfare and security of the inhabitants of the Arab territories under military occupation by Israel following the hostilities of 5 June 1967,

Recalling its resolution 237 (1967) of 14 June 1967,

Noting the report by the Secretary-General, contained in document S/8699, and appreciating his efforts in this connexion,

Deploring the delay in the implementation of resolution 237 (1967) because of the conditions still being set by Israel for receiving a Special Representative of the Secretary-General,

1. *Requests* the Secretary-General urgently to dispatch a Special Representative to the Arab territories under military occupation by Israel following the hostilities of 5 June 1967, and to report on the implementation of resolution 237 (1967);

2. *Requests* the Government of Israel to receive the Special Representative of the Secretary-General, to co-operate with him and to facilitate his work;

3. *Recommends* that the Secretary-General be afforded all co-operation in his efforts to bring about the implementation of the present resolution and resolution 237 (1967).

> *Adopted at the 1454th meeting by 12 votes to none, with 3 abstentions (Canada, Denmark, United States of America).*

Appendix XVI

Resolution 2443 (XXIII) of the General Assembly dated
19 December 1968 concerning human rights in the occupied
territories

The General Assembly,

Guided by the purposes and principles of the Charter of the United Nations and by the Universal Declaration of Human Rights,

Bearing in mind the provisions of the Geneva Convention relative to the Protection of Civilian Persons in Time of War of 12 August 1949,[15]

---

15   United Nations, *Treaty Series,* Vol. 75, No. 973, 1950.

Mindful of the principle embodied in the Universal Declaration of Human Rights regarding the right of everyone to return to his own country and recalling Security Council resolution 237 (1967) of 14 June 1967, General Assembly resolutions 2252 (ES-V) of 4 July 1967 and 2341 B (XXII) of 19 December 1967, Commission on Human Rights resolution 6 (XXIV) and Economic and Social Council resolution 1336 (XLIV) of 31 May 1968, in which these organs of the United Nations called upon the Government of Israel, *inter alia*, to facilitate the return of those inhabitants who have fled the area of military operations since the outbreak of hostilities,

Recalling the telegram dispatched by the Commission on Human Rights on 8 March 1968, calling upon the Government of Israel to desist forthwith from acts of destroying homes of the Arab civilian population in areas occupied by Israel,

Recalling also Security Council resolution 259 (1968) of 27 September 1968, in which the Council expressed its concern for the safety, welfare and security of the inhabitants of the Arab territories under military occupation by Israel, and deplored the delay in the implementation of resolution 237 (1967),

Noting resolution I on respect for and implementation of human rights in occupied territories, adopted by the International Conference on Human Rights on 7 May 1968, in which the Conference, *inter alia*:

(*a*) Expressed its grave concern for the violation of human rights in Arab territories occupied by Israel;

(*b*) Drew the attention of the Government of Israel to the grave consequences resulting from disregard of fundamental freedoms and human rights in occupied territories;

(*c*) Called upon the Government of Israel to desist forthwith from acts of destroying homes of the Arab civilian population inhabiting areas occupied by Israel and to respect and implement the Universal Declaration of Human Rights and the Geneva Conventions of 12 August 1949 in occupied territories;

(*d*) Affirmed the inalienable rights of all inhabitants who have left their homes as a result of the outbreak of hostilities in the Middle East to return, resume normal life, recover their property and homes, and rejoin their families according to the provisions of the Universal Declaration of Human Rights,

1. *Decides* to establish a special committee of three Member States to investigate Israeli practices affecting the human rights of the population of the occupied territories;

2. *Requests* the President of the General Assembly to appoint the members of the special committee;

3. *Requests* the Government of Israel to receive the special committee, to co-operate with it and to facilitate its work;

4. *Requests* the special committee to report to the Secretary-General as soon as possible and whenever the need arises thereafter;

5. *Requests* the Secretary-General to provide the special committee with all the necessary facilities for the performance of its task.

Appendix XVII

Resolution 267 of the Security Council dated 3 July 1969
concerning measures taken by Israel to change the status
of Jerusalem

The Security Council,

Recalling its resolution 252 of 21 May 1968 and the earlier General Assembly resolutions 2253 (ES-V) and 2254 (ES-V) of 4 and 14 July 1967 respectively concerning measures and actions by Israel affecting the status of the City of Jerusalem,

Having heard the statements of the parties concerned on the question,

Noting that since the adoption of the above-mentioned resolutions Israel has taken further measures tending to change the status of the City of Jerusalem,

Reaffirming the established principle that acquisition of territory by military conquest is inadmissible,

1. *Reaffirms* its resolution 252 (1968);

2. *Deplores* the failure of Israel to show any regard for the General Assembly and Security Council resolutions mentioned above;

3. *Censures* in the strongest terms all measures taken to change the status of the City of Jerusalem;

4. *Confirms* that all legislative and administrative measures and actions by Israel which purport to alter the status of Jerusalem including expropriation of land and properties thereon are invalid and cannot change that status;

5. *Urgently calls* once more upon Israel to rescind forthwith all measures taken by it which may tend to change the status of the City of Jerusalem, and in future to refrain from all actions likely to have such an effect;

6. *Requests* Israel to inform the Security Council without any further delay of its intentions with regard to the implementation of the provisions of this resolution;

7. *Determines* that, in the event of a negative response or no response from Israel, the Security Council shall reconvene without delay to consider what further action should be taken in this matter;

8. *Requests* the Secretary-General to report to the Security Council on the implementation of this resolution.

Appendix XVIII

Resolution 271 of the Security Council dated 15 September 1969 concerning arson at Al Aqsa Mosque and the status of Jerusalem

The Security Council,

Grieved at the extensive damage caused by arson to the Holy Al Aqsa Mosque in Jerusalem on 21 August 1969 under the military occupation of Israel,

Mindful of the consequent loss to human culture,

Having heard the statements made before the Council reflecting the universal outrage caused by the act of sacrilege in one of the most venerated shrines of mankind,

Recalling its resolutions 252 (1968) of 21 May 1968 and 267 (1969) of 3 July 1969 and the earlier General Assembly resolutions 2253 (ES-V) and 2254 (ES-V) of 4 and 14 July 1967, respectively, concerning measures and actions by Israel affecting the status of the City of Jerusalem,

Reaffirming the established principle that acquisition of territory by military conquest is inadmissible,

1. *Reaffirms* its resolutions 252 (1968) and 267 (1969);

2. *Recognizes* that any act of destruction or profanation of the Holy Places, religious buildings and sites in Jerusalem or any encouragement of, or connivance at, any such act may seriously endanger international peace and security;

3. *Determines* that the execrable act of desecration and profanation of the Holy Al Aqsa Mosque emphasizes the immediate necessity of Israel's desisting from acting in violation of the aforesaid resolutions and rescinding forthwith all measures and actions taken by it designed to alter the status of Jerusalem;

4. *Calls upon* Israel scrupulously to observe the provisions of the Geneva Conventions[16] and international law governing military occupation and to refrain from causing any hindrance to the discharge of the established functions of the Supreme Moslem Council of Jerusalem, including any co-operation that Council may desire from countries with predominantly Moslem population and from Moslem communities in relation to its plans for the maintenance and repair of the Islamic Holy Places in Jerusalem;

5. *Condemns* the failure of Israel to comply with the aforementioned resolutions and calls upon it to implement forthwith the provisions of these resolutions;

6. *Reiterates* the determination in paragraph 7 of resolution 267 (1969) that, in the event of a negative response or no response, the Security Council shall convene without delay to consider what further action should be taken in this matter;

7. *Requests* the Secretary-General to follow closely the implementation of the present resolution and to report thereon to the Security Council at the earliest possible date.

> *Adopted at the 1512th meeting by 11 votes to none, with 4 abstentions (Colombia, Finland, Paraguay, United States of America).*

---

16 Geneva Conventions of 12 August 1949 (United Nations, *Treaty Series*, vol. 75 (1950), Nos. 970–973).

Appendix XIX

Resolution 2535 (XXIV) B of the General Assembly dated 10 December 1969 affirming the inalienable rights of the people of Palestine

The General Assembly,

Recognizing that the problem of the Palestine Arab refugees has arisen from the denial of their inalienable rights under the Charter of the United Nations and the Universal Declaration of Human Rights,

Gravely concerned that the denial of their rights has been aggravated by the reported acts of collective punishment, arbitrary detention, curfews, destruction of homes and property, deportation and other repressive acts against the refugees and other inhabitants of the occupied territories,

Recalling Security Council resolution 237 (1967) of 14 June 1967,

Recalling also its resolution 2252 (ES-V) of 4 July 1967 and its resolution 2452 A (XXIII) of 19 December 1968 calling upon the Government of Israel to take effective and immediate steps for the return without delay of those inhabitants who had fled the areas since the outbreak of hostilities,

Desirous of giving effect to its resolutions for relieving the plight of the displaced persons and the refugees,

1. *Reaffirms* the inalienable rights of the people of Palestine;

2. *Draws the attention* of the Security Council to the grave situation resulting from Israeli policies and practices in the occupied territories and Israel's refusal to implement the above resolutions;

3. *Requests* the Security Council to take effective measures in accordance with the relevant provisions of the Charter of the United Nations to ensure the implementation of these resolutions.

1827th plenary meeting,
10 December 1969.

Appendix xx

Resolution 2546 (XXIV) of the General Assembly dated 11 December 1969 concerning violations by Israel of human rights in the occupied territories

The General Assembly,

Guided by the purposes and principles of the Charter of the United Nations,

Bearing in mind the provisions of the Geneva Convention relative to the Protection of Civilian Persons in Time of War of 12 August 1949 and the provisions of the Universal Declaration of Human Rights,

Recalling the humanitarian resolutions regarding the violations of human rights and fundamental freedoms in the territories occupied by Israel, especially Security Council resolutions 237 (1967) of 14 June 1967 and 259 (1968) of 27 September 1968, Commission on Human Rights resolutions 6 (XXIV) of 27 February 1968 and 6 (XXV) of 4 March 1969, and the relevant resolutions of the International Conference on Human Rights held at Teheran in 1968, the Economic and Social Council, the United Nations Educational, Scientific and Cultural Organization and the World Health Organization,

Further recalling its resolutions 2252 (ES-V) of 4 July 1967 and 2443 (XXIII) and 2452 (XXIII) of 19 December 1968,

Concerned that the provisions of these resolutions have not been implemented by the Israeli authorities,

Gravely alarmed by fresh reports of collective punishments, mass imprisonment, indiscriminate destruction of homes and other acts of oppression against the civilian population in the Arab territories occupied by Israel,

1. *Reaffirms* its resolutions relating to the violations of human rights in the territories occupied by Israel;

2. *Expresses its grave concern* at the continuing reports of violation of human rights in those territories;

3. *Condemns* such policies and practices as collective and area punishment, the destruction of homes and the deportation of the inhabitants of the territories occupied by Israel;

4. *Urgently calls upon* the Government of Israel to desist forthwith from its reported repressive practices and policies towards the civilian population in the occupied territories and to comply with its obligations under the Geneva Convention relative to the Protection of Civilian Persons in Time of War of 12 August 1949, the Universal Declaration of Human Rights and the relevant resolutions adopted by the various international organizations;

5. *Requests* the Special Committee to Investigate Israeli Practices Affecting the Human Rights of the Population of the Occupied Territories, established under General Assembly resolution 2443 (XXIII), to take cognizance of the provisions of the present resolution.

1829th plenary meeting,
11 December 1969.

Appendix XXI

Resolution 2628 (XXV) of the General Assembly dated
4 November 1970 concerning the situation in the Middle East
and respect for the rights of the Palestinians

The General Assembly,

Seriously concerned that the continuation of the present grave and deteriorating situation in the Middle East constitutes a serious threat to international peace and security,

Reaffirming that no territorial acquisition resulting from the threat or use of force shall be recognized,

Deploring the continued occupation of the Arab territories since 5 June 1967,

Seriously concerned that Security Council resolution 242 (1967) of 22 November 1967, which was unanimously adopted and which provides for a peaceful settlement of the situation in the Middle East, has not yet been implemented,

Having considered the item entitled "The situation in the Middle East",

1. *Reaffirms* that the acquisition of territories by force is inadmissible and that, consequently, territories thus occupied must be restored;

2. *Reaffirms* that the establishment of a just and lasting peace in the Middle East should include the application of both the following principles:

   (*a*) Withdrawal of Israeli armed forces from territories occupied in the recent conflict;

   (*b*) Termination of all claims or states of belligerency and respect for and acknowledgement of the sovereignty, territorial integrity and political independence of every State in the area and its right to live in peace within secure and recognized boundaries free from threats or acts of force;

3. *Recognizes* that respect for the rights of the Palestinians is an indispensable element in the establishment of a just and lasting peace in the Middle East;

4. *Urges* the speedy implementation of Security Council resolution 242 (1967), which provides for the peaceful settlement of the situation in the Middle East, in all its parts;

5. *Calls upon* the parties directly concerned to instruct their representatives to resume contact with the Special Representative of the Secretary-General in order to enable him to carry out, at the earliest possible date, his mandate for the implementation of the Security Council resolution in all its parts;

6. *Recommends* to the parties that they extend the cease-fire for a period of three months in order that they may enter into talks under the auspices of the Special Representative of the Secretary-General with a view to giving effect to Security Council resolution 242 (1967);

7. *Requests* the Secretary-General to report to the Security Council within a period of two months, and to the General Assembly as appropriate, on the efforts of the Special Representative and on the implementation of Security Council resolution 242 (1967);

8. *Requests* the Security Council to consider, if necessary, making arrangements, under the relevant Articles of the Charter of the United Nations, to ensure the implementation of its resolution.

Appendix XXII

Resolution 2672 (XXV) C of the General Assembly dated
8 December 1970 concerning equal rights and self-determination
of the Palestinians

The General Assembly,

Recognizing that the problem of the Palestinian Arab refugees has arisen from the denial of their inalienable rights under the Charter of the United Nations and the Universal Declaration of Human Rights,

Recalling its resolution 2535 B (XXIV) of 10 December 1969, in which it reaffirmed the inalienable rights of the people of Palestine,

Bearing in mind the principle of equal rights and self-determination of peoples enshrined in Articles 1 and 55 of the Charter of the United Nations and more recently reaffirmed in the Declaration on Principles of International Law concerning Friendly Relations and Co-operation among States in accordance with the Charter of the United Nations,

1. *Recognizes* that the people of Palestine are entitled to equal rights and self-determination, in accordance with the Charter of the United Nations;

2. *Declares* that full respect for the inalienable rights of the people of Palestine is an indispensable element in the establishment of a just and lasting peace in the Middle East.

Appendix XXIII

Resolution 2727 (XXV) of the General Assembly dated
15 December 1970 concerning violations by Israel of human
rights in the occupied territories

The General Assembly,

Guided by the purposes and principles of the Charter of the United Nations,

Bearing in mind the provisions of the Universal Declaration of Human Rights and the provisions of the Geneva Convention relative to the Protection of Civilian Persons in Time of War of 12 August 1949,[17]

Recalling Security Council Resolutions 237 (1967) of 14 June 1967 and 259 (1968) of 27 September 1968,

---

17 United Nations, *Treaty Series*, vol. 75 (1950), No. 973

Recalling also its resolutions 2252 (ES-V) of 4 July 1967, 2443 (XXIII) of 19 December 1968, 2452 A (XXIII) of 19 December 1968, 2535 B (XXIV) of 10 December 1969 and 2672 D (XXV) of 8 December 1970,

Further recalling Commission on Human Rights resolutions 6 (XXIV) of 27 February 1968,[18] 6 (XXV) of 4 March 1969[19] and 10 (XXVI) of 23 March 1970,[20] the telegram of 8 March 1968 to the Israeli authorities,[21] the relevant resolutions of the International Conference on Human Rights held at Teheran in 1968,[22] Commission on Status of Women resolution 7 (XXIII) of 9 April 1970[23] and the relevant resolutions of the Economic and Social Council, the United Nations Educational, Scientific and Cultural Organization and the World Health Organization,

Having considered the report of the Special Committee to Investigate Israeli Practices Affecting the Human Rights of the Population of the Occupied Territories,[24]

Noting with regret that the provisions of these resolutions have not been implemented by the Israeli authorities,

Gravely concerned for the safety, welfare and security of the inhabitants of the Arab territories under military occupation by Israel,

1. *Expresses its sincere appreciation* to the Special Committee to Investigate Israeli Practices Affecting the Human Rights of the Population of the Occupied Territories and to its members for their efforts in performing the task assigned to them;

2. *Calls upon* the Government of Israel to immediately implement the recommendations of the Special Committee embodied in its report,[25] and to comply with its obligations under the Geneva Convention relative to the Protection of Civilian Persons in Time of War of 12 August 1949, the Universal Declaration of Human Rights and the relevant resolutions adopted by the various international organizations;

3. *Requests* the Special Committee, pending the early termination of Israeli occupation of Arab territories, to continue its work and to consult, as appropriate, with the International Committee of the Red Cross in order to ensure the safeguarding of the human rights of the population of the occupied territories;

4. *Urges* the Government of Israel to receive the Special Committee, co-operate with it and facilitate its work;

5. *Requests* the Special Committee to report to the Secretary-General as soon as possible and whenever the need arises thereafter;

6. *Requests* the Secretary-General to provide the Special Committee with all the necessary facilities for the continued performance of its tasks;

7. *Decides* to inscribe on the provisional agenda of its twenty-sixth session an item entitled "Report (or reports) of the Special Committee to Investigate Israeli Practices Affecting the Human Rights of the Population of the Occupied Territories".

---

18 *Official Records of the Economic and Social Council, Forty-fourth Session, Supplement No. 4* (E/4475), chapter XVIII.
19 *Ibid., Forty-sixth Session*, document E/4621, chapter XVIII.
20 *Ibid., Forty-eighth Session, Supplement No. 5* (E/4816), chapter XXIII.
21 *Ibid., Forty-fourth Session, Supplement No. 4* (E/4475), para. 400.
22 See *Final Act of the International Conference on Human Rights* (United Nations publication, Sales No. E.68.XIV.2), chapter III.
23 *Official Records of the Economic and Social Council, Forty-eighth Session, Supplement No. 6* (E/4831), chapter XII.
24 A/8089.
25 *Ibid.*, paras. 145–156.

Appendix XXIV

Resolution 298 of the Security Council dated 25 September 1971
concerning measures taken by Israel to change the status of Jerusalem

The Security Council,

Recalling its resolutions 252 (1968) and 267 (1969) and the earlier General Assembly resolutions 2253 (ES-V) and 2254 (ES-V) of July 1967 concerning measures and actions by Israel designed to change the status of the Israeli-occupied section of Jerusalem,

Having considered the letter of the Permanent Representative of Jordan on the situation in Jerusalem (S/10313) and the reports of the Secretary-General (S/8052, S/8146, S/9149 and Add.1, S/9537 and S/10124 and Add.1 and 2), and having heard the statements of the parties concerned on the question,

Reaffirming the principle that acquisition of territory by military conquest is inadmissible,

Noting with concern the non-compliance by Israel with the above-mentioned resolutions,

Noting with concern further that since the adoption of the above-mentioned resolutions Israel has taken further measures designed to change the status and character of the occupied section of Jerusalem,

1. *Reaffirms* Security Council resolutions 252 (1968) and 267 (1969);

2. *Deplores* the failure of Israel to respect the previous resolutions adopted by the United Nations concerning measures and actions by Israel purporting to affect the status of the city of Jerusalem;

3. *Confirms* in the clearest possible terms that all legislative and administrative actions taken by Israel to change the status of the city of Jerusalem including expropriation of land and properties, transfer of populations and legislation aimed at the incorporation of the occupied section are totally invalid and cannot change that status;

4. *Urgently calls upon* Israel to rescind all previous measures and actions and to take no further steps in the occupied section of Jerusalem which may purport to change the status of the City, or which would prejudice the rights of the inhabitants and the interests of the international community, or a just and lasting peace;

5. *Requests* the Secretary-General, in consultation with the President of the Security Council and using such instrumentalities as he may choose, including a representative or a mission, to report to the Security Council as appropriate and in any event within 60 days on the implementation of this resolution.

Appendix xxv

Resolution 2787 (XXVI) of the General Assembly dated
6 December 1971 concerning the inalienable rights of the
Palestinians and other peoples

The General Assembly,

Reaffirming its resolutions 1514 (XV) of 14 December 1960, 1803 (XVII) of 14 December 1962, 1904 (XVIII) of 20 November 1963, 2200 (XXI) of 16 December 1966, 2535 B (XXIV) of 10 December 1969, 2625 (XXV) of 24 October 1970, 2649 (XXV) of 30 November 1970 and 2672 C (XXV) of 8 December 1970 and resolution VIII adopted by the International Conference on Human Rights held at Teheran in 1968,[26]

Solemnly reaffirming that the subjection of peoples to alien subjugation, domination and colonial exploitation is a violation of the principle of self-determination as well as a denial of basic human rights and is contrary to the Charter of the United Nations,

Concerned at the fact that many peoples continue to be denied the right to self-determination and are living under conditions of colonial and foreign domination,

Expressing concern at the fact that some countries, notably Portugal, with the support of its North Atlantic Treaty Organization allies, are waging war against the national liberation movement of the colonies and against certain independent States of Africa and Asia and the developing countries,

Confirming that colonialism in all its forms and manifestations, including the methods of neo-colonialism, constitutes a gross encroachment on the rights of peoples and the basic human rights and freedoms,

Convinced that effective application of the principle of self-determination of peoples is of paramount importance for the promotion of friendly relations between countries and peoples, the guarantee of human rights and the maintenance of peace in the world,

Affirming that the future of Zimbabwe cannot be negotiated with an illegal regime and that any settlement must be on the basis of "no independence before majority rule",

Reaffirming the inalienable rights of all peoples, and in particular those of Zimbabwe, Namibia, Angola, Mozambique and Guinea (Bissau) and the Palestinian people, to freedom, equality and self-determination, and the legitimacy of their struggles to restore those rights,

Reaffirming the Declaration on Principles of International Law concerning Friendly Relations and Co-operation among States in accordance with the Charter of the United Nations, which elaborated the principle of self-determination of peoples,

Considering that the establishment of a sovereign and independent State freely determined by the whole people belonging to the territory constitutes a mode of implementing the right of self-determination,

Further considering that any attempt aimed at the partial or total disruption of the national unity and territorial integrity of a State established in accordance with the right of self-determination of its peoples is incompatible with the purposes and principles of the Charter,

Mindful that interference in the internal affairs of States is a violation of the Charter and can pose a serious threat to the maintenance of peace,

---

26 *Final Act of the International Conference on Human Rights* (United Nations publication, Sales No.: E.68.XIV.2), p. 9.

1. *Confirms* the legality of the peoples' struggle for self-determination and liberation from colonial and foreign domination and alien subjugation, notably in southern Africa and in particular that of the peoples of Zimbabwe, Namibia, Angola, Mozambique and Guinea (Bissau), as well as the Palestinian people, by all available means consistent with the Charter of the United Nations;

2. *Affirms* man's basic human right to fight for the self-determination of his people under colonial and foreign domination;

3. *Calls upon* all States dedicated to the ideals of freedom and peace to give all their political, moral and material assistance to peoples struggling for liberation, self-determination and independence against colonial and alien domination;

4. *Believes* that the main objectives and principles of international protection of human rights cannot be effectively implemented while some States, particularly Portugal and South Africa, pursue the imperialist policy of colonialism, use force against independent African States and developing countries and peoples fighting for self-determination and support regimes that are applying the criminal policy of racism and *apartheid*;

5. *Condemns* the colonial and usurping Powers that are suppressing the right of peoples to self-determination and hampering the liquidation of the last hotbeds of colonialism and racism in the African and Asian continents and in other parts of the world;

6. *Condemns* the policy of certain States Members of the North Atlantic Treaty Organization that contribute to the creation in southern Africa of a military-industrial complex whose aim is to suppress the movement of peoples struggling for their self-determination and to interfere in the affairs of independent African States;

7. *Recalls* that it is the duty of every State to contribute through joint and independent action to the implementation of the principle of self-determination, in accordance with the provisions of the Charter, and to assist the United Nations to discharge the responsibilities vested in it by the Charter for the implementation of this principle;

8. *Urges* the Security Council as well as States Members of the United Nations or members of specialized agencies to take effective steps to ensure the implementation of the relevant United Nations resolutions on the elimination of colonialism and racism, and to report to the General Assembly at its twenty-seventh session;

9. *Resolves* to devote constant attention to the question of flagrant large-scale violations of human rights and fundamental freedoms resulting from the denial to peoples under colonial and foreign domination of their right to self-determination;

10. *Calls upon* all States to observe the principles of the sovereign equality of States, non-interference in the internal affairs of other States and respect for their sovereign rights and territorial integrity.

Appendix XXVI

Resolution 2799 (XXVI) of the General Assembly dated
13 December 1971 concerning the situation in the Middle East

The General Assembly,

Deeply concerned at the continuation of the grave situation prevailing in the Middle East, particularly since the conflict of June 1967, which constitutes a serious threat to international peace and security,

Convinced that Security Council resolution 242 (1967) of 22 November 1967 should be implemented immediately in all its parts in order to achieve a just and lasting peace in the Middle East in which every State in the area can live in security,

Determined that the territory of a State shall not be the object of occupation or acquisition by another State resulting from the threat or use of force, which is contrary to the Charter of the United Nations and to the principles enshrined in Security Council resolution 242 (1967) as well as in the Declaration on the Strengthening of International Security adopted by the General Assembly on 16 December 1970,[27]

Expressing its appreciation of the efforts of the Commission of Heads of African States undertaken in pursuance of the resolution adopted on 23 June 1971 by the Assembly of Heads of State and Government of the Organization of African Unity,

Gravely concerned at the continuation of Israel's occupation of the Arab territories since 5 June 1967,

Having considered the item entitled "The situation in the Middle East",

1. *Reaffirms* that the acquisition of territories by force is inadmissible and that, consequently, territories thus occupied must be restored;

2. *Reaffirms* that the establishment of a just and lasting peace in the Middle East should include the application of both the following principles:

(*a*) Withdrawal of Israeli armed forces from territories occupied in the recent conflict;

(*b*) Termination of all claims or states of belligerency and respect for and acknowledgement of the sovereignty, territorial integrity and political independence of every State in the area and its right to live in peace within secure and recognized boundaries free from threats or acts of force;

3. *Requests* the Secretary-General to take the necessary measures to reactivate the mission of the Special Representative of the Secretary-General to the Middle East in order to promote agreement and assist efforts to reach a peace agreement as envisaged in the Special Representative's aide-mémoire of 8 February 1971;[28]

4. *Expresses its full support* for all the efforts of the Special Representative to implement Security Council resolution 242 (1967) of 22 November 1967;

5. *Notes with appreciation* the positive reply given by Egypt to the Special Representative's initiative for establishing a just and lasting peace in the Middle East;

6. *Calls upon* Israel to respond favourably to the Special Representative's peace initiative;

---

27 General Assembly resolution 2734 (XXV).
28 A/8541-S/10403, annex I.

7. *Further invites* the parties to the Middle East conflict to give their full co-operation to the Special Representative in order to work out practical measures for:

(*a*) Guaranteeing freedom of navigation through international waterways in the area;

(*b*) Achieving a just settlement of the refugee problem;

(*c*) Guaranteeing the territorial inviolability and political independence of every State in the area;

8. *Requests* the Secretary-General to report to the Security Council and to the General Assembly, as appropriate, on the progress made by the Special Representative in the implementation of Security Council resolution 242 (1947) and of the present resolution;

9. *Requests* the Security Council to consider, if necessary, making arrangements, under the relevant Articles of the Charter of the United Nations, with regard to the implementation of its resolution.

Appendix XXVII

Resolution 2851 (XXVI) of the General Assembly dated 20 December 1971 concerning violations by Israel of human rights in the occupied territories

The General Assembly,

Guided by the purposes and principles of the Charter of the United Nations,

Bearing in mind the provisions and principles of the Universal Declaration of Human Rights, as well as the provisions of the Geneva Convention relative to the Protection of Civilian Persons in Time of War of 12 August 1949,[29]

Recalling Security Council resolutions 237 (1967) of 14 June 1967 and 259 (1968) of 27 September 1968, as well as other pertinent resolutions of the United Nations,

Having considered the report of the Special Committee to Investigate Israeli Practices Affecting the Human Rights of the Population of the Occupied Territories,[30]

Gravely concerned about the violations of the human rights of the inhabitants of the occupied territories,

Considering that the system of investigation and protection is essential for ensuring effective implementation of the international instruments, such as the fourth Geneva Convention of 12 August 1949, which provides for respect for human rights in armed conflicts,

Noting with regret that the relevant provisions of the fourth Geneva Convention of 12 August 1949 have not been implemented by the Israeli authorities,

Recalling that, in accordance with article 1 of the fourth Geneva Convention of 12 August 1949, the States parties have undertaken not only to respect but also to ensure respect for the Convention in all circumstances,

Noting with satisfaction that the International Committee of the Red Cross, after giving

---

29 United Nations, *Treaty Series*, vol. 75 (1950), No. 973.
30 A/8389 and Add.1/Corr. 1.

careful consideration to the question of the reinforcement of the implementation of the Geneva Conventions, has arrived at the conclusion that all tasks falling to a protecting Power under the Conventions could be considered humanitarian functions and that the International Committee of the Red Cross has declared itself ready to assume all the functions envisaged for protecting Powers in the Conventions,

1. *Commends* the Special Committee to Investigate Israeli Practices Affecting the Human Rights of the Population of the Occupied Territories and its members for their efforts in performing the task assigned to them;

2. *Strongly calls upon* Israel to rescind forthwith all measures and to desist from all policies and practices such as:

(*a*) The annexation of any part of the occupied Arab territories;

(*b*) The establishment of Israeli settlements on those territories and the transfer of parts of its civilian population into the occupied territory;

(*c*) The destruction and demolition of villages, quarters and houses and the confiscation and expropriation of property;

(*d*) The evacuation, transfer, deportation and expulsion of the inhabitants of the occupied Arab territories;

(*e*) The denial of the right of the refugees and displaced persons to return to their homes;

(*f*) The ill-treatment and torture of prisoners and detainees;

(*g*) Collective punishment;

3. *Calls upon* the Government of Israel to permit all persons who have fled the occupied territories or have been deported or expelled therefrom to return to their homes;

4. *Reaffirms* that all measures taken by Israel to settle the occupied territories, including occupied Jerusalem, are completely null and void;

5. *Calls upon* the Government of Israel to comply fully with its obligations under the Geneva Convention relative to the Protection of Civilian Persons in Time of War, of 12 August 1949;

6. *Requests* the Special Committee, pending the early termination of Israeli occupation of Arab territories, to continue its work and to consult as appropriate with the International Committee of the Red Cross in order to ensure the safeguarding of the welfare and human rights of the population of the occupied territories;

7. *Urges* the Government of Israel to co-operate with the Special Committee and to facilitate its entry into the occupied territories in order to enable it to perform the functions entrusted to it by the General Assembly;

8. *Requests* the Secretary-General to provide the Special Committee with all the necessary facilities for the continued performance of its task;

9. *Requests* all States parties to the fourth Geneva Convention of 12 August 1949 to do their utmost to ensure that Israel respects and fulfils its obligations under that Convention;

10. *Requests* the Special Committee to report to the Secretary-General as soon as possible and whenever the need arises thereafter;

11. *Decides* to include in the provisional agenda of its twenty-seventh session an item entitled "Report (or reports) of the Special Committee to Investigate Israeli Practices Affecting the Human Rights of the Population of the Occupied Territories".

Appendix XXVIII

Resolution of the Commission on Human Rights of the Economic
and Social Council of the UN dated 22 March 1972 concerning
violations by Israel of human rights in the occupied territories

The Commission on Human Rights,

Guided by the principles and purposes of the Charter of the United Nations, as well as the principles and provisions of the Universal Declaration of Human Rights,

Bearing in mind the provisions of the Geneva Convention relative to the Protection of Civilian Persons in Time of War of 12 August 1949,

Recalling all the relevant resolutions adopted by the various United Nations organs on the subject of the protection of the human rights of the inhabitants of the Arab territories occupied by Israel,

Recalling also that in accordance with the provisions of the Charter of the United Nations and those of the Universal Declaration of Human Rights, Member States bear a special responsibility to ensure the protection of human rights and to reaffirm faith in fundamental human rights and in the dignity and worth of the human person,

Recalling further that in accordance with article (1) of the said Geneva Convention, States Parties have undertaken not only to respect but also to ensure respect for the Convention in all circumstances,

Taking note of the reports submitted to and/or discussed in the different competent organs of the United Nations on the aforementioned subject,

Gravely concerned with all acts and policies that affect the status or the character of those occupied territories and the basic rights of the inhabitants thereof, such as:

(*a*) The declared intention to annex certain parts of the occupied Arab territories,

(*b*) The establishment of Israeli settlements on those territories and the transfer of parts of its civilian population into the occupied territories,

(*c*) The evacuation, transfer, deportation and expulsion of the inhabitants of occupied territories,

(*d*) The destruction and demolition of villages, quarters and houses and the confiscation and expropriation of property,

(*e*) The denial of the right of the refugees and displaced persons to return to their homes,

(*f*) Collective punishment and ill-treatment of prisoners and detainees,

(*g*) Administrative detention and holding prisoners incommunicado,

Noting with regret that the aforementioned acts have not been rescinded in spite of the numerous resolutions adopted on the subject,

Deploring the persistent defiance and disregard by Israel of all United Nations resolutions on the protection of human rights of the inhabitants of the occupied territories and on the preservation of the demographic composition and geographic character thereof,

Taking note of the fact that article 147 of the Geneva Convention of 12 August 1949 has considered unlawful deportation or transfer, unlawful confinement, deprivation of the rights of fair and regular trial, taking of hostages and extensive destruction and appropriation of property as grave breaches of the Convention,

Noting that the Charter of the International Military Tribunal of Nuremberg as confirmed by General Assembly resolutions 3 (I) of 13 February 1946 and 95 (I) of 11 December 1946 has considered as war crimes the "grave breaches" later enumerated in the Geneva Conventions of 12 August 1949,

Recalling its resolution 5 B (XXVI) adopted at its twenty-sixth session which considered violations of the Geneva Conventions as war crimes and an affront to humanity,

1. *Strongly calls upon* Israel to rescind forthwith all measures and to desist from all policies and practices affecting the demographic structure or the physical character of the occupied Arab territories and the human rights of their inhabitants;

2. *Calls upon* the Government of Israel to permit all persons who have fled the occupied territories or who have been deported or expelled therefrom to return to their homes without conditions;

3. *Reaffirms* that all measures taken by Israel to annex or settle the occupied territories are null and void;

4. *Calls upon* the Government of Israel – once more – to comply fully with its obligations under the Geneva Convention relative to the Protection of Civilian Persons in Time of War;

5. *Also calls upon* Israel once more to respect and implement the resolutions adopted by the Commission and other competent organs on the question of the protection of human rights of the inhabitants of the occupied territories;

6. *Requests* all States Members of the United Nations and all States parties to the Fourth Geneva Convention of 12 August 1949 to do their utmost to ensure that Israel respects the principles of human rights and fulfils its obligations under that Convention;

7. *Considers* that grave breaches of the Fourth Geneva Convention committed by Israel in the occupied Arab territories constitute war crimes and an affront to humanity;

8. *Decides* to place on the provisional agenda of its twenty-ninth session as a matter of high priority the item entitled "Question of the violation of human rights in the territories occupied as a result of hostilities in the Middle East".

Appendix XXIX

Resolution 316 of the Security Council dated 26 June 1972 condemning Israeli attacks on Lebanon

The Security Council,

Having considered the agenda contained in document S/Agenda/1650/Rev. 1,

Having noted the contents of the letter of the Permanent Representative of Lebanon (S/10715), of the letter of the Permanent Representative of Israel (S/10716), and of the letter of the Permanent Representative of the Syrian Arab Republic (S/10720),

Recalling the consensus of the members of the Security Council of 19 April 1972 (S/10611),

Having noted the supplementary information provided by the Chief of Staff of the United Nations Truce Supervisory Organization contained in the relevant documents S/7930/Add.

1584 of 26 April 1972 to S/7930/Add.1640 of 21 June 1972, and particularly S/7930/Add. 1641 to 1648 of 21, 22, 23 and 24 June 1972,

Having heard the statements of the representatives of Lebanon and of Israel,

Deploring the tragic loss of life resulting from all acts of violence and retaliation,

Gravely concerned at Israel's failure to comply with the previous resolutions of the Security Council calling on her to desist forthwith from any violation of the sovereignty and territorial integrity of Lebanon (resolutions 262 (1968), 270 (1969), 280 and 285 (1970) and 313 (1972),

1. *Calls upon* Israel to strictly abide by the aforementioned resolutions and to refrain from all military acts against Lebanon;

2. *Condemns*, while profoundly deploring all acts of violence, the repeated attacks of Israeli forces on Lebanese territory and population in violation of the principles of the United Nations Charter and Israel's obligations thereunder;

3. *Expresses* the strong desire that appropriate steps will lead, as an immediate consequence, to the release in the shortest possible time of all Syrian and Lebanese military and security personnel abducted by Israeli armed forces on 21 June 1972 on Lebanese territory;

4. *Declares* that if the abovementioned steps do not result in the release of the abducted personnel or, if Israel fails to comply with the present resolution, the Council will reconvene at the earliest to consider further action.[31]

Appendix xxx

Resolution 2949 (XXVII) of the General Assembly dated 8 December 1972 on the situation in the Middle East

The General Assembly,

Having considered the item entitled "The situation in the Middle East",

Having received the report of the Secretary-General of 15 September 1972 on the activities of his Special Representative to the Middle East,[32]

Reaffirming that Security Council resolution 242 (1967) of 22 November 1967 must be implemented in all its parts,

Deeply perturbed that Security Council resolution 242 (1967) and General Assembly resolution 2799 (XXVI) of 13 December 1971 have not been implemented and, consequently, the envisaged just and lasting peace in the Middle East has not been achieved,

Reiterating its grave concern at the continuation of the Israeli occupation of Arab territories since 5 June 1967,

---

31 Israel refused to comply with this resolution. As a result, the Security Council adopted another resolution on 21 July 1972 in which it deplored Israel's failure to comply with its previous resolution, and called upon it to return the abducted military and security personnel without delay. Israel has also ignored this resolution.

32 A/8815–S/10792.

Reaffirming that the territory of a State shall not be the object of occupation or acquisition by another State resulting from the threat or use of force,

Affirming that changes in the physical character or demographic composition of occupied territories are contrary to the purposes and principles of the Charter of the United Nations, as well as to the provisions of the relevant applicable international conventions,

Convinced that the grave situation prevailing in the Middle East constitutes a serious threat to international peace and security,

Reaffirming the responsibility of the United Nations to restore peace and security in the Middle East in the immediate future,

1. *Reaffirms* its resolution 2799 (XXVI);

2. *Deplores* the non-compliance by Israel with General Assembly resolution 2799 (XXVI), which in particular called upon Israel to respond favourably to the peace initiative of the Special Representative of the Secretary-General to the Middle East;

3. *Expresses its full support* for the efforts of the Secretary-General and his Special Representative;

4. *Declares once more* that the acquisition of territories by force is inadmissible and that, consequently, territories thus occupied must be restored;

5. *Reaffirms* that the establishment of a just and lasting peace in the Middle East should include the application of both the following principles:

(*a*) Withdrawal of Israeli armed forces from territories occupied in the recent conflict;

(*b*) Termination of all claims or states of belligerency and respect for and acknowledgement of the sovereignty, territorial integrity and political independence of every State in the area and its right to live in peace within secure and recognized boundaries free from threats or acts of force;

6. *Invites* Israel to declare publicly its adherence to the principle of non-annexation of territories through the use of force;

7. *Declares* that changes carried out by Israel in the occupied Arab territories in contravention of the Geneva Conventions of 1949[33] are null and void, and calls upon Israel to rescind forthwith all such measures and to desist from all policies and practices affecting the physical character or demographic composition of the occupied Arab territories;

8. *Calls upon* all States not to recognize any such changes and measures carried out by Israel in the occupied Arab territories and invites them to avoid actions, including actions in the field of aid, that could constitute recognition of that occupation;

9. *Recognizes* that respect for the rights of the Palestinians is an indispensable element in the establishment of a just and lasting peace in the Middle East;

10. *Requests* the Security Council, in consultation with the Secretary-General and his Special Representative, to take all appropriate steps with a view to the full and speedy implementation of Security Council resolution 242 (1967), taking into account all the relevant resolutions and documents of the United Nations in this connexion;

11. *Requests* the Secretary-General to report to the Security Council and the General Assembly on the progress made by him and his Special Representative in the implementation of Security Council resolution 242 (1967) and of the present resolution;

12. *Decides* to transmit the present resolution to the Security Council for its appropriate action and requests the Council to keep the General Assembly informed.

2105th plenary meeting, 8 December 1972

---

33   United Nations, *Treaty Series* ,vol. 75, Nos. 970–973.

Appendix XXXI

Resolutions 2963 A–F (XXVII) of the General Assembly dated 13 December 1972 on the rights of the Palestinians

A

The General Assembly,

Recalling its resolutions 2792 A (XXVI) of 6 December 1971 and all previous resolutions referred to therein, including resolution 194 (III) of 11 December 1948,

Taking note of the annual report of the Commissioner-General of the United Nations Relief and Works Agency for Palestine Refugees in the Near East, covering the period from 1 July 1971 to 30 June 1972,[34]

Taking note also of the appeal made by the Secretary-General on 20 March 1972,[35]

1. *Notes with deep regret* that repatriation or compensation of the refugees as provided for in paragraph 11 of General Assembly resolution 194 (III) has not been effected, that no substantial progress has been made in the programme endorsed by the Assembly in paragraph 2 of resolution 513 (VI) for the reintegration of refugees either by repatriation or resettlement and that, therefore, the situation of the refugees continues to be a matter of serious concern;

2. *Expresses its thanks* to the Commissioner-General and to the staff of the United Nations Relief and Works Agency for Palestine Refugees in the Near East for their continued faithful efforts to provide essential services for the Palestine refugees, and to the specialized agencies and private organizations for their valuable work in assisting the refugees;

3. *Notes with regret* that the United Nations Conciliation Commission for Palestine was unable to find a means of achieving progress in the implementation of paragraph 11 of General Assembly resolution 194 (III) and requests the Commission to exert continued efforts towards the implementation thereof and to report thereon as appropriate, but not later than 1 October 1973;

4. *Directs attention* to the continuing critical financial position of the United Nations Relief and Works Agency for Palestine Refugees in the Near East, as outlined in the Commissioner-General's report;

5. *Notes with concern* that, despite the commendable and successful efforts of the Commissioner-General to collect additional contributions to help relieve the serious budget deficit of the past year, contributions to the United Nations Relief and Works Agency for Palestine Refugees in the Near East continue to fall short of the funds needed to cover essential budget requirements;

6. *Calls upon* all Governments as a matter of urgency to make the most generous efforts possible to meet the anticipated needs of the United Nations Relief and Works Agency for Palestine Refugees in the Near East, particularly in the light of the budgetary deficit pro-

---

34 *Official Records of the General Assembly, Twenty-seventh Session, Supplement No. 13* (A/8713).
35 A/8672.

jected in the Commissioner-General's report, and therefore urges non-contributing Governments to contribute and contributing Governments to consider increasing their contributions.

B

The General Assembly,

Recalling its resolutions 2252 (ES–V) of 4 July 1967, 2341 B (XXII) of 19 December 1967, 2452 C (XXIII) of 19 December 1968, 2535 C (XXIV) of 10 December 1969, 2672 B (XXV) of 8 December 1970 and 2792 B (XXVI) of 6 December 1971,

Taking note of the annual report of the Commissioner-General of the United Nations Relief and Works Agency for Palestine Refugees in the Near East, covering the period from 1 July 1971 to 30 June 1972,[36]

Taking note also of the appeal made by the Secretary-General on 20 March 1972,[37]

Concerned about the continued human suffering resulting from the June 1967 hostilities in the Middle East,

1. *Reaffirms* its resolutions 2252 (ES–V), 2341 B (XXII), 2452 C (XXIII), 2535 C (XXIV), 2672 B (XXV) and 2792 B (XXVI);

2. *Endorses,* bearing in mind the objectives of those resolutions, the efforts of the Commissioner-General of the United Nations Relief and Works Agency for Palestine Refugees in the Near East to continue to provide humanitarian assistance, as far as practicable, on an emergency basis and as a temporary measure, to other persons in the area who are at present displaced and in serious need of continued assistance as a result of the June 1967 hostilities;

3. *Strongly appeals* to all Governments and to organizations and individuals to contribute generously for the above purposes to the United Nations Relief and Works Agency for Palestine Refugees in the Near East and to the other intergovernmental and non-governmental organizations concerned.

C

The General Assembly,

Having considered the report of the Secretary-General[38] on the effect on the inhabitants of the Gaza Strip of the continued Israeli policies and measures in the Strip,

Noting that both the Secretary-General and the Commissioner-General of the United Nations Relief and Works Agency for Palestine Refugees in the Near East have expressed great concern about the effect on Palestine refugees of these operations in which shelters in refugee camps were demolished and thousands of persons displaced, some of them to places outside the Gaza Strip,

Noting with regret the failure of Israel to comply with the provisions of General Assembly resolution 2792 C (XXVI) of 6 December 1971,

Deeply concerned at the continued measures by Israel which prejudice the rights of the population and the demographic composition and the status of the Gaza Strip,

1. *Declares* that such measures involving the physical and demographic structure in the Gaza Strip, including the destruction of refugee shelters and the forcible transfer of population, contravene the provisions of the Geneva Convention relative to the Protection of Civilian Persons in Time of War of 12 August 1949[39] as well as paragraph 7 of General

36 *Official Records of the General Assembly, Twenty-seventh session, Supplement No. 13* (A/8713).
37 A/8672.   38 A/8814.
39 United Nations, *Treaty Series,* vol. 75, No. 973.

Assembly resolution 2675 (XXV) of 9 December 1970, entitled "Basic principles for the protection of civilian populations in armed conflicts";

2. *Strongly deplores* these actions by Israel;

3. *Calls upon* Israel to desist forthwith from all measures that affect the physical structure and the demographic composition of the Gaza Strip;

4. *Calls upon* Israel to take immediate and effective steps for the return of the refugees concerned to the camps from which they were removed and to provide adequate shelters for their accommodation;

5. *Requests* the Secretary-General, after consulting with the Commissioner-General of the United Nations Relief and Works Agency for Palestine Refugees in the Near East, to report as soon as possible and whenever appropriate thereafter, but in any case not later than the opening date of the twenty-eighth session of the General Assembly, on Israel's compliance with and implementation of the present resolution.

D

The General Assembly,

Recalling Security Council resolution 237 (1967) of 14 June 1967,

Recalling also its resolutions 2252 (ES–V) of 4 July 1967, 2452 A (XXIII) of 19 December 1968, 2535 B (XXIV) of 10 December 1969, 2672 D (XXV) of 8 December 1970, and 2792 E (XXVI) of 6 December 1971, calling upon the Government of Israel to take effective and immediate steps for the return without delay of those inhabitants who had fled the areas since the outbreak of hostilities,

Having considered the report of the Secretary-General[40] of 13 September 1972 concerning the implementation of resolution 2792 E (XXVI),

Noting that the Israeli occupation authorities have persisted in changing the physical, geographical and demographic structure in the occupied territories, by the displacement of inhabitants, the destruction of towns, villages and homes, and the establishment of settlements in violation of the provisions of the Geneva Convention Relative to the Protection of Civilian Persons in Time of War of 12 August 1949[41] as well as the pertinent United Nations resolutions,

Gravely concerned about the plight of the displaced inhabitants,

Convinced that the plight of the displaced inhabitants could only be relieved by their speedy return to their homes and to the camps which they formerly occupied,

Emphasizing the necessity of full implementation of the above-mentioned resolutions,

1. *Affirms* the right of the displaced inhabitants to return to their homes and camps;

2. *Considers* that the plight of the displaced inhabitants continues since they have not yet returned to their homes and camps;

3. *Expresses its grave concern* for the failure of the Israeli authorities to take steps for the return of the displaced inhabitants in accordance with the above-mentioned resolutions;

4. *Calls once more upon* Israel immediately to take steps for the return of the displaced inhabitants;

5. *Calls again upon* Israel to desist forthwith from all measures affecting the physical, geographic and demographic structure of the occupied territories;

6. *Requests* the Secretary-General to follow the implementation of the present resolution and to report in detail thereon to the General Assembly.

---

40   A/8786.   41   United Nations, *Treaty Series,* vol. 75, No. 973.

E

The General Assembly,

Recognizing that the problem of the Palestinian Arab refugees has arisen from the denial of their inalienable rights under the Charter of the United Nations and the Universal Declaration of Human Rights,

Recalling its resolution 2535 B (XXIV) of 10 December 1969, in which it reaffirmed the inalienable rights of the people of Palestine, its resolutions 2672 C (XXV) of 8 December 1970 and 2792 D (XXVI) of 6 December 1971, in which it recognized that the people of Palestine are entitled to equal rights and self-determination in accordance with the Charter, and its resolutions 2649 (XXV) of 30 November 1970 and 2787 (XXVI) of 6 December 1971, in which it recognized that the people of Palestine are entitled to the right of self-determination,

Bearing in mind the principle of equal rights and self-determination of peoples enshrined in Articles 1 and 55 of the Charter and more recently reaffirmed in the Declaration on Principles of International Law concerning Friendly Relations and Co-operation among States in accordance with the Charter of the United Nations[42] and in the Declaration on the Strengthening of International Security,[43]

1. *Affirms* that the People of Palestine are entitled to equal rights and self-determination, in accordance with the Charter of the United Nations;

2. *Expresses once more its grave concern* that the people of Palestine have not been permitted to enjoy their inalienable rights and to exercise their right to self-determination;

3. *Recognizes* that full respect for and realization of the inalienable rights of the people of Palestine are indispensable for the establishment of a just and lasting peace in the Middle East.

[Resolution F concerns the membership of the Advisory Commission of UNRWA and is omitted from this Appendix.]

---

42   General Assembly resolution 2625 (XXV).
43   General Assembly resolution 2734 (XXV).

Appendix XXXII

Resolution 3005 (XXVII) of the General Assembly dated
15 December 1972 concerning violations by Israel of human rights
in the occupied territories

The General Assembly,

Guided by the purposes and principles of the Charter of the United Nations,

Invoking the provisions and principles of the Universal Declaration of Human Rights,

Bearing in mind the provisions of the Geneva Convention relative to the Protection of Civilian Persons in Time of War, of 12 August 1949,[44]

Recalling Security Council resolutions 237 (1967) of 14 June 1967 and 259 (1968) of 27 September 1968, as well as other pertinent resolutions of the United Nations,

Having considered the report of the Special Committee to Investigate Israeli Practices Affecting the Human Rights of the Population of the Occupied Territories,[45]

Considering that a system of investigation and protection is required for ensuring effective implementation of the international instruments, such as the aforementioned Geneva Convention of 12 August 1949, which provide for respect for human rights in armed conflicts,

Recalling that, in accordance with article 1 of that Convention, the States parties have undertaken not only to respect but also to ensure respect for the Convention in all circumstances,

Considering that implementation of the Geneva Convention of 12 August 1949 cannot and should not be left open in a situation involving foreign military occupation and the rights of the civilian population of these territories under the provisions of that Convention and in accordance with the principles of international law,

1. *Commends* the Special Committee to Investigate Israeli Practices Affecting the Human Rights of the Population of the Occupied Territories for its efforts in performing the tasks assigned to it;

2. *Strongly calls upon* Israel to rescind forthwith and desist from all such policies and practices as:

(*a*) The annexation of any part of the occupied territories;

(*b*) The establishment of Israeli settlements on those territories and the transfer of parts of an alien population into the occupied territories;

(*c*) The destruction and demolition of villages, quarters and houses and the confiscation and expropriation of property;

(*d*) The evacuation, transfer, deportation and expulsion of the inhabitants of the occupied territories;

(*e*) The denial of the right of the displaced persons to return to their homes;

3. *Reaffirms* that all measures taken by Israel in contravention of the Geneva Convention relative to the Protection of Civilian Persons in Time of War, of 12 August 1949, to settle the occupied territories, including occupied Jerusalem, are null and void;

4. *Affirms* the principle of the sovereignty of the population of the occupied territories over their national wealth and resources;

---

44 United Nations, *Treaty Series,* vol. 75, No. 973, p. 287.   45 A/8828.

5. *Calls upon* all States, international organizations and specialized agencies not to recognize or co-operate with, or assist in any manner in, any measures undertaken by the occupying Power to exploit the resources of the occupied territories or to effect any changes in the demographic composition or the geographic character or the institutional structure of these territories;

6. *Requests* all States parties to the Geneva Convention of 12 August 1949 to do their utmost to ensure that Israel respects and fulfils its obligations under that Convention;

7. *Requests* the Special Committee, pending the early termination of Israeli occupation of Arab territories, to continue its work and to consult, as appropriate, with the International Committee of the Red Cross in order to ensure the safeguarding of the welfare and human rights of the population of the occupied territories;

8. *Requests* the Secretary-General to render all necessary facilities to the Special Committee, including those required for its visits to the occupied territories with a view to investigating Israeli policies and practices affecting the human rights of the population of the occupied territories, especially:

(*a*) The measures concerning the establishment of Israeli settlements in the occupied territories and the moving into the occupied territories of an alien population, contrary to the provisions of the Geneva Convention of 12 August 1949;

(*b*) The situation concerning the annexation of any part of the territories occupied by Israel since 5 June 1967;

(*c*) The exploitation and the looting of the resources of the occupied territories;

(*d*) The changes in the physical character or demographic composition or institutional structure of these territories, including the transfer or deportation of population thereof or demolition of houses and towns therein;

(*e*) The pillaging of the archaeological and cultural heritage of the occupied territories;

(*f*) The interference in the freedom of worship in the holy places of the occupied territories;

9. *Calls upon* Israel to co-operate with the Secretary-General and the Special Committee and to facilitate their tasks;

10. *Requests* the Secretary-General to ensure the widest circulation of the reports of the Special Committee by all means available through the Office of Public Information.

11. *Requests* the Special Committee to report to the Secretary-General as soon as possible and whenever the need arises thereafter;

12. *Requests* the Secretary-General to report to the General Assembly at its twenty-eighth session on the task entrusted to him;

13. *Decides* to include in the provisional agenda of its twenty-eighth session the item entitled "Report of the Special Committee to Investigate Israeli Practices Affecting the Human Rights of the Population of the Occupied Territories".

Appendix XXXIII

Resolution of the Commission on Human Rights of the
Economic and Social Council of the UN dated
14 March 1973 concerning violations by Israel of human
rights in the occupied territories

The Commission on Human Rights,

Guided by the principles and purposes of the Charter of the United Nations, as well as the principles and provisions of the Universal Declaration of Human Rights,

Bearing in mind the provisions of the Fourth Geneva Convention of 12 August 1949, relative to the protection of civilian persons in time of war,

Recalling the pertinent United Nations resolutions on the protection of human rights and fundamental freedoms of the inhabitants of the occupied Arab territories,

Further recalling that the General Assembly in its resolution 2949 (XXVII) declared "that changes carried out by Israel in the occupied Arab territories in contravention of the Geneva Conventions of 1949 are null and void" and called "upon all States not to recognize any such changes and measures carried out by Israel in the occupied Arab territories",

Taking note of the reports of the United Nations and other international humanitarian organizations on the situation of the inhabitants of the occupied Arab territories,

Greatly alarmed by the continuation of the violations of human rights and fundamental freedoms, by Israel, in the occupied Arab territories, in particular the destruction of houses, expropriation of Arab properties, ill treatment of prisoners, pillaging of the archaeological and cultural heritage and the exploitation of natural resources,

Deeply concerned by the fact that Israel continues to establish Israeli settlements in the occupied Arab territories, encourages massive immigration to that end, continues to deport and transfer the indigenous Arab population and refuses the return of the refugees and displaced persons to their homes,

Convinced that Israel's deliberate policy of annexation and of settlement in the occupied Arab territories is in contravention of the Charter of the United Nations, the international humanitarian law, and the basic human rights and fundamental freedoms,

Deploring Israel's persistent defiance of the relevant resolutions of the United Nations and its continued policy of violating the basic human rights of the population in the occupied Arab territories,

Deplores Israel's continued grave breaches of the Fourth Geneva Convention in the occupied Arab territories which are considered by the Commission of Human Rights as war crimes and an affront to humanity,

Reaffirms that all measures taken by Israel to change the demographic structure and status of the occupied Arab territories, including occupied Jerusalem, are null and void,

Calls upon Israel to comply with its obligations under the Charter of the United Nations, the Universal Declaration of Human Rights, the principles of international humanitarian law, to abide by its obligations under the Fourth Geneva Convention and to respect and implement the relevant United Nations resolutions,

Further calls upon Israel to immediately stop the establishment of settlements in the occupied Arab territories and to rescind all policies and measures affecting the physical character and demographic composition of those territories,

Calls upon all States to do their utmost to ensure that Israel respects the principles of human rights and fundamental freedoms and that it desists from all acts and policies aimed at changing the physical character and demographic composition of the occupied Arab territories particularly through the establishment of settlements, the deportation and transfer of the Arab population,

Considers that Israel's policy of settling parts of its population, including immigrants, in the occupied Arab territories, is a flagrant violation of Article 49 of the Fourth Geneva Convention, as well as the relevant United Nations resolutions and calls upon all States and organizations not to help nor assist Israel in any way to enable it to pursue its policy of colonizing the occupied Arab territories,

Requests the Secretary-General to bring this resolution to the attention of all Governments, the competent United Nations organs, specialized agencies, regional intergovernmental organizations, and to give it the widest possible publicity and to report to the next session of the Commission on Human Rights,

Decides to place on the provisional agenda of its thirtieth session, as a matter of high priority, the item entitled "Questions of the violation of human rights in the territories occupied as a result of hostilities in the Middle East".

Addendum

While this book was with the printer, another Israeli act of aggression that violated both international law and elementary principles of civilization was perpetrated on 10 April 1973 in Beirut, the Lebanese capital. This act of aggression was committed with the assistance of Israeli commandos who had entered Lebanon with forged passports as Western European "tourists" a few days earlier. Its principal objective was the assassination of three Palestinian resistance leaders. These three leaders were murdered in their homes in the middle of the night. Unlike the assassination of representatives of the Palestine Liberation Organization by Israeli agents in Rome, Paris and Nicosia, this criminal deed was openly admitted by the Israeli Government and was even the subject of boasting by the Israeli leaders responsible.

At the Security Council, to which Lebanon submitted a complaint, the condemnation of Israel's action as constituting both a violation of the sovereignty of Lebanon and an act of state gangsterism was almost unanimous. Israel sought to justify its unjustifiable act by referring to acts of violence committed by Palestinian guerillas and by claiming that it was acting in self-defence. Such atmtepted justification, however, must be rejected. It is a distortion of law and justice to equate Palestinian acts of violence with Israel's so-called reprisals. Acts of violence committed by the Palestinians are rooted in the grave injustice inflicted on them. It is not surprising, as was pointed out in the Security Council debate by the British delegate Sir Colin Crowe, that the Palestinians sitting in their camps, often almost in sight of their former homes, should grow bitter, and that in despair some should turn to violence and extremism. Israeli violence, on the other hand, is designed to preserve the basic injustice, and to stifle the voice of the victims. From the juridical standpoint, the reprisals that Israeli military forces exercise against the Palestinians do not differ in quality from the reprisals exercised by the Nazi occupation forces against members of the French resistance movement during the Second World War. Whether it be the Germans in France, or the Israelis in Palestine, in both cases they are alien occupiers of a country that does not belong to them. The only difference is that in many cases Israeli reprisals are often aggravated by being committed on the territory of third States in violation of their sovereignty.

The question of recourse to sanctions against Israel for its repeated attacks against Lebanon engaged the attention of the Security Council. Lebanon asked the Council to use force – moral, political and legal – to end Israeli aggression. Egypt requested the imposition of a ban on economic assistance and military supplies to Israel by Member States. Soviet Russia intimated that it was ready to participate in sanctions and even to support the expulsion of Israel from the UN. A Franco-British draft resolution envisaged not only the condemnation of Israel but also a warning that if it repeated its attacks against Lebanon the Council would meet to consider what further and more effective steps or measures could be taken to ensure against their repetition.

However, owing to US opposition to any threat of sanctions against Israel, the proposed warning to Israel was abandoned in the final text of the resolution. In a somewhat weak resolution adopted on 21 April 1973, the Security Council merely deplored all acts of violence resulting in the loss of innocent lives, condemned the repeated military attacks directed by Israel against Lebanon, and called on Israel to desist forthwith from all military attacks on Lebanon. For diametrically opposed reasons, the three superpowers abstained from voting in favour of this resolution. The US Government abstained because it did not wish to condemn Israel unless the Palestinian guerillas also were condemned. Soviet Russia and China abstained because they considered that a routine condemnation of Israel's aggression without a threat of sanctions was meaningless.

The significance of this resolution lies in the insignificance of its results. This lamentable situation is the consequence of the US Government's unqualified support for Israel. This support, as is evident from several recent Security Council debates, has paralysed any effective UN action to redress the injustice done in Palestine, or even to restrain Israel's excesses and violations of international law. Uninformed (usually deliberately misinformed) internal American public opinion has not as yet been able to exercise a salutary influence such as that which helped to put an end to the war in Vietnam. The writer, however, ventures to hope that this is only a question of time, and that the UN, under the pressure of world opinion, will be able to correct the situation in Palestine by recourse to the means and principles prescribed by the Charter for the settlement of international conflicts and the redress of national injustices. A quarter of a century of tension and conflict in the Middle East should by now make it quite evident that the Palestine situation cannot be resolved except on the basis of right and justice. The costly lesson learnt by mankind from many wars, and in particular from the Second World War, is that unjust international situations must be settled in accordance with the principles of justice and international law.

INDEX